Hawkins

COMPLETE BOOK

OF

WINNING FOOTBALL DRILLS

by

GEORGE H. ALLEN

Assistant Coach
Chicago Bears

Englewood Cliffs, N. J.
PRENTICE-HALL, INC.

First printing.........May, 1959
Second printing......March, 1960

To my wife Etty and our sons
George, Gregory, and Gerald
and
to my players, who have proved
that one learns most from his
pupils.

ACKNOWLEDGEMENTS

THIS BOOK WAS DEVELOPED FOR FOOTBALL COACHES AND STUDENTS of the game who are preparing for careers in the coaching field. No claim is made by the author as to originality for many of the ideas and concepts contained in this book. Many persons, some of them unknown, have shared in developing the drills represented. The author wishes to make it clear, however, that the interpretations and applications are his responsibility.

Grateful appreciation is herewith expressed to all persons who shared in the preparation of the book. Particularly helpful has been the assistance of coaches who, through correspondence or suggestions, have made valuable contributions.

The author is grateful for the assistance of Mr. John Griffith, publisher of *Athletic Journal,* for granting permission to use many of the photographs. Paul Zimmerman, the late Henry "Red" Sanders, Vinton Rambo, Bob Homan, and the William C. Brown Company all contributed to the *Complete Book of Winning Football Drills.*

PREFACE

IN KEEPING WITH THE RAPID GROWTH OF FOOTBALL, THE *Complete Book of Winning Football Drills* represents a thorough revision and a considerable enlargement of the *Encyclopedia of Football Drills*. New chapters have been added and each chapter has been enlarged with additional drills.

In preparing this book I have kept in mind two major aims: First, and foremost, *to make the book as useful as possible*. Every drill is explained in detail, and, when feasible, is further clarified by line drawings or photographs. Thus, the book's main value is as a reference to the specific problems of teaching skills.

Second, to present and include only drills that have been *proven*. This has automatically ruled out approximately one hundred drills on hand that are interesting but not yet tested.

The present edition differs from the original text in four respects. First, it includes new drills and illustrations. Second, it contains an entirely new part on conditioning drills complete wth photographs especially prepared for each drill. Third, it presents a complete new chapter on quarterback drills. To the author's knowledge, this is the first time a complete chapter on drills to train the quarterback has appeared in print. And, finally, it includes additional material and ideas to supplement the chapter on practice organization.

GEORGE ALLEN

CONTENTS

*Each drill is listed alphabetically under
its chapter topic in the Index, page 563.*

Part 1

INTRODUCTION

1

MAKING THE
MOST OF DRILLS

Few coaches clearly realize the paramount importance of a carefully planned and organized drill schedule. *The secret of good performance at critical moments is found in drill.* No soldier ever benefited more by intensive and carefully planned drill than does the football player. It is through drill and only drill that the coach can be reasonably sure of good performance under game pressure.

The underlying principles of military drill and drill in football are the same. The striking analogy between war and football is once more made evident. Just as in war, we have the counterparts of extended-order drills, combat exercises, and field exercises, all of which it is best to follow by a brief drill at attention in order to restore smartness and control.

Drill should be of the kind that will not sap the player's vitality and which will yield him as much fun as possible. It should be executed at top speed only at intervals to maintain

3

full interest. Complete coordination of the eye, mind, and muscle should be taught at slow speed, then somewhat faster. Finally, at intervals, the individual or group should test themselves at full speed.

In conclusion, let it be said that the importance of carefully planned and skillfully organized drill *cannot be overestimated*. It is the secret of good performance. There is one caution, however, that should be followed to keep player interest: *Do not drill the individuality or initiative out of the players*. The player should be encouraged to control the drill himself. The real stars of the game of football have generally been men who drilled themselves to a high degree of excellence. Under no circumstance must the drill or the drillmaster dominate the player. If that occurs, all motivation vanishes. On the contrary, the player must be encouraged to control the drill and to rise above the coach and coaching. In this manner only is high individual excellence obtained.

2

HOW TO ORGANIZE
A PRACTICE SCHEDULE

MAKING OUT PRACTICE SCHEDULES BEFORE AND DURING THE football season is tedious work. As a rule, a practice schedule cannot be arranged for more than a week at a time. Sometimes a weekly schedule must be revised during the week. Frequently coaches overlook the importance of developing a sound practice schedule for the players. The men who are involved in the practice sessions should have an opportunity to make the best possible use of their time. The player suffers if there is laxity in planning his program for him. Following are suggestions on practice schedule organization.

Organization of drills for fundamentals

This is the most important part of the early season plan. If a coach is experienced, he will have a fairly sound plan already developed; if not, it will be necessary to decide on what drills to use and how much time to spend on them.

5

Length of practice

Not more than two hours of each day should be devoted to football practice. When the period runs longer, the player is apt to work under his optimum physical ability in order to conserve some energy for the finish. If the daily program follows a specific pattern beginning with individual drills, proceeding

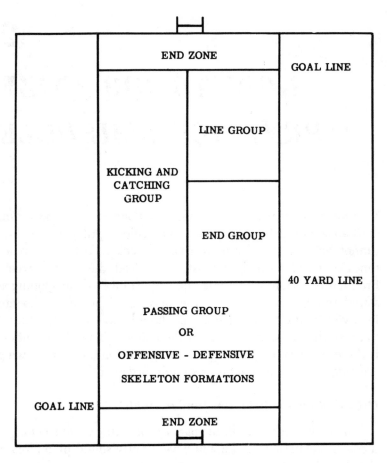

Illus. 1

to group drills, and finally to team drills, there will be no time for loafing or fooling around.

Moreover, two hours is adequate time to permit the coaching staff to devote attention to the second and third teams. Many of these players are very inexperienced and must have a great deal of coaching to be relied on in the future.

Division of practice field

If practice space permits it is well to designate specific areas of the field for certain activities. See Illustration 1, page 6. This chart may be posted on the bulletin board and the players will then be accustomed to reporting to specific areas for various types of drills. If possible, a coach should be assigned to each of these areas 15 minutes before the regular practice session begins.

Divisions of practice field by station

Another way of organizing practice is to lay out the practice field in a system of five stations grouped around a central tower. See Illustration 2, page 8. Build a movable wooden tower to serve as the hub of your activities. Detail a manager to man the tower with a stop watch, first-aid equipment, and a megaphone. It is his duty to signal the end of each 15-minute period.

Carry on all blocking drills at the first station on the dummies and sleds. Practice tackling in the pits and tackling lanes at the second station. Tackling lanes are areas lined with bags or limed markings to regulate the direction taken by the ball carrier. Provide space at a third station for several backfields to work on ball handling and timing. By having two units running in opposite directions from a common line it is possible to double practice time and conserve space. Use the fifth station as a dummy scrimmage area.

Drill the squad in the techniques of using the stations the

first time they report.   You will discover that the rapid shifting
of personnel will gain many additional minutes and assure a
better coached squad.

Daily time card

Work out and have printed a standard daily time card.   See
Illustration 3, page 9.   Divide the two hours into fifteen-
minute periods, and assign to each group within the drill divisions activities according to their specific needs.

Provide each coach and manager with a time card.   Post
several time detail cards in plain view on the locker room
bulletin board.

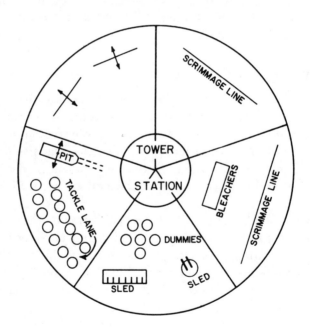

Illus. 2

Drill schedule

Another important item to be posted for the players to see each week throughout the season is a pre- and post-practice drill schedule for all. See Illustration 4, page 10.

WHITTIER COLLEGE **DAILY TIME CARD**			DATE **OCTOBER 14**		
TIME	GUARDS	TACKLES	ENDS	BACKS	CENTERS
3:30 to 3:45	←	WARM UP ON BALL	→	SHIFTING DRILLS	WARM UP ON BALL
3:45 to 4:00	BLKING OUT AT HOLE ON DUMMIES		FT. WORK DRILLS	BALL HANDLING	CHECK BLK. DRILL
4:00 to 4:15	←	CHARGING SLED	→	BALL HANDLING	CHARGING SLED
4:15 to 4:30	← 4 ON 4 →		PASS PATTERNS WITH THE BACKS		4 ON 4
4:30 to 4:45	← 2 ON 1 →		↓	↓	2 ON 1
4:45 to 5:00	PASS PROTECTION		2 ON 1 BLK. WITH WING	PASS DEFENSE	PASS PROTECT
5:00 to 5:15	←	TEAM	OFFENSIVE SCRIMMAGE LIVE		→
5:15 to 5:30	←	TEAM	DEFENSIVE SCRIMMAGE LIVE		→
5:30 to 5:45	←	DUMMIES	OFFENSIVE TEAM		→
5:45 to 6:00	←		PERFECT PLAYS TEAM		→
				GEORGE ALLEN	

Illus. 3

PRE- AND POST-PRACTICE DRILLS FOR ALL

CENTERS: At least 10 punt formation snap-backs
10 extra-point snap-backs
10 single-wing formation snap-backs
One block of each type both ways on charging sled

EXTRA POINT MEN: Ten to fifteen extra points
Six to ten field goals (no more than ten)

POINT HOLDERS: Hold ball for speed in handling and placing

KICK-OFF MEN: Ten kicks daily, no more

ENDS AND BACKS: Pass receiving—three in a group
Fifteen pass receptions, all cuts
(This is a minimum)

BACKS: Ten straight arms on any object—both arms

HALFBACKS AND FULLBACKS: Perfect footwork for all plays
Run ten times each way including all spinners

PASSERS: All types passing—speed up footwork

PUNTERS: Ten punts out of bounds to each side
Ten punts for distance
(This means a 30 kick minimum)

SAFETY MEN: Receive fifteen punts (minimum)

GUARDS AND TACKLES: Fifteen forearm shivers on charging sled
At least one of each type block, both ways on bell-bottom dummies
Concentrate on extra blocks on your weakest point

These drills are to be done daily by everyone as designated. If you can't get them done before practice, do them after practice. No one is excused. The coaches will assist you in any drill, but the responsibility to get this work done each day will rest with the individual player.

Illus. 4

Other problems

With the many fundamentals and techniques of football to be learned on the athletic field, it seems that time would not be available for any of the other phases of the game. However, these problems are of utmost importance, and they should be given a fair amount of time in the practice schedule and a record should be kept on time spent in these activities. See Illustration 5.

Number of minutes for each activity

	1st week				2nd week				3rd week				TOTAL
DATE													
CONDITIONING													
LECTURES													
TRAINING RULES													
RULES DISCUSSIONS													
CHALK TALKS													
MOVIES													
QUARTERBACK SESSIONS													
STAFF MEETINGS													
PRE-GAME DRILL													

Illus. 5

Pre-game drill

Some time before the first regular game, a pre-game warm up drill should be devised. This will go far toward eliminating confusion when the players go out on the field for the first time before a crowd, and will assure the most efficient use of the pre-game time. This should be worked into the practice time schedule about a week prior to the first game. This warm up drill should take *exactly* 20 minutes.

Have all men assemble in the end zone that has been assigned to them. The captain or coach leads the players in calisthenics. Next, the players run a few wind sprints. This is done until the players have acquired a reasonably good rhythm. Team formations come next. Full teams should run signals for four minutes. After the team formations have been run, instruct the backs and ends to run pass patterns. The kickers will practice punting with the linemen going down under the kicks to tag the safety men receiving punts. Specialists, such as place kickers or kick off men, should drill for five minutes. This will consume the full 20-minute pre-game warm up period. See Illustration 6, page 13.

Player leadership in conditioning drills

Before a team is ready to participate in a full season of hard, rugged football, the men must be in the best of physical condition. It is advantageous to the entire squad to have every man participate in five minutes of calisthenics and warming up exercises before each strenuous practice period.

A well-planned player-leadership program is highly desirable. Through this procedure, every player has the opportunity at some time to lead the squad, which gives him valuable experience. See Illustration 7, page 13.

Any convenient formation may be used in giving calisthenics. Some coaches use a large circle formation for their conditioning

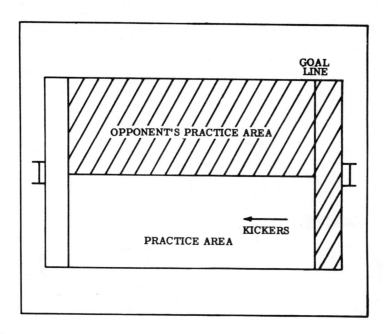

Illus. 6

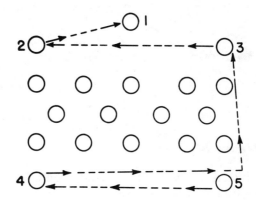

Illus. 7

COACH

drills; others use the regular three or four line squad method. See Illustration 8.

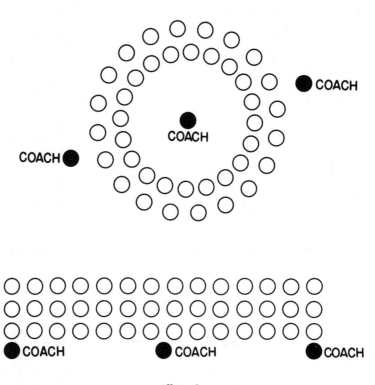

Illus. 8

Meeting schedule

Listed below is a meeting schedule for members of the varsity football squad that would appear on the bulletin board. Notice that there is a weekly shift in nights for each group. Meetings are at 7 p.m. in the school projection room. Make it a habit to be on time and help hold the length of the meetings to one hour. The topic numbers refer to the list of attached discussions.   The asterisk (°) refers to quarterback meetings scheduled for 8:30 p.m. on the dates indicated.

Week Before	Backs	Tackles	Guards	Ends	Centers	Topic
Dec. 1	M	T °	W	TH	F °	#1
Dec. 8	F °	M	T °	W	TH	#2
Dec. 15	TH	F °	M	T °	W	#3
Dec. 22	W	TH	F °	M	T °	#4
Jan. 3	T °	W	TH	F °	M	#5
Jan. 10	M	T °	W	TH	F °	#6
Jan. 17	F °	M	T °	W	TH	#7
Feb. 1	TH	F °	M	T °	W	#8

Mechanical apparatus

The major weakness in the mechanical apparatus designed and now in use is that it fails to provide life-like effects.   To include the life-like effects, both forward and lateral motion must be present.   Present day blocking and tackling apparatus does not fulfill its purpose to the author's way of thinking. *The improved apparatus must be simple in design and economical in construction.*

In our opinion "blocking armor" is one piece of apparatus that is valuable as an aid for blocking, since the wearer can react in the same way as would the defense in scrimmage.   The bulkiness of the armor is its only disadvantage because it acts as a hindrance to the wearer, resulting in a dislike for its use.

WEEKLY PRACTICE SCHEDULE

MONDAY

If we play on Saturday, Monday is a fairly easy day. We may work out in sweats. Bench men will usually scrimmage. The regulars will depart from practice early. We will always get a scout report on our next opponent. If movies are back, we will view them as a team. This is good for morale. If we play on Friday night, then Monday will be a hard workout, especially if our next contest is on Friday night. Coaches' meeting Monday night is the most important of the week. We will meet in the gymnasium office. Workout for two hours for reserves.

TUESDAY

Heavy night in the field. We should run opponent's plays that have been practiced on Monday by a reserve team. Fundamentals by positions for backs, line, and ends for *one* hour. Emphasis on defense and defensive plan for this week's game. We run two offensive units versus set defense our opponents might employ. Short meeting before practice to digest scout report and defensive plans. May show film for 15 minutes. Meeting is timed by captain and included in overall practice time. Workout for two hours on Tuesday.

WEDNESDAY

Heavy practice. Place two teams on offense and one on defense for thirty minutes. If possible, we will use a defensive team working against a scout team and a skeleton pass group for thirty minutes. Again we must devote one hour to fundamentals in breakdown work. This period is the backbone of a small college football program. We will drill approximately 15 or 20 minutes on kicking, returns, and conditioning. May conclude with relay. Workout for two hours on Wednesday.

THURSDAY

This is passing day. Two offensive teams versus one defensive team for forty-five minutes. Test pass protection and all patterns, old and new, to be used on Saturday, for thirty minutes. We will use three teams on offense rotating against a good line situation, and getting out of the hole. May have timed two-minute scrimmage.

Finish with some phase of kicking game. Workout for one and one-half hours on Thursday.

FRIDAY

Shorts or sweats, plus helmets. Backfield spend fifteen minutes on ball handling. Line, fifteen minutes on some essential fundamental they need. Review pass protection. Ends spend fifteen minutes on pass patterns and receiving. Devote remainder of practice to kick-off returns, punt returns, conversions, field goals, and punt protection. Review any new or special plays. Call squad together for Saturday instructions. Work out from thirty minutes to forty-five minutes.

SATURDAY

Day of Game.

Placement of coaches

Whenever your team is scrimmaging, whether dummy or alive, be sure that the assistant coaches have assignments. In order to view the team properly, one coach should be placed at each end of the line of scrimmage. Another coach (if staff permits) should be aligned with the backfield to check starts.

See Illustration: 9

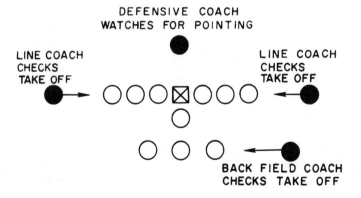

Illus. 9

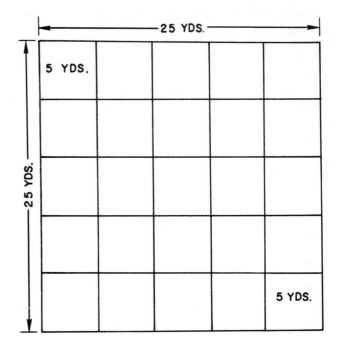

Illus. 10

Lined practice area

To improve practice organization, it is advantageous to have the practice area "lined." It helps the players, because they know exactly where to line up thus saving valuable time. With a lined area like the one shown in Illustration 10 the players always have a marker to line up on whether offense or defense is being taught. This method outlines five-yard squares for twenty-five yards.

Organization of practice field drills

Another method of saving time is to use yard lines as divisions for practice drills. The players would start on the forty-yard line and proceed into the end zone. See Illustration 11. The junior varsity and reserve squads are working in the opposite direction.

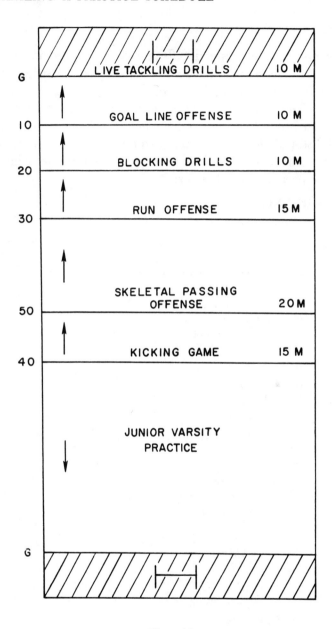

Illus. 11

Check sheet

Because of the many details involved in preparation of a squad, it is necessary to have a check list. Every assistant coach should have a copy of the check list in meetings and on the practice field. By having it on the practice field, the coach can circle the item that may have been overlooked. Without a check-list, practice organization can become a hit-or-miss proposition. The check-list below helps us determine what our practice periods should cover:

A. KICKING GAME
    1. *Punting Game*
        (a) Kicking
        (b) Receiving punts
        (c) Receiving punts inside 10-yard line
        (d) Punt protection
        (e) Punt coverage
        (f) Punt returns
        (g) Blocking punts
        (h) Rules
    2. *Kick-Off*
        (a) Alignment
        (b) Coverage
        (c) Return
        (d) Rules
    3. *Conversion*
        (a) Protection
        (b) Kicking conversion
        (c) Running conversion
        (d) Passing conversion
        (e) Rules

B. PASSING GAME
    1. *Offense*
        (a) Protection
        (b) Play assignments
        (c) Coverage
        (d) Rules

    2. *Defense*
      (a) Rushing passers
      (b) Delaying receivers
      (c) Coverage of flankers and men in motion
      (d) Individual assignments

C. RUNNING GAME
    1. Offensive plays
    2. Downfield blocking
    3. Ball carrying
    4. Ball handling
    5. Laterals
    6. Line blocking
    7. Trap blocking
    8. Block backers
    9. Blocking code
  10. Goal-line offense

D. DEFENSE
    1. Individual assignments—line fundamentals
    2. Play of linebackers
    3. Secondary play
    4. Live tackling
    5. Spread defense
    6. Goal-line defense

E. GENERAL
    1. Recovering fumbles
    2. Stance and starts
    3. Game strategy
    4. Consideration for squad morale
    5. Rules

NOTE:

There is never enough practice time devoted to *rules.*

Scrimmage day

Watching the Iowa team prepare for its Rose Bowl victory over Oregon State, I liked its organization for a scrimmage day.

This was a Friday practice before a Tuesday game. Head Coach Forest Evashevski followed the offense and kept a record of the calls.

A. CALISTHENICS (15 minutes)
  1. Led by co-captains
  2. Good warm-up

B. CALL SQUAD TOGETHER
  1. Announce two teams
  2. Extras on sidelines

C. OFFENSIVE TEAM (No. 1)
  1. Takes ball on own 20-yard line and two coaches officiate
  2. Scrimmage under game conditions

D. TEAM NO. 2
  1. Runs Oregon State offense
  2. Uses Oregon State defense

E. PUNTS, Team No. 1 returns

F. CONVERSIONS

G. FIELD GOALS

H. HEAD COACH keeps chart on quarterbacks

Grading sheet

I made up this grading sheet for the Los Angeles Rams' offensive ends and found it to be effective.

See Illustration: 12

X-Y-Z GRADE SHEET

GAME ——————
DATE ——————

NAME ——————

RUN	PASS	LEFT END				Y				RIGHT END			
		PASS		RUN		PASS		RUN		PASS		RUN	
		strong	weak	strong	weak	strong	weak	strong	weak	strong	weak	strong	weak
				on	off			on	off			on	off
1													
2													
3													
4													
5													
6													
7													
8													
9													
10													
11													
12													
13													
14													
15													
16													
17													
18													
19													
20													
21													

RUNNING
Total Plays ——————
Total points ——————
Bonus points ——————
Score ——————

PASSING
Total Plays ——————
Total points ——————
Bonus points ——————
Score ——————

Illus. 12

Friday workout

Watching Green Bay, under Lisle Blackbourn, work out on
Friday for a Sunday game (which would correspond to a
Thursday workout in college), I liked their practice program,
which was planned as follows:

A. CALISTHENICS
B. ENDS & BACKS..................Passing with No. 1 Quarterback.
C. LINE WITH No. 2
      QUARTERBACK ....Running plays.
                                      Practicing take-off.
                                      Special plays.
                                      Quarterback's alternate.
D. DEFENSIVE BACKS .. ..Pass-defense drills.
                                      Long-pass drill for one back only.
                                      Deflection drill.
E. OFFENSIVE TEAM ....vs....Expected defense in secondary and
                                      line.
                                      Emphasis both on running and
                                        passing, ½ each.
F. PLATOONS ....Use men for dummies.
G. KICKING DRILLS ....Kickoffs
                                      Conversions
                                        Field Goals
                                        Punt Returns
H. SIGNALS—ALL PASSING ONLY.
I. SHOWERS

Three practices daily

I have heard that necessity is the mother of invention and
in 1953 we were forced to alter our pre-season practice program. We liked the "three-a-day" program so well that we
have used it ever since that date. Most of all, our players like
the arrangements of workouts. Sid Gillman, a fine organizer,

introduced three practices a day with the Rams, and both players and coaches were pleased with the program.

We believe it has much to offer.

ORGANIZATION SCHEDULE
THREE PRACTICES DAILY

A. PURPOSES
1. For limited pre-season practice period before first contest.
2. For coaching staff that is small numerically or composed of part-time assistants.
3. For large squad that would be difficult to handle collectively with a limited coaching staff.

B. TIME TABLE OF THREE-A-DAY SESSIONS
1. First Day.
   (a) AM lecture: 9:00-9:55.
   (b) Practice as full team: 10:00-12:00.
   (c) PM lecture: 3:00-3:55.
   (d) Practice as full team: 4:00-6:00.
   (e) On first day entire team will drill both AM and PM.

2. Second Day.
   (a) AM lecture: 9:00-9:25.
   (b) Backs plus ends and two centers: 9:30-11:00.
   (c) PM lecture: 2:30-2:55.
   (d) Entire squad, including AM men: 3:00-4:30.
   (e) Line drills on plays practiced in AM.
   (f) Twilight lecture: 6:00-6:10.
   (g) Interior line plus two PM centers: 6:15-7:45.
   (h) Drills on plays for following day.

C. PRACTICE SCHEDULE VARIATIONS
1. AM, entire team; PM, backs and ends with two centers; Evening, interior line with two centers who did not work in the AM session.
2. AM, interior line; PM, backs and ends with two centers; evening, entire team with two other centers.
3. AM, entire team; PM, interior line; evening, backs and ends with two other centers.

D. DRILL PROGRAM IMMEDIATELY FOLLOWING
   CALISTHENICS
   1. Calisthenics.
      (a) Circle run, both directions.
      (b) Six 100-yard dashes, half speed.
   2. Drills.
      (a) Ends: Footwork drill.
      (b) Backs: Two-line drills with one and two footballs.
      (c) Interior line: Take-off drill on ball with cadence.

E. DRILLS BY POSITIONS
   1. Line.
      (a) One-on-one.
      (b) Hit and react.
   2. Backs.
      (a) Production drill.
      (b) Technique drill.
   3. Ends.
      (a) Individual route.
      (b) One-on-one.

One coach for 125 candidates

Sometimes a coach is required to handle a large group of men alone. This often happens in high school during spring practice when his assistants are assigned to the various spring sports. Ed Austin at Mark Keppel High School was faced with this problem. He had to handle 125 boys alone for a portion of spring practice. His practice organization follows:

It should be noted that Mark Keppel employs the single wing and the drills are made up of the fundamentals needed to make the offense effective.

1. Start practice in rows of ten. Have them line up at double arm interval and step forward to a line.
2. Have them set in the line stance or a backfield stance.
3. Check the stance and remove the players who need considerable help. They report to a senior who has a good line stance.

4. The remainder on a command step forward, run 10 yards and line up again facing the *opposite* direction.

5. The next line steps up and gets set on a command and then runs through the first line and falls in behind it.

6. As each line comes forward, make corrections as quickly as possible. Boys who need special attention report to the senior. The senior works with them until he feels they can get back in the line. See Illustration 13.

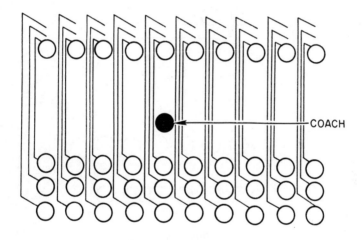

Illus. 13

7. The players move forward and keep the blank spots filled so that only one line is not complete. Run everybody until their stances are good.

8. Next, they all cross step with the left foot and then cross step with the right foot. This is from a line stance. Backfield men use similar technique when running a sweep.

9. Then run a pull-out drill for linemen or a cross step drill as backfield men run out past the end of the line. They loop and run to form a new line. Go right first and then left coming back. See Illustration 14.

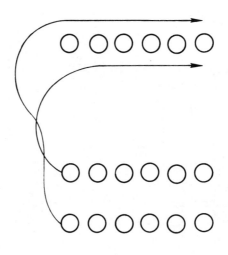

Illus. 14

10. In single-wing football it is important that all backs, ends, and guards know how to cut at 90-degree angles without pointing until they actually cut. This is accomplished by use of the military flank step. Use two lines for this drill and have them run a pattern starting with a walk. Have them speed up as they gain confidence and ability. See Illustration 15.

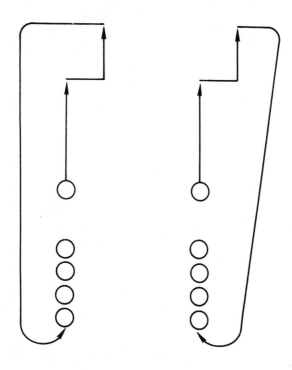

Illus. 15

11. This allows both right and left cuts. Lay out a line to follow and force them to cut without drifting. This drill produces continuous action.
12. Next comes blocking through drill. Explain and demonstrate before they execute. Line up five lines of tall bags *held* at a 45 angle pointed towards the line of players.
13. The blockers come at walk, dip their shoulders and lift with their legs on the bags. The weight of the bag will force good position with the legs up under the body.
14. Run everyone through with the same men holding. Then send the front row out to hold while the holders go to the end of the line. Then go all through this procedure again.
15. Go one way on the right shoulder and come back on the left side.

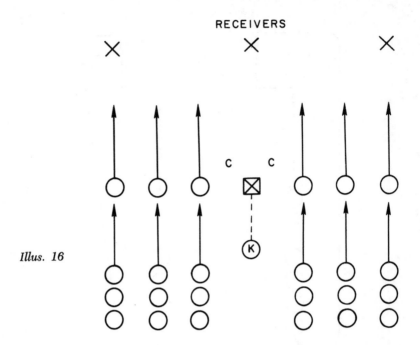

Illus. 16

16. Practice kicking by having the players line up in lines of six behind the kicker. The centers are out in front in a group and take turns snapping the ball. See Illustration 16.
17. Each kicker adjusts his depth to the center's ability to snap the ball.
18. Use three rows of backs to receive.
19. The first line moves forward and lines up in spread punt formation and goes down to cover the kick. They tag the receivers or hold off on a fair catch.
20. The receiver runs the ball back to the center and then follows the next wave going downfield to cover.
21. This drill provides the following:
    (a) Kicking practice for all the kickers.
    (b) Receiving practice in congested areas.
    (c) Teaches the players that if they run hard they can beat the ball.

(d) Speeds everything up because the men stay at the other end of the line and get ready for the next kick while the ball is in the air.

(e) After the lines are all down at the other end of the field the receivers become kickers, if possible, and the kickers become receivers.

(f) The centers start going down with the lines, when the numbers work out, so that the last center goes down with the last line.

22. The above schedule should consume one hour of practice time.

23. Next, break them up into touch football games for twenty minutes, plus ten minutes for organizing teams.

24. Send all players in except specialists: punters, kick-off men, field goal men, receivers, and holders. Let them work with or without centers for thirty minutes depending upon your goal for that practice.

25. As the squad progresses, eliminate stance drills and separate line from backs. Have passing drills for the ends and backs.

26. This is important. When working with a large squad a good rule to follows is: *Anyone who fools around or insists on loafing leaves the field, but can try out again the next afternoon.*

27. Passing drills are replaced by pass defense drills.

28. Touch football games for the backs and ends become passing and pass defense games.

29. Next, all drill time is reduced and touch football is replaced by a team organization schedule. The players run teams against the bags while pass protection is explained.

30. This latter phase leaves a large group of players watching, but interest can be held if it is used as a *demonstration* period instead of merely talking, or a drill on plays by one or two teams. Remember you have 125 players.

FILM EXCHANGE CHART

A problem in pro football involves the exchange of film. Since each team plays the other twice, and all are allowed to switch pictures, organization of a film exchange chart is essential.

Illustration 17 is only the first page of a three page chart.

FILM EXCHANGE (Pictures to be received)

SEPT. 17: for Sept. 29 Preparation

PHILADELPHIA EAGLES		Promised	Rec'd.	Reminder	Returned
Steelers — Eagles	Sept. 2	Sept. 15	Sept. 19		Sept. 30
°Eagles — Bears	Sept. 8	Sept. 11			
49'ers — Eagles	Sept. 22	Sept. 23			

SEPT. 26: for Oct. 6 Preparation

SAN FRANCISCO 49'ers

	Promised	Rec'd.	Reminder	Returned
°49'ers — Giants	Aug. 18		√	√
°49'ers — Browns	Sept. 1		√	√
°49'ers — Cards	Sept. 7	Sept. 8	√	√
°Cards — 49'ers	Sept. 29	Sept. 30		

OCT. 3: for Oct. 13 Preparation

DETROIT LIONS

°Giants — Lions	Sept. 22	Sept. 23
°Lions — Colts	Sept. 29	Oct. 3
°Packers — Lions	Oct. 6	Oct. 7

OCT. 10: for Oct. 20 Preparation

CHICAGO BEARS

Eagles — Bears	Sept. 8	Copy
Colts — Bears	Oct. 6	
°49'ers — Bears	Oct. 13	

Illus. 17

° Duplicate to be made before returning film.

Defensive practice

When Buddy Parker was coaching the Detroit Lions, his practice program for a Thursday was to emphasize defense. I found his organization to be different, but very effective. The day I visited practice, the Lions were preparing to meet the Los Angeles Rams, and had an excellent workout. Below is a partial schedule:

1. Run six 100-yard runs at half speed to warm up.
2. Take calisthenics for stretching.
3. Kicking game follows:
    (a) Ends covering
    (b) Kick-offs
    (c) Conversions
    (d) Field goals
4. Pass defense every day.
5. Run Lions' patterns vs Rams' defense.
6. Team defense (Lions) with ends and middle line backer; ends rush against the offensive backs.
7. Pass defense against Rams' patterns.
8. One unit on defense and number one quarterback throws passes in opponents' patterns. This provides him with added practice and keeps tempo up.
9. Six 50-yard runs for line across field at half speed.
10. Agility drills for line across field.
11. Defensive shield drill.
    (a) Roll out
    (b) Pursue
    (c) Inside
12. Showers.

Part II

THE OFFENSIVE GAME

3

THE RUNNING GAME

Twist, turn, lunge, plunge, but keep going.

—Robert Zuppke

RUNNING IS ONE OF THE MOST IMPORTANT PHASES OF THE GAME of football. If a player is unable to run well he will be ineffective in the other skills necessary to play. Bierman believes that running is of prime importance:

In the first place, football is a game of movement. To get anywhere, the ball, that tricky, slippery prolate spheroid of cowhide, must be pushed over the other fellow's goal line . . . all else is of no avail until this important factor has been licked. To lick it adequately, the team on offense has some running to do. By the same token, of course, the team on defense must run to thwart the offense. *Running is the basic fundamental of the game.*[1]

Discussions by football coaches attending the 1953 Whittier College Coaching Clinic conducted by the author indicated

---

[1] By permission from *Winning Football,* by B. W. Bierman, p. 8. Copyright, 1937. McGraw-Hill Book Company, Inc.

that the great majority of coaches present believed that running played the *most* important part in carrying on a practice session.

Running can become drudgery if not properly organized. Since a player has to run to get in good condition, he might just as well do his running in an interesting manner and at the same time learn basic skills and team play.

Not all drills should be practiced each day, but the time should be allotted to specific drills according to the need set up by the coaches at the beginning of each week. A record of the time spent on each drill should be kept on a practice time chart. See Illustration 18a.

Number of minutes for each drill

	1st week					2nd week					3rd week					TOTAL
DATE																
SIGNAL DRILL																
SKELETON DRILL																
DUMMY SCRIMMAGE																
ACTUAL SCRIMMAGE																
CADENCE DRILL																
PULL-OUT DRILL																
SQUARE DRILL																

Illus. 18a

1. HOW TO DRILL FOR STANCE

The purpose of this drill is to stress the importance of a proper stance and to practice that stance.

INSTRUCTIONS:

(1) Everything in football begins with a balanced stance. No matter how much strength or speed a back might possess, it will be wasted without a good stance. All backfield men *must* develop the proper stance, whether it be the three-point stance, four-point stance, or crouch.

(2) After the warm-up drill, line the backs up according to positions and examine their stance. In this manner any suggestions made to one fullback will be heard by all the fullbacks.

(3) After examining each back's stance, have the players take several starts on a signal.

(4) This is a must drill early in the season. Two minutes a day is sufficient to inspect the stance of four complete backfields.

(5) It is also a good check-up drill late in the season when the players tend to become careless.

(6) The formation shown in Illustration 18b, which shows a shifting drill, can also be used in checking stance.

Illus. 18b. Shifting Drill. Quarterback stationed in front of backfield gives cadence and orders shifting right or left.

2. HOW TO DRILL FOR COMPETITION IN WARM-UP

The object of this drill is to provide a ball-handing warm-up for the backs.

INSTRUCTIONS:

(1) This practice stunt has been called "Allen's Alley."

(2) The players should form groups of five or six which run in circles with the players spaced about 10 yards apart.

(3) Each group uses one ball. The players should throw it around the circle in any direction, and to any man in the group.

(4) Derive competition by having each group complete as many passes as possible in a one-minute period.

(5) No player is allowed to return the ball to a player he received it from.

(6) Everyone must keep moving. No one may stop to catch the ball.

(7) Appoint one player in each group to count the number of *completed* passes.

(8) Have a manager keep time with a stopwatch.

(9) This is an excellent competitive warm-up drill.

(10) See Illustration 19a; see 19b for another warm-up drill.

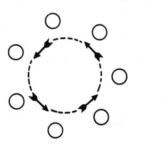

Illus. 19a

COACH

Illus. 19b. Warm-Up Drill for Backs and Ends. Divide the group equally, half as ball carriers and half as receivers. The ball carriers run forward and hand off to the receivers. Begin at slow pace and finish at top speed. When the backs become proficient at handing off and receiving, two or three balls may be used.

3. HOW TO DRILL FOR THE TAKE-OFF

All coaches are interested in the three- and five-yard speed of the backfield men. This drill is designed to improve the take-off ability of the backs.

INSTRUCTIONS:

(1) Station the two best backfields in opposite directions.

(2) Each unit has a center with one football.

(3) A coach is stationed between the two backfields.

(4) The backfields run in alternating sequence. Each unit runs five yards and returns.

(5) The coach can view both units and offer suggestions without moving.

(6) This is also an excellent conditioning drill if the distance is increased to 15 yards.

(7) The drill should be used all season.

(8) See Illustrations 20a and 20b, page 42.

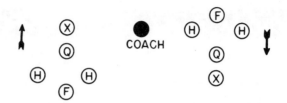

Illus. 20a

Illus. 20b

4.   HOW TO DRILL FOR CARRIAGE OF THE BALL

Backfield men who do not hold the ball properly are in constant danger of fumbling.   The object of this drill is to teach backs proper carriage of the football.

INSTRUCTIONS:

(1) Station two defensive linemen on the line of scrimmage. Position them in the area for an off-tackle run.

(2) Locate a center on offensive with three footballs.

(3) Have the backs line up at a depth of five yards and assume their stance.

(4) A coach stationed in the backfield and outside of the defense gives the snap signal.

(5) The ball carrier receives a pass from center and runs between the two defensive linemen.

(6) As the ball carrier comes between the linemen, they try to knock the ball out of the grasp of the ball carrier by punching at the ball or grabbing the ball or an arm.

(7) This drill should be run to both right and left side.

(8) See Illustrations 21a and 21b.

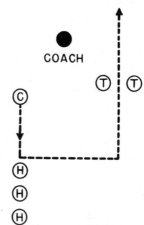

Illus. 21a

Illus. 21b. Drill for Eliminating Fumbles. Quarterback calls a series of plays that require each back in turn to run between two linemen, who slam the dummies at him as he goes through.

5. HOW TO DRILL FOR FUMBLE PREVENTION

The object of this drill is to aid the runners in avoiding fumbling habits. The following drill is effective in teaching a back to hold tightly to the ball.

INSTRUCTIONS:

(1) The players form two lines about two yards apart.

(2) Use five men in each line.

(3) Each ball carrier runs the gantlet while the men in the line attempt to snatch the ball.

(4) No. 1 runs the gantlet and then takes his position next to 14. No. 5 moves behind 4, and so on, as the entire line moves up. Runners hold ball with *one* hand only.

(5) See Illustrations 22a and 22b.

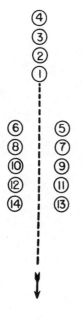

Illus. 22a   Illus. 22b

6. HOW TO DRILL FOR FALLING WITH THE BALL

The purpose of this drill is to teach the ball carriers to fall with the ball correctly.

INSTRUCTIONS:

(1) Two bags are lined up five yards apart.

(2) The bags should stand alone, needing no one to hold them up.

(3) Each ball carrier runs through the bags and executes evasive action as if he were being tackled. After getting past the second bag he deliberately falls to the ground, cupping the ball and pulling it into his body.

(4) Use two footballs so that the waiting man always has a ball ready. The ball carrier passes back to the second man in line after each try.

(5) See Illustration 23.

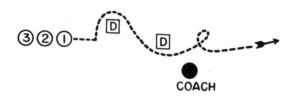

Illus. 23

7. HOW TO DRILL FOR RECOVERING THE BALL

The purpose of this drill is to teach the players how to fall on the football and how to scoop it.

INSTRUCTIONS:

(1) The center, with a football, is the instigator of this drill.

(2) The other players are stationed in the lines facing the center.

(3) The center tosses the ball to both sides.

(4) Each time that the center tosses the ball he calls "offense" or "defense" to specify the maneuver to be executed.

(5) If the signal is "offense," then the player scoops up the ball and runs with it.

(6) If the signal is "defense," then the player falls on the ball and secures it as a recovered fumble.

8. HOW TO DRILL FOR BALL HANDLING

The purpose of this drill is to teach the backfield men the correct method of receiving the ball and to practice starting on a signal.

INSTRUCTIONS:

(1) Line up a center with three footballs. Have ready a complete backfield.

(2) The quarterback calls signals.

(3) He hands off to each back, one at a time, with as little delay as possible.

(4) The ball carriers receive the hand-offs and run, using dodging tactics, for 10 yards.

(5) Repeat the drill for 20 minutes.

(6) Use as many units like this as is feasible.

(7) See Illustration 24.

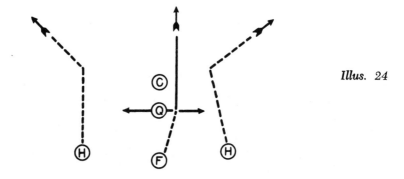

Illus. 24

9. HOW TO DRILL FOR MULTIPLE BALL HANDLING

The purpose of this drill is to teach the players ball handling. This is an excellent warm-up drill for all backfield men.

INSTRUCTIONS:

(1) The players are divided into groups of eight. In each group, two lines of four players are placed so that they face each other.

(2) No. 1 hands off to 2, 2 to 3, 3 to 4, and so on until the end of the line.

(3) After each player has passed the ball, he stops at the position occupied by the player to whom he passed. Thus the formation is kept.

(4) When 8 receives the ball, he passes it back to 7, 7 to 6, 6 to 5, etc.

(5) The first time around the ball should be handed to the next player as the ball carrier goes by at full speed.

(6) The second time it should be flipped when he is a yard away.

(7) The third time when he is three yards away.

(8) The players enjoy this drill, and competition can be arranged in groups.

(9) See Illustration 25.

Illus. 25

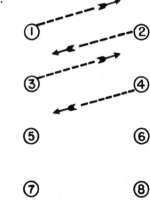

10. HOW TO DRILL FOR REVERSE HANDLING

The purpose of this drill is to teach the players ball handling for the reverse.   In addition, it provides extra running.

INSTRUCTIONS:

(1) The backfield men line up behind the offensive center.

(2) Two lines of players (backs) station themselves so that they are in position to play offensive end.

(3) The snap goes to No. 1 who gives the ball to 3 as he goes by. No. 2 starts running and times himself so as to receive the ball from 3 as they go past each other.   The exchange takes place behind 1.

(4) They line up again at the end of the lines to keep the drill moving.

(5) This may be used as a warm-up drill.

(6) See Illustration 26.

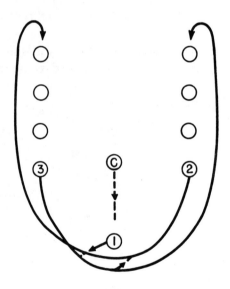

Illus. 26

11. HOW TO DRILL FOR END AROUND

The real purpose of this drill is to provide the backs with more ball handling and to develop skill on the end around.

INSTRUCTIONS:

(1) The players line up with the ball handler behind the center and two lines of backs.

(2) One line behind the offensive halfback.

(3) One line behind the offensive end.

(4) The snap goes to No. 1 who gives the ball to 2.

(5) No. 2 stops, whirls and passes to 3, who is in line with the center.

(6) No. 2 goes to the end of line *B* so as to keep the lines even.

(7) This drill should be worked from both the left and right sides.

(8) See Illustration 27.

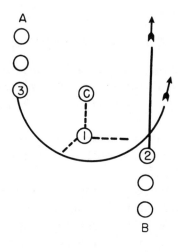

Illus. 27

12. HOW TO DRILL FOR PITCH-OUTS

The purpose of this drill is to provide practice in ball handling and practice pitch-outs.

INSTRUCTIONS:

(1) The ball handler is lined up behind the center.

(2) The ball receivers are located in the normal halfback's position.

(3) The center snaps the ball to No. 1, who receives it at a regular signal count.

(4) No. 2 starts from a position far enough back so that he does not make 1 wait for him. No. 1 throws a sidearm pitch out as 2 goes by at full speed.

(5) No. 1 runs parallel to 2, and 2 passes it back to 1 just as they go past center.   No. 1 must be ready for a quick start.

(6) See Illustration 28.

13. HOW TO DRILL FOR SPINNING

In a single-wing type of offense, it is necessary to develop a spinner series to create deception.   The purpose of this drill is to provide practice in faking and hiding the ball.

INSTRUCTIONS:

(1) Two offensive centers are employed in this drill.

(2) The two backs who do the most spinning are the fullback and left halfback.

(3) Place these two men together *every day* and have them drill spinning. Footwork is of prime importance.

(4) Fullbacks spin to the right, stepping with the right foot first.   Left halfbacks spin to the left, stepping with the left foot first.

(5) This is an absolute *must* drill for spinning backs.

(6) See Illustration 29.

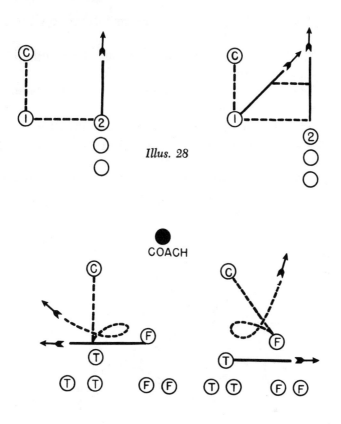

Illus. 28

COACH

Illus. 29

14. HOW TO DRILL FOR THE LATERAL PASS

The object of this drill is to provide training in ball handing for the backs. It is also a good warm-up drill.

INSTRUCTIONS:

(1) Form two lines of players about eight yards apart.

(2) The *two* front men, one of them with the ball, run down the field 30 yards and return.

(3) They make as many lateral passes as they can during the run.

(4) A player should run three or four steps with the ball before he returns the pass to the other player.

(5) The receiver of the pass must be sure he is *behind* the passer when the ball is thrown.

(6) This drill may be used to conclude practice, with the manager recording the number of good passes made by each pair.

(7) A variation of this drill is to have *six* players spread out. They take the ball down the field and back, using as many lateral passes as they wish.

(8) See Illustration 30.

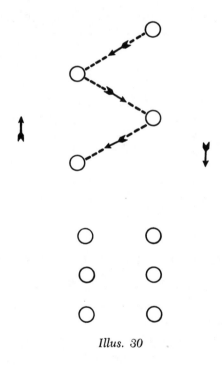

Illus. 30

15. HOW TO DRILL FOR RECEIVING PITCH-OUTS

The purpose of this drill is to teach the ball carrier to accept the ball from the quarterbacks and initiate a run. Also, it will teach the backs how to hold the ball and how to cut up-field.

INSTRUCTIONS:

(1) The center and quarterback line up to begin a play.

(2) The halfback and fullback take the regular offensive positions.

(3) The quarterback takes the ball from the center and alternates pitch-outs to the backs. The runners go about five yards beyond the line of scrimmage and cut.

(4) Defensive halfbacks can be placed in the secondary to simulate a tackler, and thus give the ball carrier a hurdle to evade.

(5) The coach should observe the carriage of the ball each time.

16. HOW TO DRILL FOR DECEPTION

In modern football, faking and deception is a must. This drill is designed to improve deception in the backfield.

INSTRUCTIONS:

(1) Line up one complete backfield with a center and two footballs.

(2) Place another backfield on defense in a selected area.

(3) The backfield on defense will grade the offensive back-field on technique, carriage of the ball, take off, and deception.

(4) A third backfield is huddled and ready to go on offense.

(5) Three units rotate in rapid sequence.

(6) With this competitive drill the coach can get better results than by projecting himself on the scene.

(7) Often the men will pick up valuable cues that a coach might overlook.

(8) The drill motivates the players to do a better job of fooling the enemy.

(9) If running the reverse, place the backs in a position normally occupied by the defensive right tackle and right end.

(10) See Illustration 31.

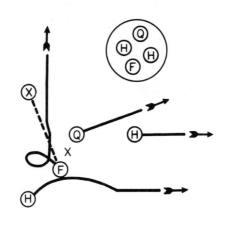

X-DESIGNATES EXCHANGE

Illus. 31

17. HOW TO DRILL FOR BALL EXCHANGING BE-TWEEN THE FULLBACK AND WINGBACK

The purpose of this drill is to develop a smooth exchange be-tween the fullback and the wingback.

INSTRUCTIONS:

(1) The secret of precise ball handling is "breakdown work" —division of the backs into pairs for practice.

(2) Place the fullbacks and wingbacks together in pairs without a center.

(3) The fullback has a ball in his hands.

(4) They go through the mechanics of faking and handing off at half speed. These are the *only two* mechanics they drill on.

(5) The fullback holds the ball and also counts cadence.

(6) Add a center as soon as the players are ready for one.

(7) Five minutes of this drill each day will improve the backfield's timing.

(8) A coach rotates from one group to another making com-ments.

(9) See Illustration 32.

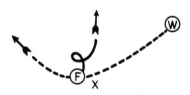

X-DESIGNATES EXCHANGE

Illus. 32

18. HOW TO DRILL FOR BALL EXCHANGING BE-TWEEN THE TAILBACK AND FULLBACK

The purpose of this drill is to develop a smooth exchange between the fullback and the tailback.

INSTRUCTIONS:

(1) Place the fullbacks and tailbacks together in pairs without a center.

(2) The fullback has a ball in his hands.

(3) They go through the mechanics of faking and handing off at half speed.   These are the *only two* mechanics they drill on.

(4) The fullback holds the ball and also counts cadence.

(5) Add a center as soon as the players are ready for one.

(6) Five minutes of this drill each day will improve the backfield's timing.

(7) A coach rotates from one group to another making comments.

(8) See Illustration 33.

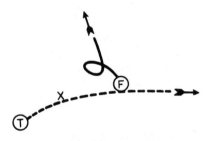

X-DESIGNATES EXCHANGE

Illus. 33

19. HOW TO DRILL FOR BALL EXCHANGING BE-TWEEN CENTER AND QUARTERBACK

T-formation quarterbacks are the life line of the "T." The purpose of this drill is to perfect the center-quarterback exchange.

INSTRUCTIONS:

(1) Line up three centers and three quarterbacks.

(2) Drill them together as often as possible, both before and after squad practice.

(3) Have the quarterback take the ball in his right hand alone.

(4) He should not use two hands until he can master the exchange with one.

(5) This will insure correct position of the hands, because he cannot accept the ball with one unless it is correct.

(6) After the quarterback has mastered the one-hand exchange, allow the use of the left hand.

(7) See Illustration 34.

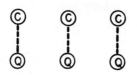

Illus. 34

20. HOW TO DRILL FOR BUCK LATERAL PITCH-OUTS

This drill can be applied to any quarterback mechanic whether in T or single-wing formation. The object is to train and develop inexperienced quarterbacks in the fundamentals of the buck lateral series.

INSTRUCTIONS:

(1) Start drilling quarterbacks on a basketball court rather than the football field.

(2) Have the quarterbacks wear basketball shoes because they provide greater traction in performing pivots.

(3) The long lateral to the tailback can be thrown more accurately indoors due to lack of air resistance.

(4) When the quarterback becomes familiar with his mechanics by drilling with the coach, add a center and three backs.

(5) Fifteen minutes indoors are much more valuable than the same time outdoors.

21. HOW TO DRILL FOR RUNNING FORM

The purpose of this drill is to enable the backs to develop powerful running forms with a solid base, from which they can change directions quickly.

INSTRUCTIONS:

(1) The backs who are going to carry the ball line up single file.

(2) These ball carriers run downfield and straddle an imaginary plank 18 inches wide.

(3) After running a short distance (10 yards), they should break to the right or left and repeat breaking several times.

(4) This drill is especially good for straight-line runners.

(5) See Illustration 36.

22. HOW TO DRILL FOR HANDING OFF

The purpose of this drill is to practice handing off to a single receiver.

INSTRUCTIONS:

(1) Station a center on offense with two footballs.

(2) Place a quarterback behind the center in his regular T-formation position.

(3) Line up one receiver, and have the quarterback run through this drill for five minutes.

(4) Place another halfback in the backfield and the quarterback can alternate to either side.

(5) It is the responsibility of the men receiving the ball to take it from the quarterback, rather than the latter going out and giving it to the receivers.

(6) Tell the quarterbacks to handle the ball as if it were a "big bubble."

(7) See Illustration 35.

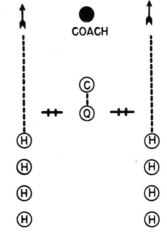

Illus. 35

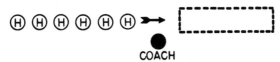

Illus. 36

23. HOW TO DRILL RUNNING LOW

The purpose of this drill is to teach the ball carriers to drive low and hard. Practice in running under control so that it would be possible to change directions is also obtained.
INSTRUCTIONS:
(1) Place two portable posts eight yards apart with a rope across them.   Arrange the posts so that the rope can be set at three different heights.

(2) The rope should be adjustable from three to three and one-half feet from the ground.

(3) Station a dummy on the other side of the rope about five yards back.

(4) Pass the ball to the backs who are lined up single file.

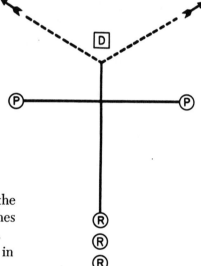

(5) The back plunges into the line and under the rope. He then side-steps the dummy either to the right or left.

(6) A second set of portable posts may be placed beyond the dummy.

(7) This is better than the old method of tieing a clothes line between the goal posts.

(8) A center is optional in this drill.

(9) See Illustration 37a (right).

24. HOW TO DRILL FOR DRIVING POWER

The object of this drill is to develop driving power on the part of the ball carrier.
INSTRUCTIONS:
(1) Stack together a dozen dummies. Always attempt to

keep them in as circular a formation as possible.

(2) Place five players on the perimeter of the circle to replace the dummies when they are knocked down.

(3) Each ball carrier plows through the dummies, attempting to blast them apart and at the same time maintain his balance.

(4) After plowing through, No. 1 passes back to 2 and takes 7's place.   No. 4 goes to the rear of the running line, while 5 to 1 reset the dummies.

(5) See Illustration 37b; see 37c for another driving-power drill.

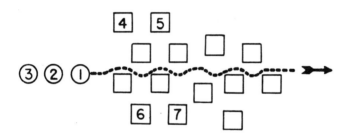

Illus. 37b

Illus. 37c.   Fireman's Carry.   Run ten yards and reverse positions.

25. HOW TO DRILL FOR OPEN-FIELD RUNNING

The object of this drill is to teach the ball carriers open-field tactics such as spinning, weaving, dodging, straight-arming, and ball changing.

INSTRUCTIONS:

(1) The dummies are lined up in a tandem about seven yards apart.

(2) One player must hold each bag.

(3) If air dummies are used the players can work on fundamentals because they can be moved around.

(4) The players holding the bags can lift and maneuver them to create life-like situations.

(5) Ball carriers use straight-arm, weaving tactics, as well as ball changing, as they cut.

(7) See Illustration 38.

26. HOW TO DRILL FOR THE STRAIGHT-ARM

The purpose of this drill is to develop and perfect use of the straight-arm and to practice ball-changing ability.

INSTRUCTIONS:

(1) The bags are lined up about seven yards apart.

(2) Five bags to the line are used.

(3) The ball carrier runs in a weaving fashion through the bags.

(4) As he approaches each bag he executes a straight-arm maneuver.

(5) He may use the straight-arm as a thrust on the dummy, or a thrust and lever for a reverse pivot.

(6) Use as many units as feasible.

(7) See Illustration 39.

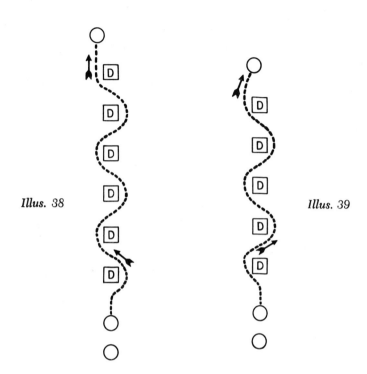

Illus. 38   *Illus. 39*

27. HOW TO DRILL FOR PIVOTING

The purpose of this drill is to practice driving through a hole and pivoting away from tacklers. It will provide practice for the linebackers in stalking the runner as he comes through the hole.

INSTRUCTIONS:

(1) Place two dummies or inactive players about five feet apart on the line of scrimmage.

(2) Station an active linebacker between them and five yards back.

(3) The ball carrier drives through the hole between the dummies, lowers his shoulders, contacts the linebacker with his forearm and attempts to pivot away from him.

(4) This same drill may be used with a blocker going ahead of the ball carrier.

(5) This is an excellent drill for the linebackers as well as the playing backs.

(6) See Illustration 40.

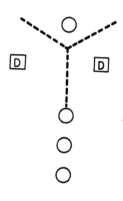

Illus. 40

28. HOW TO DRILL FOR SIDESTEPPING AND STIFF-ARMING

The object of this drill is to teach the ball carriers to stiff-arm and side-step tacklers.

INSTRUCTIONS:

(1) Station a man wearing shoulder pads and head gear in a semi-crouch position. He should be facing the line of ball carriers.

(2) Place the ball carriers in a straight line.

(3) Give the first and second man in line a football.

(4) The ball carrier runs toward the defensive man with the protective equipment.

(5) As the runner approaches the defensive man, he goes either to the right or left side.

(6) The defensive man moves forward as a tackler, but *without* actually tackling.

(7) The runner tries to get his hand on the head gear or shoulder pads as he executes his right or left movement.

(8) The runner then passes the ball back to the man next in line.

29. HOW TO DRILL FOR OFFENSIVE MANEUVERS

The purpose of this drill is to teach the ball carriers to become proficient in various maneuvers that will enable them to dodge tacklers.

INSTRUCTIONS:

(1) Split the ball carriers into two groups.

(2) Each group has a coach lined up behind it.

(3) First, have all the ball carriers practice these maneuvers in a group: (a) Simple side step with straight-arm, (b) The cross-over, (c) The limp leg, and (d) The pivot.

(4) Then have the ball carriers individually carry the ball and execute these maneuvers, one at a time.

(5) Have them begin by executing the side step with a straight-arm. Next they use the cross-over, and so forth.

(6) After these drills have been practiced three or four times, make them more complicated.

(7) Have the ball carrier fake, change the ball from one arm to the other, straight-arm, and pivot.

(8) Have the backs run directly at the coach on these drills.

(9) The coach should make it as complicated and difficult as he can for the runner to dodge him.

30. HOW TO DRILL FOR DODGING

This drill is designed to develop dodging ability and maneuverability on the part of the ball carrier.

INSTRUCTIONS:

(1) Scatter a dozen dummies in prone positions.

(2) The dummies should be fairly close together.

(3) Each ball carrier runs through the maze of dummies, striving for speed and sureness of balance.

(4) Use as many groups of dummies as feasible.

(5) See Illustration 41.

31. HOW TO DRILL FOR STUNTS

The object of this drill is to provide practice in the change of pace, stiff-arm, cut-back, and pivot. These maneuvers are must skills for backs to master.

INSTRUCTIONS:

(1) Divide the squad of backs evenly.

(2) Form two lines facing each other, 10 yards apart.

(3) The offensive man runs straight at the defensive man and performs one of the stunts in attempting to get away from the tackler.

(4) This drill can be used in regular scrimmage style or dummy fashion.

(5) Linemen may be used in this drill as a means of improving their coordination.

(6) Practicing backfield stunts is a player's own responsibility. Each back should devote at least five minutes on individual stunts. This should be done in addition to the time allowed on the daily schedule.

(7) See Illustration 42.

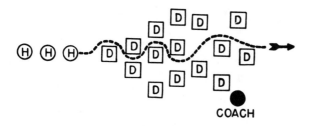

Illus. 41

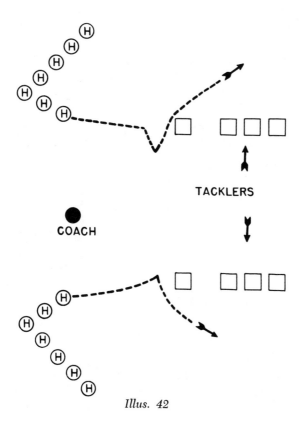

Illus. 42

32. HOW TO DRILL FOR HARDER-RUNNING BACKS

Many backs think they are running hard when actually they are not.   They may be running fast, but not with power.   This drill is designed to develop that power.

INSTRUCTIONS:

(1) Station two *linemen* (tackle) on defense with dummies.

(2) The dummies are held against each other at the base, and the holders face slightly toward the ball carrier.   The dummies make a "V" opening which is at a height comparable to the ball carrier.

(3) Have the holders grasp their *arms* around the dummy near the top, rather than hold on by the handles.

(4) Line up ball carriers five yards from the dummies and have them attempt to split the dummies.

Illus. 43a

(5) It is very embarrassing for the ball carrier if he fails to break through or, worse still, if he bounces off on his back.

(6) The holders have a rough job and should be changed every fifth man.

(7) There is little danger of injury in this drill.

(8) It is a good morale drill for linemen versus backs.

(9) See Illustrations 43a and 43 b.

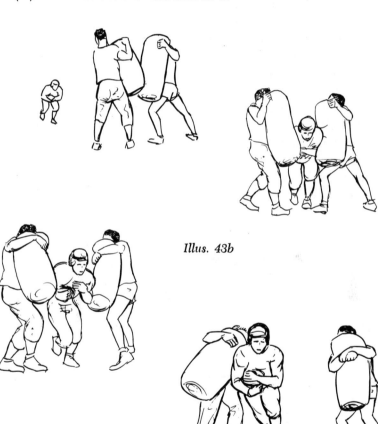

Illus. 43b

33. HOW TO DRILL FOR ALERT BALL-RUNNING

The fullback often doesn't hit the correct hole after spinning and thus doesn't make adequate yardage.   The purpose of this drill is to allow the fullback to pick the holes as they open, forcing him to keep his eyes open.

INSTRUCTIONS:

(1) Line up one complete offensive team.

(2) Place eight dummies on defensive to represent a six-man line and two linebackers.

(3) Any play is called where the fullback keeps the ball, but without his knowing what play has been signaled.

(4) The remainder of the men know the exact play.

(5) The ball is centered to the fullback who makes his fake to the tailback.   He must run under control until he sees the hole opening and goes for that spot.

(6) With this drill the fullback will keep his eyes open because he isn't sure where the hole will be.

(7) See Illustration 44.

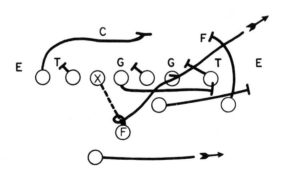

Illus. 44

34. HOW TO DRILL FOR CROSS-STEPPING

All backs must learn to run hard and be able to use different maneuvers to break open. The object of this drill is to teach backfield men cross-stepping for open-field running.

INSTRUCTIONS:

(1) Line up two rows of four automobile tires.

(2) Single tires should be used in this drill.

(3) Place the tires about two feet apart.

(4) In this drill, the left foot steps into tire No. 1, the right foot swings across into tire No. 2, the left foot crosses back into tire No. 3, and on through in that order.

(5) This tire drill is most useful during the first two weeks of practice. It may be used as a "limbering up" drill throughout the season.

(6) Boxes or ropes may be substituted for tires.

(7) See Illustration 45.

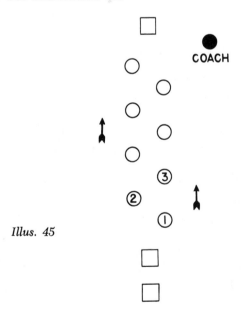

COACH

Illus. 45

35. HOW TO DRILL FOR KNEE ACTION

The purpose of this drill is to develop high knee action when running.

INSTRUCTIONS:

(1) Secure some old automobile tires and have the backs run through them daily.

(2) Place the tires about one yard apart and piled three deep so that the backs will have to bring the knees up high in order to step out of the tires.

(3) The players should line up and take turns running through the tires.

(4) The left foot should step into the first tire, the right foot into the second tire, and on through in that order.

(5) Linemen may be used in this drill. They enjoy this type of practice and it helps to develop the body balance.

(6) See Illustration 46.

36. HOW TO DRILL FOR CHANGING DIRECTION

The purpose of the drill is to provide training for the backfield men in changing directions as they run.

INSTRUCTIONS:

(1) Place 10 tires in an even zig-zag on the field, so that they are not in a straight line. Arrange the tires one yard apart.

(2) Stack another tire on top of each. Therefore, 20 tires are necessary to make the 10 stacks.

(3) This added height makes the backs lift their knees when running.

(4) Have the backs run at top speed and score a point against any back who steps on a tire.

(5) Add a third tire to the stock to make the drill more difficult.

(6) See Illustration 47.

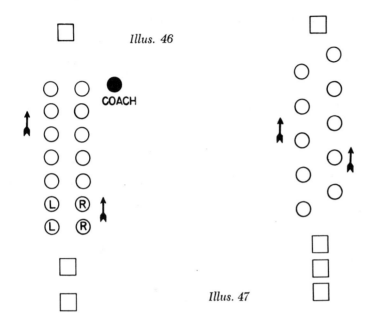

Illus. 46

COACH

Illus. 47

37. HOW TO DRILL FOR THE AGILITY RUN

This drill is a test to measure the speed, agility and endur-ance of a man carrying a football.

INSTRUCTIONS:

(1) The course is shown in the illustration.

(2) Players will stand upright on each of the marked *X*'s on the course.

(3) The ball will be centered from a specified mark, five yards forward and one yard to the left of the starting position.

(4) The ball carrier will start from a two-point, semi-erect stance (backfield stance).

(5) The ball will be snapped on the signal, "one!" preceded

by the signal "Ready, hike, one!" given by an official scorer.

(6) A stopwatch will be started by the scorer on the verbal hike signal "one!"

(7) The stopwatch will be stopped when the ball carrier crosses the finish line.

(8) In case of a bad center pass or fumble, subsequent trials will be allowed until the ball carrier gets a fair start in the opinion of the scorer.

(9) The raw score will be the time in seconds taken to traverse the entire course.

(10) See Illustration 48.

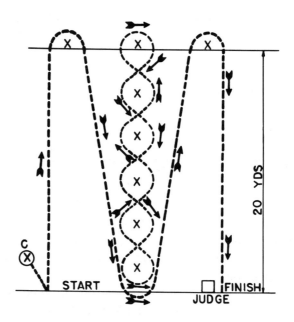

Illus. 48

38. HOW TO DRILL FOR THE HELMET RUN

The purpose of this drill is to keep the backfield men low when running signals.

INSTRUCTIONS:

(1) Locate a center on offensive with a complete backfield.

(2) Place five or six helmets beyond the line of scrimmage at intervals of five yards.

(3) The ball carrier is required to reach down and touch the helmets with his free hand.

(4) Stress speed and body balance.

(5) When the backs complete the drill in one direction, have them turn around and repeat it in the opposite direction.

(6) This is a good drill for keeping backs low as well as training for balance and sprinting. It requires no mechanical equipment. Helmets are always available.

(7) See Illustration 49.

Illus. 49

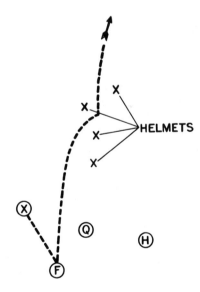

39. HOW TO DRILL FOR THE STRAIGHT-ARM MACHINE

The purpose of this drill is to develop the straight-arm. Although not difficult to learn, it has become a forgotten maneuver. The straight-arm can change an average back into a good one.

INSTRUCTIONS:

(1) This machine (see illustration) was constructed by Scott Ramsey, superintendent of buildings and grounds at Whittier College. The players call this machine the "Frontal Lift."

(2) An old helmet is attached to the horizontal arm of the machine to simulate an opponent's head. The helmet also provides a target for the ball carrier's hand.

(3) An automobile tire is placed around the base. The tire prevents the runners from getting too close and provides foot protection if they do.

(4) The machine and tire are painted white to improve their appearance.

(5) The players run right up to the machine and push off from the tire as they apply the straight-arm.

(6) As the players practice straight-arming, they can also drill on the pivot dodge.

(7) The pivot dodge resembles the reverse turn in basketball.

(8) The player runs up to the machine and places the heel of his hand against the helmet. He then turns away from the machine, pivoting on his *outside* leg.

(9) If straight-arming is done with the right hand, the pivot is on the *left* leg; swing the right leg back and around to the left.

(10) Stress *low* body position when making the pivot, so that when the turn is completed the weight is forward. This

forces the ball carrier to lunge ahead and away from the grasp of the opponent.

(11) See Illustration 50.

Illus. 50

40. HOW TO DRILL FOR PICKING UP THE FEET

Many backs run with little or no knee action.   Backs of this type will often stumble over a lineman's foot when going through an opening in the line.   The purpose of this drill is to train the backs to lift up their feet.

INSTRUCTIONS:

(1) Lay two rows of six dummies on their sides approximately three feet apart.   If the dummies are "bell bottom" shaped, place the bell ends in alternating positions.

(2) On a signal from the coach the backs run through these dummies at top speed.

(3) Once through they repeat the drill from the other end.

(4) Place the dummies closer together to make the drill more difficult.

(5) If the backs fail to pick up their feet, they will stumble and fall.

(6) Two minutes a day of this will get the backs in the habit of picking up their feet.

(7) A stopwatch may be used to create group competition.

(8) See Illustration 51.

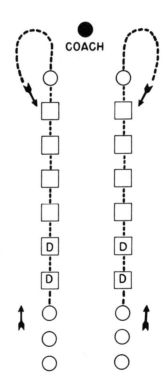

Illus. 51

41. HOW TO DRILL FOR KEEPING THE EYES OPEN

Most fumbles in the backfield result from taking the eyes off the ball. This drill is designed to force the player to keep his eyes open.

INSTRUCTIONS:

(1) Use this drill when practicing ball handling.

(2) Paint one-inch numbers in white on four footballs.

(3) Omit the number 1 and start with 2. One is too easily recognized. Use 2, 3, 4, 5, or 7.

(4) As the ball reaches the player's hands, he must call out the number.

(5) If the back keeps his eyes on the ball, he can always call the correct number.

(6) These four balls should be used for ball handling and pass receiving only.

(7) See Illustration 52.

Illus. 52

42. HOW TO DRILL FOR PLUNGING

This is a short yardage drill to improve the "drive" of a back to score or make the necessary yard for a first down.

INSTRUCTIONS:

(1) Backs must be drilled in short yardage situations.

(2) Place three bell-bottom dummies tightly together.

(3) Locate the dummies three yards from the goal line.

(4) Station a fullback three yards behind an offensive center.

(5) The center snaps the ball and the player plunges into the apex of the three dummies.

(6) Stress starting quickly, body balance, leverage, and continual leg action even in the air.

(7) With practice, the backs can become quite skilled in this maneuver.

43. HOW TO DRILL FOR BALANCE AND ELUSIVE-NESS

Backfield candidates continually need training on balance and elusiveness. The purpose of this drill is to develop these two qualities.

INSTRUCTIONS:

(1) Use this drill when practicing ball-handling drills.

(2) The ball carrier must complete this cycle after he receives the ball:

(a) Step over a fallen dummy to represent some lineman's feet.

(b) Run three yards and touch a helmet on the ground to represent running low and keeping body balance.

(c) Step inside of a tire and fade away, to represent the cross-over step in avoiding an open field tackler.

(3) Three backfields are rotated in this drill, with each returning to the starting position.

(4) Change the obstacle sequence after the backs become proficient.

(5) Insure that the players always run under full speed.

(6) The players find this drill interesting and profitable.

44. HOW TO DRILL FOR STARTING POWER

The backs should always have a warm-up drill after calisthenics. The purpose of the drill is to develop the starting power of the backfield candidates.

INSTRUCTIONS:

(1) It is wise to warm up by practicing starts on the ball. The coach may act as a center and snap the ball.

(2) Line up the backs according to positions. For example, all fullbacks, all quarterbacks, and so on.

(3) This creates competition to discover the fastest starting back at each position.

(4) The backs assume their offensive stance and take off for five yards.

(5) If a player jumps the ball, he should do five push ups.

(6) Each group takes off when the coach moves the ball.

(7) Two minutes each day after calisthentics as a final warm-up will improve the backfield take-off tremendously.

(8) See Illustration 53.

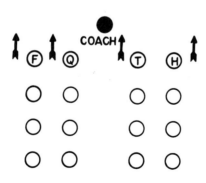

Illus. 53

45. HOW TO DRILL FOR STARTING AN END RUN

The purpose of this drill is to develop fast starting on an end run.

INSTRUCTIONS:

(1) Place a center on offense with three footballs.

(2) Position a quarterback behind the center.

(3) Line up several backs in single file.

(4) Back No. 2 should start when the ball is snapped from center, and No. 1 should pass it to him by throwing an underhand lateral.

(5) The extra backs should line up behind No. 2 and move up to take their turns.

(6) When No. 2 returns from his run, he should take a position at the end of the line.

(7) Alternate quarterbacks in this drill.

(8) See Illustration 54.

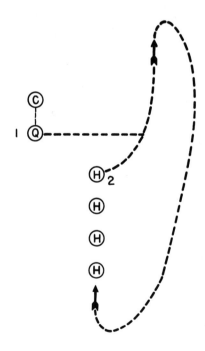

Illus. 54

46. HOW TO DRILL FOR THE STADIUM RUN

The object of this drill is to run the entire squad with emphasis on conditioning the ankles and knees.

INSTRUCTIONS:

(1) This is definitely an early-season drill that should be used during the first week of practice.

(2) Place a double row of 10 automobile tires up the aisles of the stadium.

(3) Have the players run up and down the aisles stepping into these tires.

(4) No football shoes are worn on this drill.

(5) This drill may be used to conclude practice during the first week.

47. HOW TO DRILL FOR FOOTWORK IN SPINNING

Many hours are devoted to teaching a fullback to spin properly. The purpose of this drill is to provide specialized practice in footwork training for the fullback.

INSTRUCTIONS:

(1) This drill is valuable for the inexperienced fullbacks. It simplifies the spinning technique and allows them to learn spinning in a shorter time.

(2) Have three life-sized outlines of the human foot made on paper.

(3) Have these three outlines brought to double size and cut from heavy white canvas.

(4) Place these "footprints" on the ground in the correct position for the spin.

(5) The inexperienced fullback must hit these prints with his feet as he spins.

(6) No center is needed in this drill until the footwork is mastered.

(7) The fullback becomes accustomed to these footprints

and learns the correct footwork in a short time, forming fewer bad habits.

(8) Add the center and complete backfield after the full-back has confidence in his spinning.

48.   HOW TO DRILL FOR PRECISION TIMING

The object of this drill is to improve the timing of the entire backfield.   It will reveal how much time it takes to have each back arrive at a specific hole.

INSTRUCTIONS:

(1) Run entire backfields through the play pattern without the ball.

(2) Check with a stopwatch the exact time it takes for a specific back to arrive at the correct spot.

(3) Change the steps taken to make up the deficiency discovered, or begin the take-off sooner.

(4) Work the backs in the same units of four as much of the time as is practicable.

(5) Stress running harder!

(6) See Illustration 55.

Illus. 55

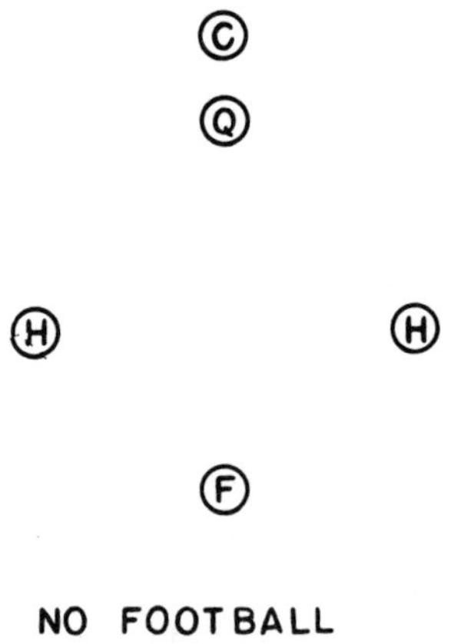

NO FOOTBALL

49. HOW TO DRILL FOR SPEED BY TIMING

The object of this drill is to find out the exact speed of every player on the squad in a complete uniform, both with and without a football.

INSTRUCTIONS:

(1) Line up the players according to positions on the goal line.

(2) Run two players at a time.

(3) Have two stopwatches and get both players' times.

(4) The backs start from their backfield stance and the linemen from their three-point stance.

(5) The coach starting the players uses an arm signal to the timers.

(6) Every player should be timed in the following distances: 25, 50, 75, and 100 yards, all dashes.

(7) Time the backs with and without a ball.

(8) Time the squad at the conclusion of practice in place of wind sprints.

(9) Post the results on the bulletin board.

50. HOW TO DRILL FOR PARTIAL OFFENSE

The object of this drill is to practice running plays on one side of the line only and to provide ball-handling and running practice for the backs against live competition.

INSTRUCTIONS:

(1) Station an offensive center with two footballs on the line of scrimmage.

(2) Line up one left guard on offense.

(3) A full backfield is lined up behind the center.

(4) Place an end on defense.

(5) Drill on all running plays to the left side only.

(6) The defensive end should be relieved when necessary.

(7) The same drill may be used on the right side.

(8) See Illustration 56.

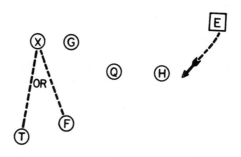

Illus. 56

51. HOW TO DRILL FOR TWO AND THREE

This drill is designed to perfect plays hitting through a particular hole.

INSTRUCTIONS:

(1) Line up a center, left guard, right guard, right tackle, and right end on offense (single wing unbalanced right).

(2) Locate four players in the backfield.

(3) Have the quarterback call all plays designed to go through holes 2 and 3.

(4) This drill may be dummy or live. If live, place two guards, a tackle, an end, and a linebacker on defensive.

(5) By constant drilling on these two holes the players will perfect the key blocks and the ball carriers will develop timing.

(6) The backfield coach should be located behind the offense and to the right.

(7) See Illustration 57.

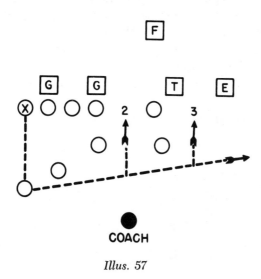

Illus. 57

52. HOW TO DRILL FOR ASSEMBLY LINE SIGNALS

The object of this drill is to develop ball-handling techniques. It is also an excellent drill to train and develop the voices of all the quarterbacks.

INSTRUCTIONS:

(1) This is an excellent signal drill to accustom all the backs to the cadence of each quarterback.

(2) Line up three or four complete backfields, depending upon the number of players.

(3) Give each backfield a center with one football.

(4) The backfields are spaced about 10 yards apart to avoid collisions.

(5) Have *one* quarterback call the play and cadence for the *four* backfield units.

(6) After 15 plays assign another quarterback to take over.

(7) Give each quarterback an opportunity to call signals.

(8) Create competition with units on fumbles.

(9) One coach can view the entire drill and make suggestions that will apply to all.

(10) This is one of the smartest and most precise drills in football.

(11) See Illustrations 58a and 58b.

Illus. 58a

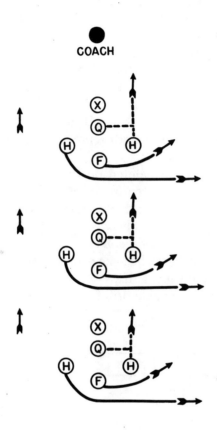

Illus. 58b

53. HOW TO DRILL FOR BACKFIELD ALIGNMENT

In every offensive formation, backfield alignment is important. The object of this drill is to provide practice for exact backfield alignment.

INSTRUCTIONS:

(1) Without proper spacing in the backfield, timing is disrupted. If the backs are too close together, fumbles may result. If they are too far apart, deception may be lost.

(2) Fasten a canvas strip (10 inches wide) to the ground by long spikes. The length represents the positions occupied by the seven linemen.

(3) Numbers are painted on the canvas so that the backs may hit the correct offensive holes.

(4) Measured strips of canvas are placed in the backfield to insure exact spacing between the backs. These are also fastened down with long spikes.

(5) After the backs become accustomed to the correct spacing, remove the canvas strips.

(6) This is a valuable drill for a new coach installing a new system.

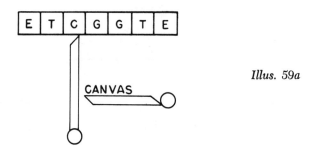

Illus. 59a

(7) The drill also provides a checkup late in the season when the players may become careless on alignment.

(8) See Illustrations 59a and 59b.

Illus. 59b

54. HOW TO DRILL FOR THE SQUARE

This is known as the back square drill. This drill is designed to help the backs and center coordinate as a unit to develop backfield footwork and ball handling.

INSTRUCTIONS:

(1) Four backfields and four centers are used to execute this drill.

(2) Squads 1 and 3 face the goal posts at opposite ends of the field.

(3) Squads 2 and 4 face the sidelines.

(4) The coach stands in the center of the square formed by the four squads.

(5) The coach calls the play numbers he wishes to see and watches the execution of the plays by each squad.

(6) After each play the squads return to their original positions.

(7) This drill can be altered for two or three backfields if the total number is less than 16.

(8) See Illustration 60.

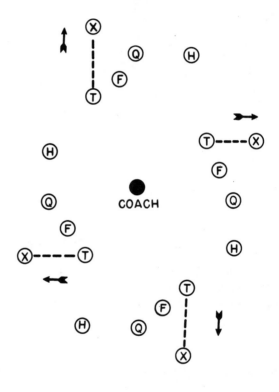

Illus. 60

55. HOW TO DRILL FOR CIRCULATION

The idea behind this series of drills is to improve backfield running techniques. These drills are to be perfomed at conclusion of practice.

INSTRUCTIONS:

(1) Three men at a time run ten yards straight ahead at full speed from backfield stance, Illustration 61a.

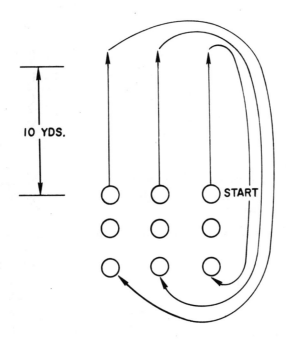

10 YDS.

START

Illus. 61a

(2) Back pedal for ten yards—three apiece. Same procedure as in number (1).

(3) Objective—Run at two dummies, cut sharply at full speed and twist through. Do five each way. See Illustration 61b.

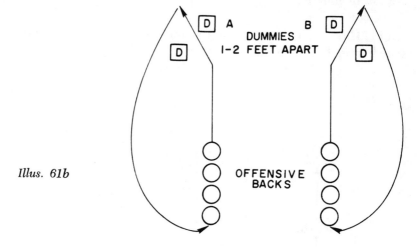

Illus. 61b

(4) Run hard with three pivots to each side. Illustration 61c.

(5) Run over dummies with high knee action five times. Illustration 61d.

(6) This improves open field running. See Illustration 61e.

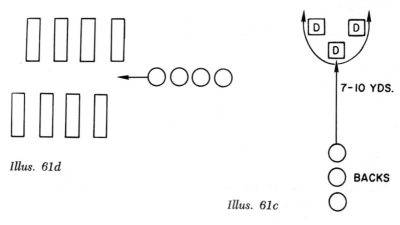

Illus. 61d

Illus. 61c

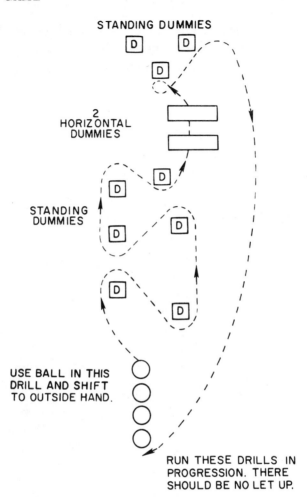

STANDING DUMMIES

2
HORIZONTAL
DUMMIES

STANDING
DUMMIES

Illus. 61e

USE BALL IN THIS
DRILL AND SHIFT
TO OUTSIDE HAND.

RUN THESE DRILLS IN
PROGRESSION. THERE
SHOULD BE NO LET UP.

56. HOW TO DRILL FOR LOWERING THE BOOM

*The object of this drill is to develop power and toughness in
the ball carriers as well as to improve carriage of the ball.*

INSTRUCTIONS:

(1) Place four dummies in a shape of a diamond. Station
the four biggest linemen to hold these bags.

(2) Have the backs line up in front of the diamond.

(3) On a signal have them run hard at the first dummy and contact it as if they were meeting a tackler.

(4) Have them hit hard and spin off each dummy.

(5) See Illustration 62.

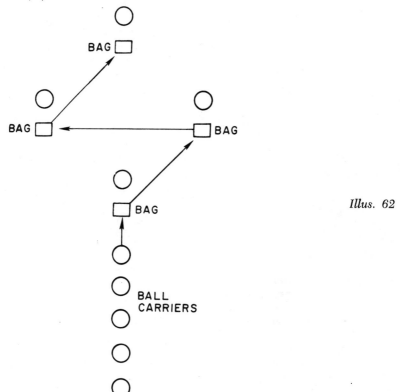

Illus. 62

57. HOW TO DRILL FOR BACKFIELD TAKE-OFF

The object of this drill is to provide practice for all the back-field men so that they can improve their take-off. This is a good warm-up drill after calisthenics.

INSTRUCTIONS:

(1) Place the backs in four lanes five yards apart.

(2) Station a coach in front of the backs to point directions and give commands to take off. Pointing is better than giving

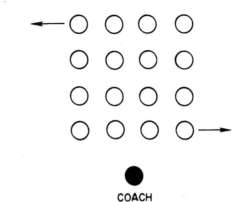

Illus. 63

COACH

the verbal commands of "Right" or "Left," and avoids the confusion of several backs colliding. Have the backs go on the word "hike."

(3) Change directions frequently and offer suggestions as the drill proceeds.

(4) Insist on a good push off and a step with the lead foot in the direction indicated.

(5) The backs must go at full speed.

(6) See Illustration 63.

58. HOW TO DRILL FOR ONE ON ONE

The purpose of this drill is to coordinate offense and defense. It is one of the better drills in football.

INSTRUCTIONS:

(1) Use six standing dummies on offense.

(2) Place a dummy on its side between the halfback and the quarterback. This will force the quarterback forward.

(3) Place a center, halfback, quarterback and offensive lineman on offense. The offensive lineman will place his hands on the front end of the dummies.

(4) Station the defensive lineman one yard from the offensive man. The coach will give the starting count, etc.

(5) Have the waiting offensive lineman count the number of steps the offensive man takes after he has made contact. This keeps the men more alert and exerts pressure on them to do a good job.

(6) See Illustration 64.

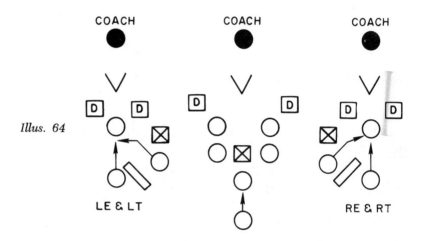

Illus. 64

59. HOW TO DRILL FOR FUMBLE PREVENTION

This drill is designed to force the backfield men to carry the ball properly.

INSTRUCTIONS:

(1) Have five linemen form a circle. Allow approximately two yards between each lineman.

(2) Place a back inside the circle with a football.

(3) The back must try to get out of the circle without losing the football.

(4) The linemen may grab arms, may grab the ball, but they do not tackle.

(5) See Illustration 65.

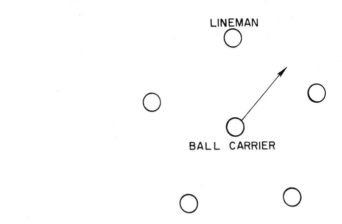

Illus. 65

Coaching hint that may be helpful—Tell your backs that tension on the ball should not be extremely forceful—but firm until the whistle blows.

60. HOW TO DRILL FOR THREE ESSENTIALS

This drill is designed to provide multiple practice for offensive backs in three essentials: Ball handling, running hard, and proper carriage of the football.

INSTRUCTIONS:

(1) Place a center, a quarterback, and a halfback on offense.

(2) Place three dummies horizontally on the ground to force the halfback to pick up his feet.

(3) Station two defensive players on the ground in front of the first dummy. These men may contact with the ball carrier and force him to keep driving.

(4) Locate a tackler two yards behind the last dummy. The ball carrier attempts to avoid the tackler.

(5) See Illustration 66.

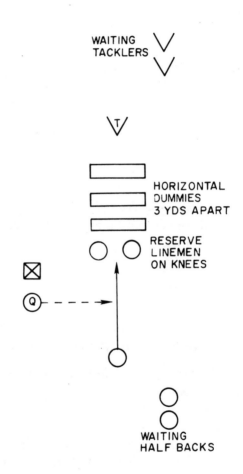

Illus. 66

61. HOW TO DRILL FOR FROSH BALL HANDLING

The purpose of this drill is to practice ball handling and also to emphasize proper carriage of the football.

INSTRUCTIONS:

(1) Set up a regular defensive line. Use freshmen on defense.

(2) Place a center and the first string backfield on offense.

(3) Have the offense run all plays against this defensive line.

(4) The defensive linemen grab at the ball and try to force the backs to fumble as they come through the line.

(5) See Illustration 67.

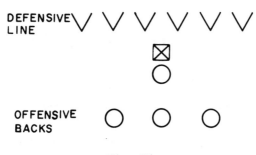

Illus. 67

62. HOW TO DRILL FOR FUMBLE PREVENTION

The purpose of this drill is to make the backs conscious of protecting the football.

INSTRUCTIONS:

(1) Line up one center and a fullback on offense. Any back may be used.

(2) Have two defensive men stationed within two yards of the back receiving the ball.

(3) As soon as he receives the ball, the other two men try to take it away from him.

(4) See Illustration 68.

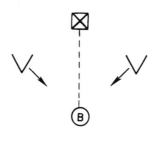

Illus. 68

63. HOW TO DRILL FOR HARDER RUNNING BY BACKS

The purpose of this drill is to provide motivation during the ball handling period for backs to run harder.

INSTRUCTIONS:

(1) Take one complete backfield with a center and line up on the opposing ten-yard line.

(2) Instruct the quarterback to call scoring plays in this area.

(3) This will give added incentive to the men while running into the end zone. Stress timing and take off.

(4) Station two or four men with air dummies. These men give the runner a jolt with the bag and try to knock him off balance. They also go for the ball.

(5) Have men alternate hitting the ball carrier so that he can learn to run hard and yet keep balance when hit unexpectedly from the side.

(6) A large blocking dummy may be placed on the ground to teach the back to pick up his feet.

64. HOW TO DRILL FOR THE HAND-OFF

The purpose of this drill is to work three groups simultaneously and save time.

INSTRUCTIONS:

(1) Place three quarterbacks and three centers on offense as indicated.

(2) Use a canvas line with the offensive splits marked on it to help the backs.

(3) Station a dummy and holder on defense.

(4) Have the quarterbacks go from one group to another.

(5) See Illustration 69.

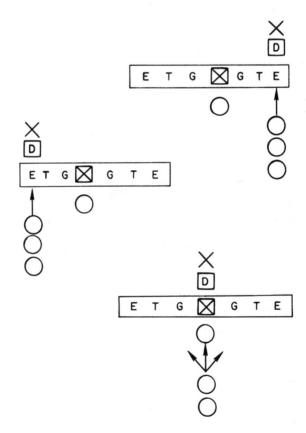

Illus. 69

65. HOW TO DRILL FOR THE SNEAK

The object of this drill is to practice offensive football as well as teaching the defensive man recognition and reaction.

INSTRUCTIONS:

(1) This is a fine drill and will only take a few minutes several times per week to prove valuable.

(2) Place a center and a quarterback on offense.

(3) Station a defensive man to play over the center. The defensive man may do anything he wishes to stop the play.

(4) The quarterback runs sneaks to either side. This is good training for him.

(5) This is a good post-practice drill for three minutes.

(6) See Illustration 70.

Illus. 70

66. HOW TO DRILL FOR VEERING

Veering is a valuable stunt used to best advantage by full-backs.

INSTRUCTIONS:

(1) Veering is easily practiced by stationing several players on a line across the field, ten yards apart.

(2) The backs may then weave through these men on alternate sides.

(3) Many different stunts can be practiced as a part of this procedure.

(4) Later—the stationary men may be permitted to tackle, putting the executions of the various stunts under fire. Thus the backs learn to get both hands on the ball in a tackle and to double up as they hit the ground.

(5) See Illustration 71.

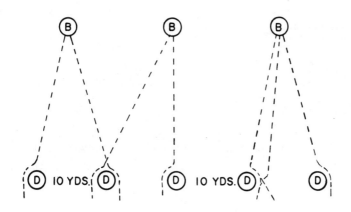

Illus. 71

67. HOW TO DRILL WITH HURDLES

The purpose of this drill is to give the quarterback practice in spinning within an area enclosed by hurdles.

INSTRUCTIONS:

(1) This is a drill Jim Bonder used to guide the quarterbacks with their pivots.[1]

(2) Arrange four hurdles longwise—one at two o'clock, five o'clock, seven o'clock, and ten o'clock.

---

[1] James B. Bonder, *Fundamentals of the T Formation* (Dubuque, Iowa), William C. Brown Company, 1956, pp. 82-83.

(3) The quarterback then practices his spins in the enclosed area for a few minutes every day.

(4) See Illustration 72.

Illus. 72

68. HOW TO DRILL IN THE PIVOT PIT

The purpose of this drill is to practice pivoting in a specially designed pivot pit.

INSTRUCTIONS:

(1) Use an area of the practice field 20 yards wide and seven yards deep.

(2) In the center of the 20 yards place an upright marker. (small plank)

(3) Nail four aluminum strippings a yard long and one inch wide on two-by-three-inch boards. Aluminum is desirable because it will not rust and is easily visible.[2]

(4) Sink the boards into the ground so that the aluminum strippings show and are flush with the ground surface.

---

[2] *Ibid.*, pp. 82-83.

(5) Place strippings approximately one yard back of the upright post so that they will fall about the same position as the quarterback's feet when he has completed his various pivots.

(6) Have the quarterback line up facing the upright marker and then pivot right or left. His swinging foot should come as close as possible to the aluminum strippings placed for that particular pivot.

(7) See Illustration 73.

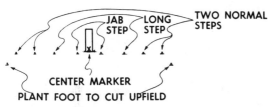

A pivoting pit for the split "T" pivots.

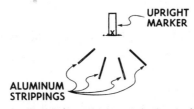

You now have a permanent pivoting pit where all your quarterbacks can master their spins.

Illus. 73

69. HOW TO DRILL FOR THE TUBE

The purpose of this drill is to improve leg drive.

INSTRUCTIONS:

(1) Use two inflated inner tubes tied together. The second tube is tied with a piece of rubber-covered rope two feet from the first tube.

(2) Tie the first tube to a pole, tree or some stationary object. Place a piece of hose around the tube to prevent the rope from cutting it.

(3) Have your best back step into the second tube and place it around his waist. Place a ball under his arm and tell him to start running.

(4) The player must maintain a good running base, stay low, and dig hard.

(5) The "grinder" will test the player's legs and most will tire in a few seconds.

(6) The "grinder" teaches the importance of a wide base in running which makes it harder for a back to get knocked off his feet.

70. HOW TO DRILL FOR GOING IN MOTION

The purpose of this drill is to practice in going in motion and to save time.

INSTRUCTIONS:

(1) Line up all fullbacks single file behind each other.

(2) Line up all the right halfbacks single file behind each other.

(3) Line up all the left halfs single file behind each other.

(4) Upon a predetermined signal have all the left halfs go in motion. Have them continue until they hear another predetermined number when they plant and turn up field.

(5) Do same with right halfs and have the fullbacks go in motion to both sides.

(6) See Illustration 74.

Illus. 74

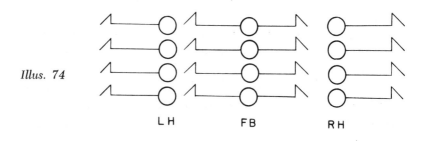

LH   FB   RH

71. HOW TO DRILL FOR POSITION STARTS

The purpose of this drill is to practice backfield starts under observation of the backfield coach.

INSTRUCTIONS:

(1) Have all the backs line up according to position in groups of three or four.

(2) Start one group at a time so that you can examine their footwork in starting.

(3) See Illustrations 75a and 75b.

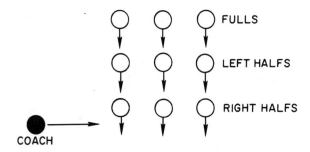

Illus. 75a

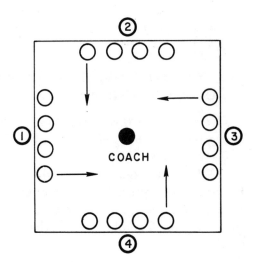

Illus. 75b

72. HOW TO DRILL FOR "SUICIDE ROW"

The purpose of this drill is to improve on the old run, the gauntlet drill, and combine both offense and defense. Primarily designed to prevent fumbles.

INSTRUCTIONS:

(1) Line A is ball carriers.

(2) Lines B & C are tacklers. Each player is five yards behind the player in front of him.

(3) The lines are three yards apart.

(4) The ball carriers run between lines B & C.

(5) Coach X secretly designates who is to do the tackling. This is unknown to the ball carrier.

(6) Two men could be in on the tackle, or one man could fake at the ball carrier and the other tackle him.

(7) See Illustration 76.

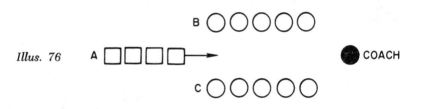

Illus. 76

73. HOW TO DRILL FOR QUARTERBACK CADENCE AND PIVOTING

The purpose of this drill is to give the quarterback practice in receiving the ball, pivoting, faking and cadence.

INSTRUCTIONS:

(1) Place an equal number of centers and quarterbacks on footballs that are located in a straight line.

(2) Have the quarterback at ball A call the pivot and the snap number. The other quarterbacks pick up his cadence for rhythm.

(3) When the ball is snapped, each quarterback pivots for the play called in order to get uniformity of position. He also uses the necessary jokes in the play.

(4) Rotate after each pivot, A to D, D to C, C to B, and B to A in order for quarterbacks to become accustomed to the individual style of each center.

(5) See Illustration 77.

Illus. 77

A	B	C	D
⊠	⊠	⊠	⊠
Ⓠ	Ⓠ	Ⓠ	Ⓠ

74. HOW TO DRILL FOR FUMBLE PREVENTION

The purpose of this drill is to lessen the probability of fumbling in a game.

INSTRUCTIONS:

(1) During the calisthenic period when stressing grass drills see that each back has a football.

(2) When the backs practice a series of rapid falls (simulated tackle falls) insist the ball carriers protect the ball.

(3) If there are not enough footballs, let the backs take turns holding the balls available.

75. HOW TO DRILL FOR FUMBLE PREVENTION

The purpose of any fumble drill is to prevent losing the ball.

INSTRUCTIONS:

(1) Any drill that involves blocking or tackling and to which a ball carrier can be added. Make sure that he has a football.

(2) This is as close to game conditions as possible and it is essential the ball carrier protect the ball when going down.

76. HOW TO DRILL FOR FUMBLE PREVENTION

No one can guarantee that a team will not fumble, but various drills may reduce the probability.

INSTRUCTIONS:

(1) In ball handling sessions use a very smooth, almost slippery ball. This ball should be of standard size and weight.

(2) Using this smooth ball forces the backs to be more conscious of looking the ball into their hands and more careful in exchange and carriage.

77. HOW TO DRILL FOR FUMBLE PREVENTION

The idea of this drill is to have backs actually practice receiving bad passes from the center.

INSTRUCTIONS:

(1) Have a center with several footballs line up.

(2) Station a tailback or fullback approximately 4 yards behind the center.

(3) The center will snap the ball high, low, right or left.

(4) In order to catch these different passes, added concentration is needed.

78. HOW TO DRILL FOR FUMBLE PREVENTION

The purpose of this drill is to make the ball carrier conscious of protecting the ball as he goes thru the line.

INSTRUCTIONS:

(1) Line up a complete team as necessary to run signals.

(2) Place two extra men at the hole the ball carrier is to run through.

(3) These men would represent a small gauntlet for the ball carrier to run through.

(4) The entire backfield and line benefit by working on timing.

79. HOW TO DRILL FOR FUMBLE PREVENTION

This drill is designed to help prevent a player from dropping or fumbling the ball through sheer carelessness.

INSTRUCTIONS:

(1) Inform the ends and backs the penalty for fumbling through carelessness.

(2) When the occasion arises give the player a used football and have him bounce it against the fence 100 times, catching it each time on the rebound and placing it under his arm in *proper* carrying position.

(3) Penalties such as this cure men of persistent faults much more quickly than any amount of scolding.

Fumble prevention note

In all of these drills have the runners carry the ball the same as under game conditions. In other words, allow the runners to use only one hand on the ball, etc.

4

THE BLOCKING GAME

Blocking paves the way.
—Bernie Bierman

BLOCKING IS THE FIRST PRINCIPLE IN OFFENSIVE PLAYING. FULLY 90 per cent of all offensive action is used in blocking. It is the essence of good football. Therefore, it is the first rudiment which a lineman must master, and too much attention cannot be given by the coach to this branch of linemanship.

Successful blocking must be taught in the first three weeks of the season and during spring practice. In order to teach players how to block, drills are necessary to perfect endurance and technique. A considerable portion of the practice program should be devoted to the teaching of these fundamentals, since blocking is the backbone of all good football teams. Care must be taken to make this part of the practice program as interesting as possible.

Many coaches use their own drills and techniques in teaching fundamental blocks. A record of the time spent on each block should be kept on the drill time study chart. See Illustration 78, page 116.

In this chapter, emphasis is placed on the two basic blocks: (1) the shoulder block, and (2) the cross body block. The drills outlined are primarily to teach these two blocks. All other blocks are secondary or relative to these two and originate from different situations that arise on a football field.

Many drills in this chapter involve more than just blocking. Rather, they may embrace several of the major fundamentals. As a result, it has been difficult to determine in just what category some of the drills belong. For the purpose of organization, the author has attempted to place them categorically according to their primary objective. Since at least 90 per cent of all offensive action and energy in football is used in blocking, this explains why the greatest proportion of drills fall under the chapter entitled "The Blocking Game."

1. HOW TO DRILL FOR THE BOX METHOD STANCE

Distribution of weight on the balls of both feet and comfort in assuming a stance is difficult for most inexperienced linemen. The purpose of this drill is to help teach linemen the proper stance.

INSTRUCTIONS:

(1) A square is drawn on the ground with lime approximately two and one-half feet on each side.

(2) The lineman places one foot in the rear corner, and the other foot in the middle of the opposite side.

(3) Place the right hand down to correspond with the rear foot. The other arm is resting across the front knee.

(4) Five minutes daily during the first two weeks of practice should be devoted to examining the linemen's stance.

(5) See Illustration 79.

Number of minutes for each drill

	1st week					2nd week					3rd week					TOTAL
DATE																
SHOULDER BLOCK																
REVERSE SHOULDER BLOCK																
LONG-BODY BLOCK																
REVERSE LONG-BODY BLOCK																
DOWNFIELD BLOCK																
CROSS BLOCK																
PASS AND PUNT BLOCK																
SKELETON BACKS																
TWO-ON-ONE DRILL																
THREE-ON-ONE DRILL																
FOUR-ON-ONE DRILL																

Illus. 78

Illus. 79

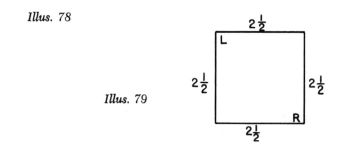

2. HOW TO DRILL FOR LEVERAGE

The purpose of this drill is to provide the linemen with practice in obtaining leverage in blocking.

INSTRUCTIONS:

(1) Station one complete offensive line (seven men) in three-point stances.

(2) Locate defensive line (seven men) one yard away.

(3) Linemen alternate on quick shoulder charges with emphasis on dipping under the defenders' hands and lifting.

(4) Stress a low tail and lifting with legs.

(5) Practice both right and left shoulder blocks.

(6) Coach calls the starting signals.

(7) See Illustrations 80a and 80b.

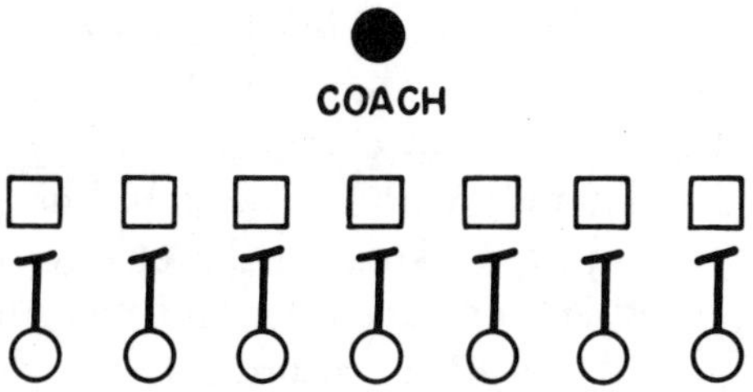

Illus. 80a

COACH

Illus. 80b

3. HOW TO DRILL FOR THE SHOULDER BLOCK

The purpose of this drill is to teach the players the funda-mentals of the shoulder block. This drill gives the boy the confidence he does not get when he is trying to learn the block on live competition.

INSTRUCTIONS:

(1) Pair off two men, one man holding a dummy and one man located in front of it, in a three-point stance.

(2) The men rotate after each block.

(3) Use as many units of two as is feasible.

(4) If the player is going to take the bag to the left, jolt the bag with the left shoulder, stepping simultaneously with your right foot. This is just the opposite if you are going to take the bag to the right.

(5) A good rule for this type of block is *inside* foot, *out-side* shoulder.

(6) Concentrate on the initial charge.

(7) Work the bag laterally with the neck and head.

(8) If the player is just working on the charge, take the bag straight back, using first one shoulder and then the other.

(9) Stress keeping the head up in order to see the target and have him keep the back straight.

(10) Work for a good lift with the upper arm, keeping the elbow even with the shoulder to provide more blocking sur-face.

(11) See Illustration 81.

Illus. 81   COACH

4. HOW TO DRILL FOR QUICKNESS

The purpose of this drill is to teach the players to charge quickly and at the same time to develop the shoulder block.
INSTRUCTIONS:

(1) Line up several dummies as in a scrimmage position with about two yards separating each bag.

(2) Assign a player to each dummy.

(3) Use as many dummies as is feasible.

(4) The coach tells the players who are going to charge and block to move it right, left, or back on a designated count.

(5) Players must concentrate on quick take-offs and the cadence of the coach.

(6) The players learn to react quickly if drilled on a count.

5. HOW TO DRILL FOR THE RUNNING SHOULDER BLOCK

The object of this drill is to train guards and tackles in pulling out to block ends and linebackers, or to trap opponents.
INSTRUCTIONS:

(1) The left guards and right guards line up in two rows, single file, with the space of one man between the two files.

(2) The tackles divide left and right and assume the defensive end positions in single file.

(3) A coach is stationed behind the tackles to give signals.

(4) On a starting signal, the lead guards pull. The left guards file to the left and right file to the right and practice blocking the lead tackles.

(5) These four men drop to the ends of their respective lines and the next set of guards executes the same block on the next set of tackles, and so on.

(6) On the second round, the left guards line up in the

right file and drill to the right file and pull to the right. The right guards line up in the left file and pull to the left.

(7) The guards take the defensive end positions. The tackles take their respective offensive positions and the drill is repeated in its entirety.

(8) The tackles take the defensive linebackers' positions and the guards pull out and block as before.

(9) The guards become the defensive linebackers and the tackles pull and block.

(10) With one-platoon football, this is a good drill for the interior linemen.

(11) See Illustration 82.

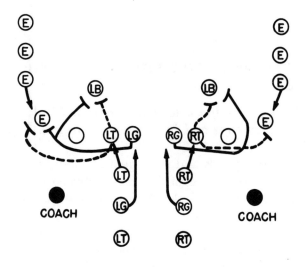

Illus. 82

6. HOW TO DRILL FOR DETAIL IN THE RUNNING SHOULDER BLOCK

The object of this drill is to perfect the techniques of the guards and tackles in pulling out of the line to trap-block an opponent.

INSTRUCTIONS:

(1) Pair off two men, one holding the dummy and one located directly in front of it with an offensive stance.

(2) Drill first on one shoulder and then the other.

(3) Hit first from a distance of one yard, then two yards. Gradually move back to five and 10 yards. Work quickly, but do not overlook details.

(4) Just before the player blocks the dummy, have him give a head fake to simulate straightening up the opponent.

(5) Stress placement of the feet (well spread), head up, and back straight.

(6) Aim the head right at the middle of the bag and just as contact is made, slide the head to the side. Let the shoulders do the work.

(7) The boys that come up with "strawberries" on their cheeks are usually doing it correctly.

7. HOW TO DRILL FOR THE REVERSE SHOULDER BLOCK

The purpose of this drill is to teach the players the fundamentals of the reverse shoulder block. It also gives the men confidence that they would not get when trying to learn to block in live competition.

INSTRUCTIONS:

(1) Pair off two men, one holding a dummy and one lined up either to the right or left, in a three-point stance.

(2) Stress that the reverse shoulder block is almost like pivoting into the opponent.

(3) Work from the right side of the bag. Shoot the head across the front of the dummy and hit with the right shoulder.

(4) Drive the dummy laterally along the line of scrimmage.

(5) Insist on the players' getting their heads across quickly.

(6) If this block is applied correctly, the offensive man is actually helping the opposing linemen to take himself out of the play.

8. HOW TO DRILL FOR THE NEAR FOOT AND NEAR SHOULDER BLOCK

The purpose of this drill is to teach the fundamentals of the near foot, near shoulder block. It also gives the players the confidence they do not get when they are trying to learn this block on live competition.

INSTRUCTIONS:

(1) Pair off, one man holding the bag and one lined up in an offensive stance.

(2) Line up on either side of the bag. Line up either to the right or left side of the bag.

(3) The block is used as a fill-in block by the tackle when the guard pulls out.

(4) Step with the foot nearest the bag and hit with the near shoulder.

(5) Contact must be made on the first step.

(6) The motion is like a jab in boxing.

(7) Concentrate on quickness.

(8) Keep the head between the bag and the ball.

9.   HOW TO DRILL FOR THE CROSS-BODY BLOCK

The purpose of this drill is to teach the players the fundamentals of the cross-body block.   This is important in gaining confidence for the players before sending them against live competition.

INSTRUCTIONS:

(1) Pair off two men.   One man holds the bag and one is lined up in front of the bag in a three-point stance.

(2) Men rotate after a right-side and left-side block.

(3) Use as many units as is possible for the coaching staff to handle.

(4) The blocker starts the raise as if he were going to make a shoulder block.

(5) If blocking to the right side, the blocker would:

(a) Shoot the right hand across the bag, about chin level, (b) Contact the bag with the right hip, and (c) Drive against the bag, using a crab-like motion.

(6) Insist the men work on speed, power and follow through.

(7) This block may be executed from a stationary or running position.

(8) Errors to watch for in the cross-body block:

(a) Leaving the feet too soon, (b) Keeping arms too close to body, (c) Making contact too low, and (d) Hesitating before making contact.

10.   HOW TO DRILL FOR BLOCKING IN THE LINE

The purpose of this drill is to provide the linemen, from tackle to tackle, with practice in blocking (closing) holes where men pull out to form the interference.

INSTRUCTIONS:

(1) One offensive line, from tackle to tackle, is lined up in

scrimmage position.   Place one lineman in the backfield to represent a back.

(2) Have a complete line placed on defense.   In place of the ends, use two tackles or guards.   These linemen get a great kick out of playing defensive end and vary their defensive maneuvers to confuse the guards who are pulling out to block them.

(3) The coach faces the offensive team but is behind the defensive team so that he can give hand signals to the offense.

(4) The defensive men are informed that their sole duty is to try to get through the holes where men pull out.   They try to get the man receiving the ball.

(5) The ball carrier does not move after he gets the ball, merely standing as a target for the defensive men to shoot at.

(6) By hand signals the coach can indicate a regular group of plays such as off-tackle; inside tackle, quicks, plays over center, and pass protection.

(7) See Illustration 83.

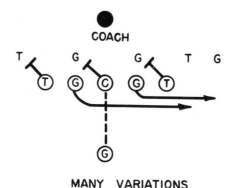

MANY   VARIATIONS

Illus. 83

11. HOW TO DRILL FOR SUCCESSION

The real purpose of this drill is to condition the men early in the season. It also enables the coach to pick out player weaknesses in the various blocks.

INSTRUCTIONS:

(1) Place three bags, one behind the other, approximately 10 yards apart.

(2) The coach can have as many groups of these bags as he can handle. Three or four is usually sufficient.

(3) One player will hold each bag.

(4) The other players will line up one behind the other, five yards away from the first bag.

(5) Any type of block may be used in this drill, but the best procedure is a shoulder block, right and left, and a head-on tackle.

(6) To start the drill, the first player in each line will begin in a three-point stance.

(7) When the whistle is blown the boys will charge forward hitting the first bag with a right shoulder block. They will drive until the whistle is blown again.

(8) At this stage they will charge the second bag, hitting it with their left shoulder, again driving with their left shoulder until the whistle is blown. The last maneuver will be a head-on tackle. When the whistle is blown for the fourth time all the players will rotate. The players all move up a bag. The player who was holding the first bag will go to the end of the line and await his turn to block and tackle.

(9) See Illustrations 84a and 84b.

Illus. 84a

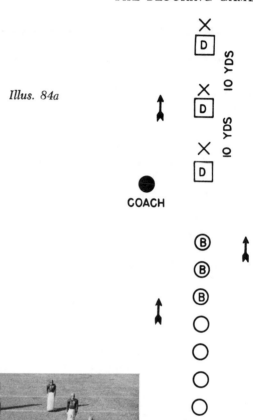

Illus. 84b

12. HOW TO DRILL FOR REVERSE CROSS-BODY BLOCK

The object of this drill is to teach the players the funda-mentals of the reverse cross-body block. This is a dummy drill that builds confidence before going against live competition.

INSTRUCTIONS:

(1) Pair off, one man holding the bag and one lined up on either side of the bag.

(2) The blocker should be one man removed from the bag.

(3) The blocker begins his motion as if he were going to make a cross-body block.

(4) If the blocker is to the right of the bag he will:

(a) Make contact with the right hip, (b) Whip the legs around to the rear of the bag, (c) Keep his body between the bag and the ball carrier, using a crab-like motion, and (d) Have reversed the position of the feet and head.

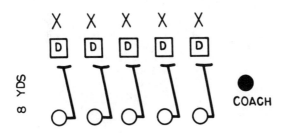

Illus. 85a

13. HOW TO DRILL FOR TRAP BLOCKING

The purpose of this drill is to develop speed and skill for the offensive linemen in pulling and executing a trap block.

INSTRUCTIONS:

(1) The bags are located in a line with one man holding each bag.

(2) The blockers are lined up in their offensive stance and in a straight line.

(3) On the whistle, the players who have their backs to the coach pull out right or left. They run 10 yards and execute a right or left shoulder block on the bags.

(4) Competition is gained by noting who is the first to reach his bag.

(5) The coach should watch for pointing or pulling out too soon.

(6) See Illustrations 85a and 85b.

Illus. 85b

14. HOW TO DRILL FOR THE PULL OUT AND TRAP

This drill is designed to accomplish three fundamentals:
(a) Enable the coach to work on the pull out; (b) Enable the
coach to work on the trap block; (c) Enable the coach to work
on the fill-in blocks.

INSTRUCTIONS:

(1) Two dummies are lined up, one as a defensive guard
and one as a defensive tackle.

(2) One dummy, the guard, is on the line of scrimmage.
The other bag, the tackle, is across the line of scrimmage to
simulate being trapped.

(3) One player holds each bag, and rotates after each drill.

(4) Station two offensive linemen side by side, one a guard
and one a tackle.

(5) The guard pulls out and traps the defensive tackle.

(6) The tackle works on his fill-in block:

   (a) The reverse shoulder block.

   (b) The near foot, near shoulder block.

   (c) The reverse cross-body block.

(7) During the drill the coach should concentrate on:

   (a) Proper pulling method.

   (b) Proper trap block with the guard's head behind
the trapped tackle (if the guard is pulling to his right, he
should hit the trapped man with his right shoulder).

(8) See Illustration 86.

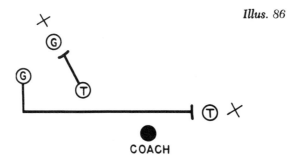

Illus. 86

COACH

15. HOW TO DRILL FOR LOW TRAP BLOCKING

Many times the defensive man will charge across the line and drop to the ground. The trapper will not adjust to this situation and fail on his block. The object of this drill is to develop the trapper so that he can execute his block.

INSTRUCTIONS:

(1) Locate the guards and tackles who trap on the line of scrimmage.

(2) Place them in two rows, single file so that both players pulling left and right can practice pulling and trap blocking at once.

(3) Station two players on defense and have each one hold a dummy.

(4) The players pull on a signal from the coach standing behind the defense.

(5) As the trappers approach to block, the man holding the dummy either pushes it over on the ground or holds it erect.

(6) The trapper must react to the situation and make his block.

(7) If he drops the dummy to the ground, the bellbottom end should be facing the trapper.

(8) This drill should be run live after several turns on the dummies.

(9) See Illustration 87.

Illus. 87

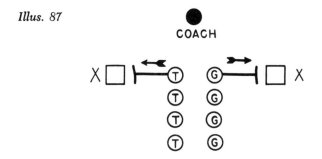

COACH

16. HOW TO DRILL FOR PULLING OUT AND LEADING

This drill accomplishes three things: (a) it enables the coach to work on pulling; (b) it enables the coach to work on blocking the linebacker; (c) it enables the coach to work on closing-the-hole blocks.

INSTRUCTIONS:

(1) Two bags are lined up. One represents a defensive guard and the other a linebacker.

(2) This drill occupies four men who rotate each time a block is made.

(3) Two offensive linemen are in line, one as a tackle and one as a guard.

(4) The guard pulls out and blocks the linebacker.

(5) The tackle works on closing the hole with a near foot, a near shoulder block, a reserve shoulder block, or a reverse cross-body block.

(6) During the drill the coach should concentrate on:

(a) Proper pulling out method.

(b) Proper turning downfield.

(c) Proper shoulder block on the linebacker.

(d) Proper closing of the hole.

(7) See Illustration 88.

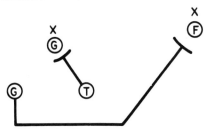

Illus. 88

17. HOW TO DRILL FOR BLOCKING LINEBACKERS

The purpose of this drill is to provide practice for developing blocks on linebackers.

INSTRUCTIONS:

(1) Place two players on defense (holding dummies) to represent linebackers.

(2) Station two more players on the line of scrimmage with *hand* dummies.

(3) Line up the blockers single file. Have them charge between the players holding the hand dummies and block left and right.

(4) The players holding the hand dummies make it difficult for the blockers to run between them.

(5) Locate a coach on defense to call out right or left so that the blockers must adjust to the signal.

(6) See Illustration 89.

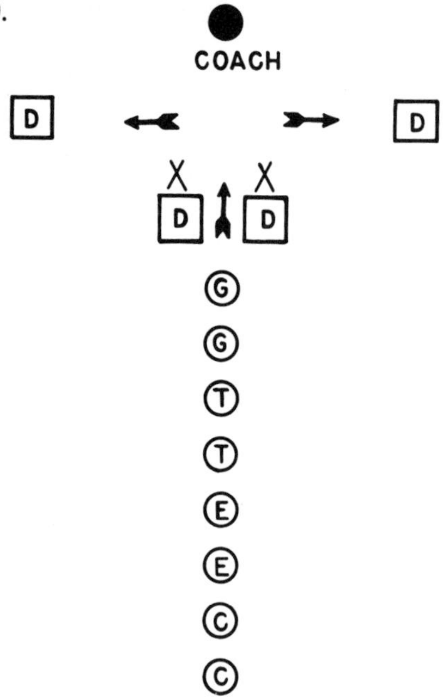

Illus. 89

18. HOW TO DRILL FOR BLOCKS ON LINEBACKERS

*The purpose of this drill is to give pulling linemen practice
in blocking the linebacker.   It will also provide defensive work
for the linebacker.*

INSTRUCTIONS:

(1) This is an excellent drill for both the linebacker and
the guard.

(2) Use a center, three ball carriers, and six linemen.

(3) Alternate the pattern: Linebacker to right guard, right
guard to left guard, left guard to linebacker.

(4) The ball carrier will make his cut according to the
direction of the block executed by the guard.

(5) See Illustration 90.

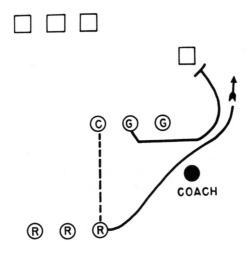

Illus. 90

19. HOW TO DRILL FOR PULLING THROUGH THE HOLE

The object of this drill is to teach the offensive linemen to pull out and turn upfield through the hole.

INSTRUCTIONS:

(1) The players are lined up in groups of eight in their regular offensive stances.

(2) The players count off from one to eight.

(3) On the signal, the odds pull right or left and turn upfield through the hole left vacant by the man removed from them.

(4) The evens then execute the same maneuvers, both right and left.

(5) See Illustration 91.

COACH

Illus. 91

20. HOW TO DRILL FOR CUTTING OFF THE LINE-BACKER

The object of this drill is to give the linemen practice in leaving the line and cutting off the linebacker without live contact. This is a good warm-up drill for linemen.

INSTRUCTIONS:

(1) The players are lined up and count off by threes.

(2) Have them assume their offensive stances.

(3) On a signal, the No. 1 players charge forward, quickly coil and turn in to cut off an imaginary linebacker coming across to meet the play.

(4) The No. 2 and 3 players check-block in the line.

(5) Nos. 2 and 3 perform the same maneuvers as No. 1.

(6) The same routine is repeated to the other side.

(7) See Illustration 92.

21. HOW TO DRILL FOR LINE INTERFERENCE

The object of this drill is to give the men practice in pulling out of the line and in turning as they swing upfield in the interference.

INSTRUCTIONS:

(1) The players are lined up facing the coach.

(2) Starting at the left of the line (as the coach faces them) count off in threes.

(3) The command is given "No. 1's down (left or right foot forward) and pull to the right."

(4) When No. 1 pulls out, he runs behind Nos. 2 and 3 up the field for at least 10 yards.

(5) After he has done his running he comes back into the line in the same place he had before and No. 2 pulls around Nos. 3 and 1.

(6) The men must keep on the run to and from the line.

(7) See Illustration 93.

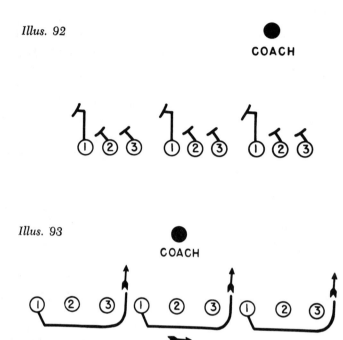

Illus. 92

COACH

Illus. 93

COACH

22. HOW TO DRILL FOR THE POST BLOCK

The purpose of this drill is to provide groups of linemen practice in developing the post block.

INSTRUCTIONS:

(1) Select the 12 best offensive linemen and divide them into groups of six.

(2) Station a defensive man in front of the offensive blocker.

(3) Have the defensive man charge directly through the blocker.

(4) The blocker must hold his ground and break the charge of the defensive man.

(5) The line coach and his assistant may view the entire group.

(6) Alternate men after four blocks.

(7) See Illustration 94.

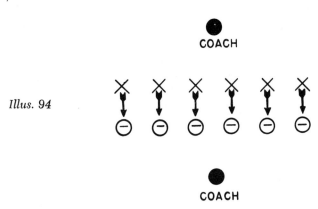

Illus. 94

23. HOW TO DRILL PIVOT BLOCKS

The objective of this drill is to practice pass-protection blocking for a pulling lineman, a blocking back, and a fullback.

INSTRUCTIONS:

(1) Place a center on offensive with two footballs.

(2) Station a pulling lineman next to center.

(3) Place two ends on offense, but have them alternate. First the left end and then the right end run downfield for passes.

(4) Locate an end and tackle on defensive to rush the passer.

(5) Station a passer, a blocking back, and a fullback in the offensive backfield.

(6) On the snap of the ball, the tackle and end rush the passer.

(7) The fullback always blocks the end on the left side. When the defense changes to the other side, the blocking back contacts him.

(8) The lineman (guard) blocks the tackle by riding him out with a pivot block.

(9) Occasionally have the center pull and block the tackle to the left side. This helps keep him honest.

(10) Receivers alternate going for passes.

(11) Passer is timed by coach and must step up into the cup to throw.

(12) This drill is a great help to the passer in stepping into the cup and anticipation in throwing.

(13) See Illustration 95.

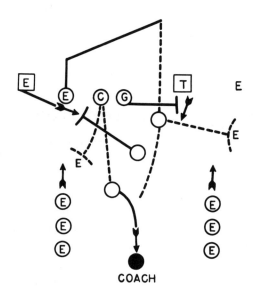

Illus. 95

24. HOW TO DRILL FOR BLOCKING ENDS

The object of this drill is to give the players practice in blocking ends.

INSTRUCTIONS:

(1) The players are divided into two groups and placed in two lines forming a 45-degree angle.

(2) The two lines interchange as they work. After a man has blocked, he becomes an end. The opposite is true of those who have been ends.

(3) On a signal, the men pull out of the line (right) and get in position fast to make their block.

(4) As each blocker comes up, he is first a pivot man for the blocker to line up on. Then after the man pulls out, he moves over and becomes the blocker while the teammates behind take turns becoming the pivot.

(5) The men may use shoulder blocks and then body blocks.

(6) The emphasis is upon pulling out, without pointing, and upon blocking form.

(7) This is a fine drill to teach players open field blocking where an interferer may meet a defensive man just after he passes the line of scrimmage.

(8) See Illustration 96.

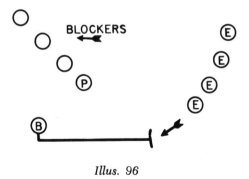

Illus. 96

25. HOW TO DRILL FOR DUMMY PASS PROTEC-
TION

The objective of this drill is to practice pass protection and check blocks without contact.

INSTRUCTIONS:

(1) Any number of players may be used in this drill.

(2) If nine men are used on offense, nine men should be placed on defense.

(3) At a signal from the coach, the No. 1 men drop out and protect the passer against imaginary rushers from left or right.

(4) The others check-block in the line, then take their turn in blocking.

(5) See Illustration 97.

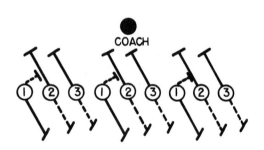

Illus. 97

26. HOW TO DRILL FOR CROSS BLOCKING

The purpose of this drill is to provide cross-blocking practice for the linemen.

INSTRUCTIONS:

(1) Linemen pair off in defensive and offensive groupings.

(2) Linemen alternate positions in counter clockwise directions.

(3) ○ represents offensive men.

(4) □ represents defensive men.

(5) A coach is stationed near the action to offer suggestions.

(6) See Illustration 98.

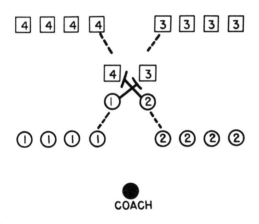

Illus. 98

27. HOW TO DRILL FOR OBSERVATION

The object of this drill is to develop the ability to be observing and alert and to increase proficiency in various types of blocks.

INSTRUCTIONS:

(1) Locate the bags in a line with the blockers in front of each bag.

(2) Each bag requires a man to hold and maneuver it.

(3) Blockers should be approximately three yards from the bags.

(4) Each blocker walks away from the boy opposite him while his personal bag tender plays "cat in the corner" by exchanging positions with some other tender.

(5) On the whistle, the blockers turn around, scan the bags for their own bag tender and throw a block on the new bag held by their man.

(6) Use as many units as feasible.

(7) See Illustration 99.

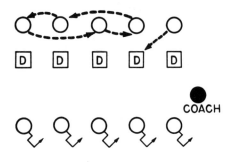

Illus. 99

28. HOW TO DRILL FOR FOLLOW THE LEADER

*The purpose of this drill is to develop blocking proficiency.
The blockers may use any type of block.*

INSTRUCTIONS:

(1) The bags are located in a line six yards apart.

(2) One player must hold each bag.

(3) Use as many bags as is feasible.

(4) The blockers assume their offensive stance.

(5) On a whistle, the blocker and runner of each group
start forward toward the bags.

(6) The blocker blocks in or out, using a shoulder or body
block.

(7) The runner follows the blocker and cuts to the proper
side.

(8) See Illustration 100.

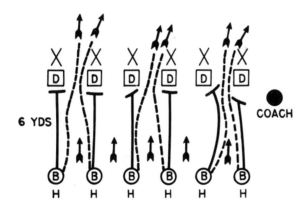

Illus. 100

29.   HOW TO DRILL FOR BACKFIELD BLOCKS

The idea behind this drill is to provide practice for the quarterback and the right half in blocking.

INSTRUCTIONS:

(1) A center and two complete backfields are needed on offense.

(2) One backfield runs all plays to the right and the other backfield runs all plays to the left.

(3) Four ends can alternate as linebackers and ends on defense.

(4) Run plays at top speed to obtain proper timing.

(5) A valuable drill for the quarterback and right halfback.

(6) See Illustration 101.

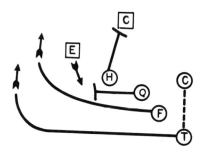

Illus. 101

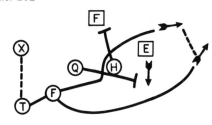

30. HOW TO DRILL FOR SET UP BLOCKING

The purpose of this drill is to teach offensive line blocking under simulated game conditions, utilizing a defensive alignment on the ball carrier.

INSTRUCTIONS:

(1) This drill is used with any number of units that may be feasible.

(2) Place a ball carrier closely behind an offensive lineman. Place a defensive lineman and a linebacker similarly.

(3) Only two play signals are given by the coach:

(a) One finger means that the ball carrier runs directly up to the defensive man and veers right.

(b) Two fingers means that the ball carrier veers left.

(4) In each case the offensive lineman blocks the defensive man accordingly—with the right or left shoulder.

(5) See Illustration 102.

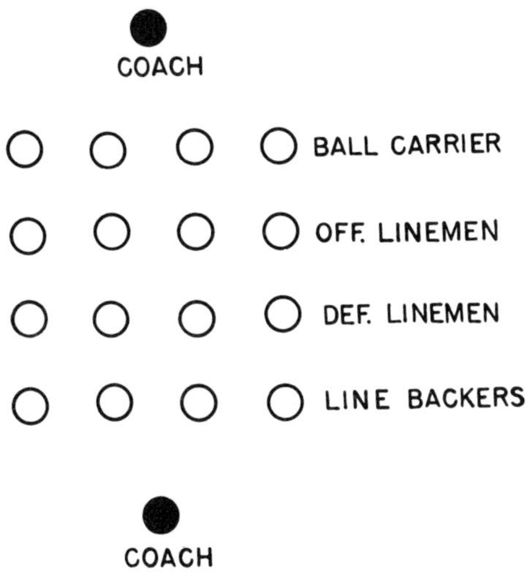

COACH

○ ○ ○ ○ BALL CARRIER

○ ○ ○ ○ OFF. LINEMEN

○ ○ ○ ○ DEF. LINEMEN

○ ○ ○ ○ LINE BACKERS

COACH

Illus. 102

31. HOW TO DRILL FOR OUTFLANKING THE DE-FENSE

The purpose of this drill is to give blockers practice in out-flanking a defender. This block is used when the offensive man has the defender flanked and desires to turn him toward the center.

INSTRUCTIONS:

(1) Place three blockers with three ball carriers on offense.

(2) Have two centers to snap the ball to the backs.

(3) Locate six linemen on defense—three with each group. Ends are preferred here.

(4) Station the blocker five yards outside the defensive man.

(5) Have blocker drive head and shoulder past defender and keep contact.   Watch for clipping.

(6) The ball carrier fakes in and runs wide outside.

(7) Blockers need practice in this type of drill to develop timing when blocking an opponent they have outflanked.

(8) See Illustration 103.

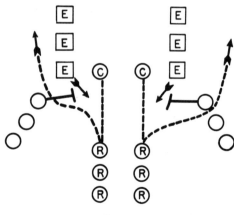

Illus. 103

32. HOW TO DRILL FOR REACTION

The purpose of this drill is to help speed up the reaction time of the players. Also to develop body balance and maneuverability.

INSTRUCTIONS:

(1) Arrange the dummies in a triangular shape about five yards apart with the apex of the triangle away from the blocker.

(2) Station three men to hold each of the dummies.

(3) The blocker assumes his offensive stance.

(4) Coach blows his whistle and the blocker starts forward. One man performs each time.

(5) When the blocker gets to the "cross roads," the coach designates 1, 2, or 3. The player then charges that bag and executes a particular maneuver.

(6) The players rotate so that each gets a chance to block and hold the dummies.

(7) See Illustration 104.

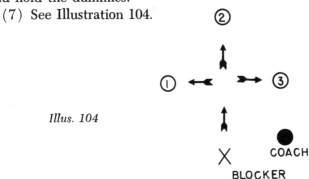

Illus. 104

COACH

X

BLOCKER

33. HOW TO DRILL FOR REACTION IN CHARGING

The purpose of this drill is to teach the linemen to make their offensive charge and then to react quickly—to make a tackle.

INSTRUCTIONS:

(1) Place the offensive linemen in a straight line.

(2) Locate two dummies about one foot apart. These bags are held by players.

(3) Station two other dummies behind these first two dummies and three yards on their outside. These dummies are also held by players.

(4) Use as many of these units as is feasible for the size of the coaching staff.

(5) The offensive lineman makes his charge, driving his head between the dummies and bringing his arms and shoulders into action.

(6) On the whistle, he rolls out of these dummies by a pivot step and works toward the secondary set of dummies where he throws a tackle on the bag that has been called or designated.

(7) Instead of using the whistle, the coach may yell "right" or "left" and the player responds accordingly.

(8) See Illustration 105.

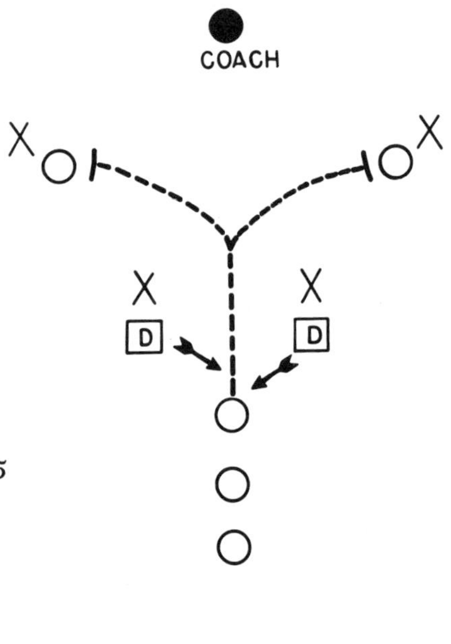

Illus. 105

34. HOW TO DRILL FOR REACTION AFTER BLOCKING

The purpose of this drill is to teach the players to react quickly after blocking. This drill is also designed to train and condition players so that they will not be on the ground after making a block.

INSTRUCTIONS:

(1) Station the players in a line.

(2) Place one bag on the line of scrimmage.

(3) Locate three other bags about five yards behind this bag and arrange them parallel to the line of scrimmage.

(4) Number these bags, starting from the left, one, two, and three.

(5) The player runs five yards to reach the first bag where he executes a shoulder or cross-body block.

(6) At the instant of the block, the coach yells "one," "two," or "three." The player must immediately jump to his feet and react toward the appropriate bag where he executes another block or tackle, as the case may be.

(7) Use as many of these units as the coaching staff will allow.

(8) See Illustration 106.

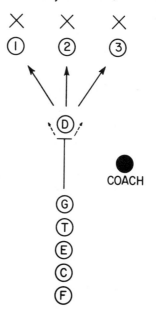

Illus. 106

35. HOW TO DRILL FOR ONE-ON-ONE

The object of this drill is to provide line blocking practice for the entire line. This one-on-one blocking drill is among the best drills in football.

INSTRUCTIONS:

(1) Line up the players in two lines facing each other about four yards apart. It is better to have the men paired according to weight.

(2) Start with the No. 1 line blocking with the right shoulder and the No. 2 line in a defensive position with the *right leg forward* for the right shoulder block.

(3) The coach commands "Ready . . . hike," and the first man in line No. 1 blocks the first man in line No. 2 until the coach signals "Position." On this signal both men return quickly to their original positions.

(4) The coach goes to the next pair and repeats the command.

(5) When the coach reaches the end of the line he turns around and No. 2 line blocks and No. 1 takes the defensive position.

(6) This is repeated until all the men have blocked three times with each shoulder.

(7) Demonstrate for the whole group, then go into the drill.

(8) Do not waste time with each individual.

(9) Have the men watch each other for technique.

(10) See Illustration 107.

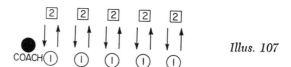

Illus. 107

36. HOW TO DRILL FOR TWO-ON-ONE

The purpose of this drill is to get the linemen accustomed to the type of work they will be called upon to do when the actual scrimmage begins.

INSTRUCTIONS:

(1) The players are located in a line facing the coach.

(2) The players are then numbered off by threes.

(3) No. 1 faces Nos. 2 and 3, stays low, and on the command to charge braces against 2 and 3 to provide resistance.

(4) Then practice double-teaming with short driving steps.

(5) The man on defense does not try to break through but he does try to hold the two offensive men so that they will have to put real drive into their charge.

(6) It is a good idea to rotate the men after every three charges.

(7) See Illustration 108.

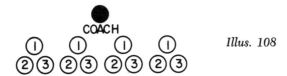

Illus. 108

37. HOW TO DRILL FOR THREE-ON-ONE

The object of this drill is to develop both offensive and defensive proficiency with the linemen.

INSTRUCTIONS:

(1) This drill involves offensive blocking, pulling out, three-on-one blocking, two-on-one blocking, and one-on-one blocking. It is a good drill to develop defensive ability for the one man on defense.

(2) The players line up in groups of four with three on offense, in a three-point stance, and one on defense in a defensive stance.

(3) Use as many groups as the coaching staff can handle.

(4) The coach, standing behind the defense, will signal to the three offensive men on the line of scrimmage:

(a) Designate two men to take the defensive lineman either right, left, or straight back.

(b) Designate all three to gang up on him.

(c) Designate two to pull and the remaining offensive linemen to trap the defensive charger.

(5) See Illustration 109.

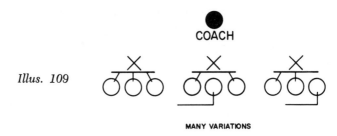

Illus. 109

MANY VARIATIONS

38.   HOW TO DRILL FOR FOUR-ON-ONE

If a coach has four guards and he desires to know quickly who are the most capable, this drill will accomplish that objective.

INSTRUCTIONS:

(1) Place a center on offensive with three other guards.

(2) Station the other guards on defensive between two dummies.

(3) Assign a reserve back to run the ball behind the offensive men.

(4) The defensive guard tries to cover the territory between the dummies. If he can hold his ground he is doing a great job.

(5) This drill offers seven different operations: (a) Initial

1. The Initial Formation	*2. Two-on-One from the Left*
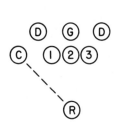	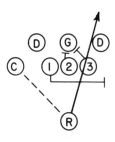

No. 3 does a hard shoulder block, No. 2 being the post. The guard on the left, No. 1, pulls.

3. The Wedge	*4. Reaction to a Trap*
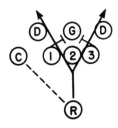	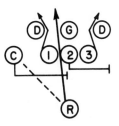

The offensive men three-on-one the defensive guard and try to drive him back. The ball carrier takes a snap from the center, runs up to the wedge, and breaks to either side.

The middle guard pulls to the right; both of the outside men step toward the guard as if they are going to block, then break away. The center snaps the ball, pulls, and traps the guard.

Illus. 110

formation, (b) The wedge, (c) Two-on-one left, (d) Two-on-one right, (e) Trap reaction, (f) Center trap, (g) Pass reaction, and (h) Confidence drill.

(6) See Illustration 110, in eight parts.

5. *Reaction to a Pass*   6. *Confidence Drills*

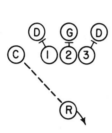   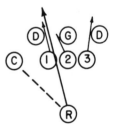

Both of the outside men turn out, the middle man steps in, hits and blocks for the passer. The back shows the pass, and the defensive man is timed on recognizing it and reaching for the passer. He tries to get to the passer and tackle him.

To restore the defensive man's confidence, let the No. 2 man block the guard himself one way or the other. No. 1 and No. 3 go through.

7. *Two-on-One from the Right*

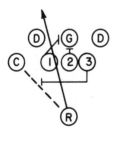

No. 1 does a hard shoulder right with No. 2 acting as a post. The guard on the right, No. 3, pulls and trap-blocks. The runner goes behind the trap.

These include just about every type of block a defensive lineman will encounter. Together, they make a great toughening-up drill. Put the tackles through the same drill.

Illus. 110 (cont'd)

39. HOW TO DRILL FOR THE 1-3-5 PULL OUT

This drill has four objectives: (a) *To develop speed in getting out of the line;* (b) *To check on men pointing when they are to pull out of the line;* (c) *To accustom men to running interference with others preceding and following them;* (d) *To teach the interference to turn upfield and not widen toward the sideline.*

INSTRUCTIONS:

(1) Five players participate in this drill and line up as an offensive line ready for scrimmage.   Have a waiting group of players formed in another line.

(2) A standing bell-bottom dummy is placed at the end of the five players, next to No. 5.

(3) On a signal, Nos. 1, 3, and 5 pull out and run as indicated.   Nos. 2 and 4 hold until the second signal is given and break downfield.   They may also pull.

(4) The linemen in the formed lines await their turn.

(5) The coach stands back and a little to the outside of the dummy where he is in position to check the form of the men pulling out.

(6) The lane between the dummy and the coach allows just enough room for one man to go through and this represents about the width of a line the interferers may expect in a game.

(7) Competition may be developed by the men who are running interference trying to slap each others' tails after they swing past the line of scrimmage.

(8) The men should never be allowed to shove slower men.

(9) The players must move into position quickly so that this drill does not lag.

(10) See Illustration 111.

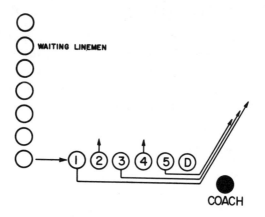

Illus. 111

40. HOW TO DRILL FOR SLED BLOCKING

The object of this drill is to teach the offensive linemen to block and charge as a unit with cadence.

INSTRUCTIONS:

(1) Locate the entire offensive line of seven men in position in front of a heavy blocking sled.

(2) Place a second- or third-string quarterback to the rear of these players to call the starting signals.

(3) Have the quarterback start the signals with a low count, two or three, and then work up to seven or eight.

(4) Strive to have all seven linemen hitting at the identical time.

(5) Alternate right and left shoulders.

(6) Alternate as many offensive units as is desirable.

(7) For variation, have all the linemen pull left or right after blocking the sled.

41. HOW TO DRILL DOWNFIELD BLOCKING TO TIME WITH THE BACKFIELD

Downfield blocking is one of the most difficult phases of football to teach. It demands a terrific selling job from the coach. The purpose of this drill is to provide practice for the linemen in downfield blocking by drilling with the backfield.

INSTRUCTIONS:

(1) Place dummies downfield in the position of defensive backs.

(2) Have the key downfield blockers on one side of the line stationed with the offensive center.

(3) As the backs are practicing ball handling and deception, the downfield blockers drill with them.

(4) This is a helpful drill for both the backfield men and linemen.

(5) See Illustration 112.

42. HOW TO DRILL FOR DOWNFIELD BLOCKING

The purpose of this drill is to teach the players the rudiments of downfield blocking without live competition. This drill also develops open-field running ability for the backfield.

INSTRUCTIONS:

(1) The dummies are lined up on a diagonal line about 15 yards downfield.

(2) The blockers and ball carriers are lined up in four lines. The blockers assume a three-point stance.

(3) Nos. 1, 2, and 4 are blockers and have assigned dummies to contact.

(4) No. 3 is the ball carrier and follows a predesigned course.

(5) No. 3 may receive the ball from a center or start with it in his hands.

(6) This drill can be used with variations.

(7) See Illustration 113a; see 113b for another downfield blocking drill.

Illus. 112

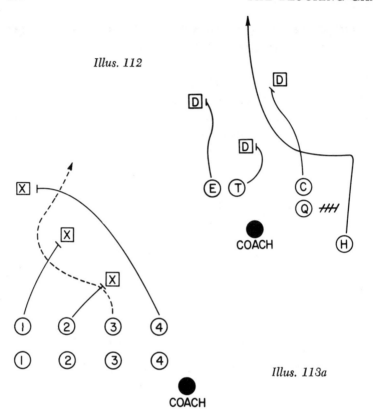

Illus. 113a

Illus. 113b. Downfield Blocking.   Left side goes down first, then right side, on signals from coach.

43. HOW TO DRILL DOWNFIELD BLOCKING FOR PULLING LINEMEN

The purpose of this drill is to teach downfield blocking for pulling linemen who lead plays from an end run to inside tackle.

INSTRUCTIONS:

(1) Station the offensive line of seven men in their three-point stances.

(2) The defensive players, either holding dummies or being "live" as the case may be, are lined up in the three defensive positions representing: (a) Defensive end, (b) Defensive halfback, and (c) Defensive linebacker.

(3) There are no defensive linemen in this drill.

(4) The offensive linemen who are not pulling out of the line practice dummy check blocks to screen off the defensive men in order that the interference cannot spot ball carriers and pulling men too readily.

(5) The defensive men are constantly changing their positions so the interference will have to hustle to block them.

(6) After the players have mastered the fundamentals of this drill, "live bait" may be substituted for the dummies.

(7) See Illustration 114.

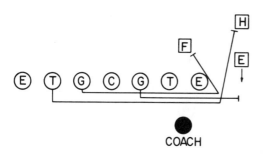

COACH

Illus. 114

44. HOW TO DRILL FOR COMPETITIVE DOWN-FIELD BLOCKING

The object of this drill is to make a game out of the live downfield blocking drill.

INSTRUCTIONS:

(1) Place defensive men in a regular 6-2-2-1, 5-3-2-1, or other common defensive alignment.   Run regular plays against them.

(2) Five linemen, a quarterback and two halfbacks are used on offensive.

(3) If the downfield blockers can keep the defensive men from tackling the ball carriers, the offense is credited with one point.

(4) If the defense makes the tackle or even gets into position where they should have made the tackle, but missed, the defense is awarded one point.

(5) The game continues until one side amasses 10 points.

(6) The losers must carry the dummies in at the end of the practice and out again the next day.

(7) See Illustration 115.

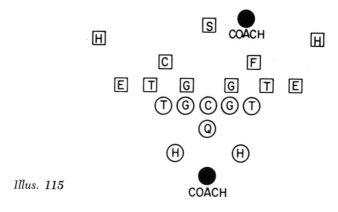

Illus. 115

45. HOW TO DRILL FOR TIMING

The idea behind this drill is to run the offensive without the danger of injury, but at the same time gaining much-needed polish and timing. It is especially effective when running new plays in order to concentrate on the play rather than physical contact.

INSTRUCTIONS:

(1) Locate the dummies in a simulated defensive situation, using a five, six, seven, or any predesigned defense.

(2) One man will be assigned to hold each bag.

(3) This drill can be worked effectively with three teams.

(4) To start the drill, one team will hold the bags in a defensive formation, one team will run a play, and the other team will be in a huddle.

(5) When the play is finished all teams change positions. The team that held the bags will form into a huddle. The team that ran the play will hold the bags, and the team that was in the huddle will run the next play.

(6) During this drill the coach should concentrate on: (a) Proper take-off, (b) Perfection in execution of the play, (c) Proper technique in individual blocking assignments, (d) The defensive man bringing the bag across the line of scrimmage.

(7) This drill coordinates many individual drills.

(8) See Illustration 116.

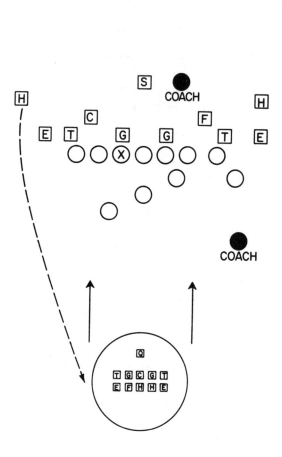

Illus. 116

46. HOW TO DRILL FOR LINE COHESION AND TIM-ING

The purpose of this drill is to develop exact offensive timing for the linemen.

INSTRUCTIONS:

(1) Station the No. 1 line (minus ends) on offensive.

(2) Place six dummies on defense to be held by players who will not take part in this drill.

(3) Station the No. 2 line behind the first line. The No. 2 line will run the same play as the No. 1 line.

(4) The linemen are to count cadence in this drill with a reserve quarterback.

(5) There are no backfield men except a spare lineman who is located in the backfield to give the center a target.

(6) Practice running all plays against the dummies, working for precision.

(7) Teams alternate after each play.

(8) Drill should last 15 minutes.

(9) See Illustration 117.

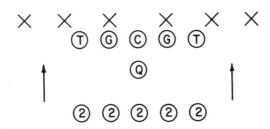

Illus. 117

47. HOW TO DRILL FOR SPOT SCRIMMAGE

The object of this drill is to conduct a contact scrimmage without using all of the available men.

INSTRUCTIONS:

(1) An offensive team is lined up in scrimmage position.

(2) A defensive team is likewise located on the line of scrimmage.

(3) Certain players on the defensive team are designated to be active on each play.

(4) The procedure is for the coach to call out, for example, "Ends active!"

(5) The quarterback would then call a play inside or outside of end.

(6) Another might be, "Secondary active!"

(7) The quarterback would then call a pass play.

(8) If the coach called "Right side active!" the play would be directed to that side of the line.

(9) The final step is to make all members of each side active in full-scale scrimmage.

(10) See Illustration 118.

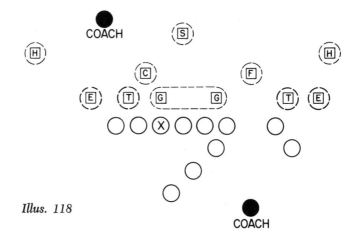

Illus. 118

48. HOW TO DRILL FOR SKELETAL SCRIMMAGE

The object of this drill is to provide competition between the seven best linemen on the squad when the coach has a good first line and only a fair second line. With this drill you can provide competition between the first and second lines. Also, two scrimmages may be going on at once.

INSTRUCTIONS:

(1) Line up the right side of your first line against the left side of the first line.

(2) Line up the right side of the second line against the left side of the second line.

(3) Allow one side to be on offense for 15 minutes and then let the other side be on offense for the same amount of time.

(4) Run the regular offensive plays against standard defense.

(5) This drill is also adaptable to large squads where various coaches can conduct their own separate drills. Very few players will be idle in this plan.

(6) See Illustrations 119a, 119b, and 119c.

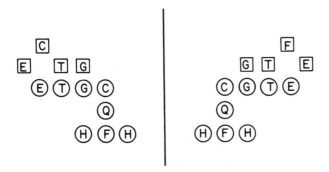

Illus. 119a

Illus. 119b

Illus. 119c

49. HOW TO DRILL FOR ROTARY SCRIMMAGE

The object of this drill is to provide practice for three or four defensive players at a time and to give the backs practice in executing plays at full speed.

INSTRUCTIONS:

(1) Place the first-string line on offense and the second-string line on defense.

(2) The first backfield runs offensive plays and the second backfield holds dummies downfield.

(3) Name two linemen and one or two (as the case may be) linebackers "live."

(4) The remainder of the positions on defense are dummies being held by players on defense.

(5) The three or four "live" defensive men may work any kind of defense that they wish.

(6) The offensive men run any plays of their choosing at the defensive men.

(7) The blockers not blocking the "live" men will block the appropriate dummies, including those downfield.

(8) The coach should see that the dummies are hit at full speed.

(9) The "live" men on defense may be varied.

(10) Switch the defensive men to the offense, and vice versa.

(11) See Illustration 120.

50. HOW TO DRILL FOR MORALE

There are times when a coach needs some drill that will pick up the morale of the players.   That is the purpose of this drill.
INSTRUCTIONS:

(1) Morale drills should possess much speed and one or two men in action at one time.

(2) Use three large standing bell-bottom dummies.

(3) Station the dummies in the pattern of a triangle.

(4) Position players in a single-file line. Each man attempts to knock down all three dummies with a rolling open field block.

(5) The amusing positions often resulting from this drill should entertain the players and restore them to good spirits.

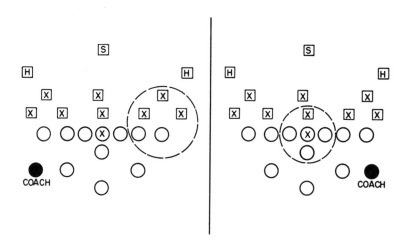

Illus. 120

51. HOW TO DRILL FOR DUMMY SCRIMMAGE

The purpose of this drill is to teach timing and finesse of play situations without actual contact. It will simulate game conditions while developing the offense.

INSTRUCTIONS:

(1) The dummies are lined up to simulate a five-, six-, or seven-man line.

(2) ◯ indicates the offensive men.

(3) ✕ indicates dummies being held by players.

(4) Drill is accomplished by running two plays against the dummies.

(5) One or two teams may be on offense.

(6) The players holding the bags remain on defense until the drill is completed.

(7) See Illustration 121.

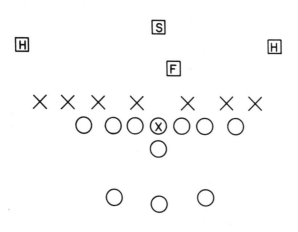

Illus. 121

52. HOW TO DRILL THE ROTATION PLAN

The object of this drill is to provide rapid blocking practice for the complete line. It will give each lineman defensive training.

INSTRUCTIONS:

(1) Station two offensive lines and two defensive lines.

(2) A coach stands behind the defensive players and gives hand signals to the offensive blockers to block in or out.

(3) A reverse shoulder block may be used when blocking out.

(4) Assign four blockers and defensive men in each line.

(5) Rotation plan: Players in Line 1 go to Line 2. Players in Line 2 go to Line 3. Players in Line 3 go to Line 4. Players in Line 4 go to Line 1.

(6) See Illustration 122.

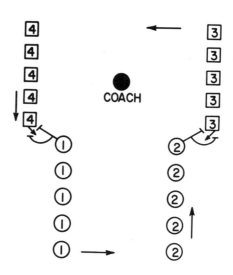

Illus. 122

53. HOW TO DRILL FOR TRIANGLE BLOCKING AND TACKLING

This is a combination drill that features both offense and defense.

INSTRUCTIONS:

(1) Place three dummies in a triangle five yards apart.

(2) Have three men holding the dummies.

(3) Three files of players are needed. Two act as blockers and the other as ball carriers.

(4) Position tacklers five yards downfield and have them alternate one at a time.

(5) Blockers may block any one of the three dummies, except one blocker must always block the lead dummy.

(6) The runner follows his blockers closely. This will improve reactions of ball carriers because they never know which way the blockers will contact the dummies.

(7) The tackler downfield approaches as far as the lead dummy and attempts to tackle the ball carrier.

(8) Insist that the blockers drive five yards after making contact.

(9) See Illustration 123.

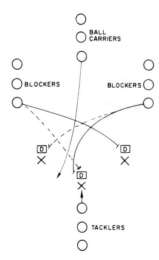

Illus. 123

54. HOW TO DRILL FOR CHARGING, BLOCKING AND TACKLING

This sled is the next best thing to live practice. The purpose of the Crowther sled is to save time and improve practice organization.

INSTRUCTIONS:

(1) One of the finest pieces of mechanical equipment ever devised for both offensive and defensive drills is the Rae Crowther two man sled. Rae Crowther, a former line coach at University of Pennsylvania, also designed a seven-man sled.

(2) Drills of all types can be used on the two-man Crowther sled. They are too numerous to mention, and almost every conceivable drill can be employed with the sled.

(3) See Illustration 124.

Illus. 124

(4) Do the same for the left guard.

(5) This is good practice to have the players go in and "dig 'em out."

(6) The lines will be more shallow when trapping for the counter play.

(7) See Illustration 127.

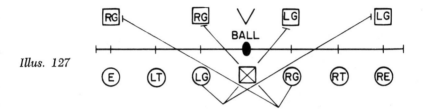

Illus. 127

58. HOW TO DRILL FOR DOWNFIELD BLOCKING

The purpose of this drill is to stress and teach downfield blocking by the offside line.

INSTRUCTIONS:

(1) Place a complete unit on offense to run any plays the quarterback calls except passes.

(2) The defensive on-side line is always playing dummy.

(3) The off-side line plays full speed and goes for blocks downfield.

(4) Place a complete unit on defense. The secondary plays at full speed.

(5) See Illustration 128.

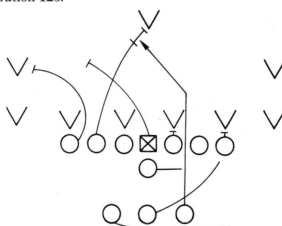

Illus. 128

59. HOW TO DRILL WITH SEVEN DUMMIES

The purpose of this drill is to practice downfield blocking with seven linemen and seven dummies.

INSTRUCTIONS:

(1) Align seven bell-bottom dummies.

(2) Place a complete offensive line five yards away from the dummies.

(3) On a command by the reserve quarterback have the offensive men release and execute their blocks.

(4) See Illustration 129.

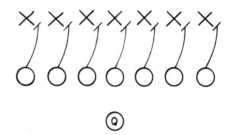

Illus. 129

60. HOW TO DRILL BACKSIDE BLOCKING

The purpose of this drill is to teach downfield blocking with half lines.

INSTRUCTIONS:

(1) Use three or four half lines on offense against one team on defense.

(2) The defensive team employs the same defenses that your opponent is expected to use.

(3) Place dummies eight yards from the ball and forward of the line of scrimmage.

(4) The defensive is "full speed" and they make it difficult for the offensive linemen to release.

(5) See Illustration 130.

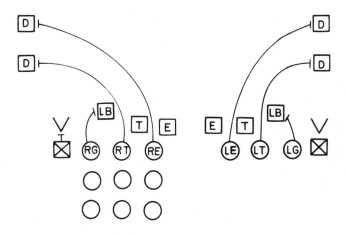

Illus. 130

61. HOW TO DRILL FOR THE SHOULDER BLOCK

The purpose of this drill is to practice the shoulder block under game conditions.

INSTRUCTIONS:

(1) Station five blockers on offense.

(2) Place five players on defense.

(3) Locate a coach behind the defensive players to give hand signals indicating the direction he wants the offense to block.

(4) Have the players practice both right and left shoulder blocks.

(5) Every player on the squad can take part in this drill.

(6) See Illustration 131.

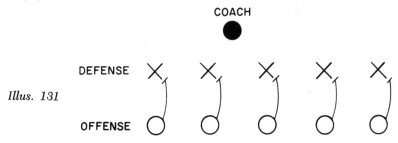

Illus. 131

62. HOW TO DRILL FOR ASSEMBLY-LINE BLOCKING

This is a production drill for teaching blocking in the shortest possible time after the men have acquired the fundamentals.

INSTRUCTIONS:

(1) Line up players in two lines facing each other about four yards apart.

(2) It is better to have men paired according to weight.

(3) Start with A line blocking with a right shoulder and.B line in a defensive position with the right leg forward for right shoulder block.

(4) The coach commands, "Ready . . . charge" and first man in A line blocks first man in B line until coach signals "position." On this signal both men return as quickly as possible to their original positions.

(5) The coach may make a comment and go to the next pair and repeat the command.

(6) When the coach reaches the end of the line he turns around and B line blocks and A line takes the defensive position.

(7) This is repeated until all men have blocked three times with each shoulder. (More or less as the coach desires.)

(8) Do not waste too much time with each individual.

(9) Demonstrate for whole group, then go into drill. Have men watch each other for technique.

(10) See Illustration 132.

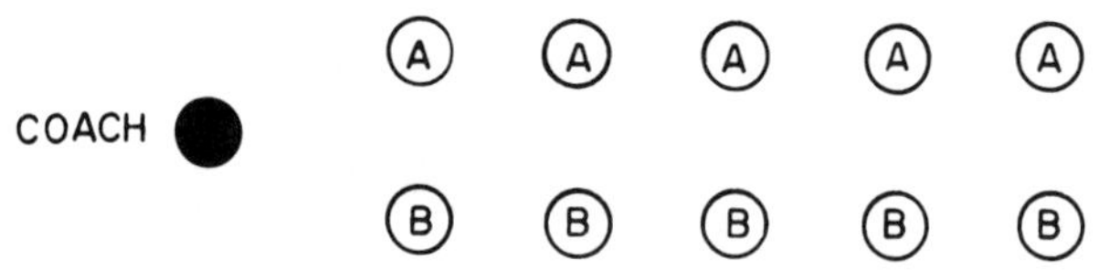

Illus. 132

63. HOW TO DRILL FOR UNIFIED CHARGING

The purpose of this drill is to provide practice for the linemen to develop a quick unified charge on offense.

INSTRUCTIONS:

(1) Place the offensive center, with the ball, exactly one-half yard ahead of the other linemen.

(2) Locate on the right of the center those men who normally play on the right of the center, and on the left those who normally play on the left.

(3) Position one lineman five yards back to receive the ball.

(4) As the ball is snapped the linemen take four short, fast steps forward, keeping the back parallel to the ground with the legs well under the body.

(5) On the last step have them dive forward flat on the ground.

(6) Backfield men may also be used in this drill.

(7) Select a soft grassy spot for this drill.

(8) See Illustration 133.

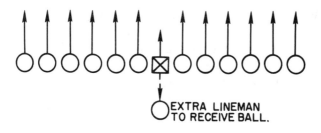

Illus. 133

5

THE KICKING GAME

The punt is the most important play in football.

—Fielding H. Yost

A GOOD KICK IS AN INDISPENSABLE PART OF THE OFFENSE. AN average kick, properly used, can do wonders. Even a mediocre punt skillfully used is a tremendous strength to either offense or defense.

Most of the "breaks" that pave the way to scores in close games result in one way or another from kicks. The break may be a very long kick, a short kick, a blocked kick, a kick out of bounds, or a poorly placed kick. It may be a fumbled punt or a long return. In any event, the favorable position from which one team or the other scores in a closely contested game is usually traceable to a kick or a play growing out of it. In many closely contested games (under normal conditions) each team will kick between seven and 10 times. Therefore, one team has approximately fourteen to twenty opportunities, consisting of kicking and receiving the ball, to gain yardage or put itself in a favorable position on the field. Judging from

180

this it would seem that the team with the better kicking game has a distinct advantage.

Kicking in combination with a good running attack should land the offensive team within striking distance at least two or three times in a game. The score then can be effected either by the rushing game, the place kick, or the pass.

This chapter outlines many drills used in the kicking game. The majority of drills that exist on the kicking aspect of the game (they are relatively few) usually involve the entire team working as a unit—such as protecting the kicker, either punter or place kicker, while he is executing his kick. This type of drill is one in which several fundamentals are drilled at once.

This is one aspect of the football game, and a very important one, where there is a dire need for more efficient drills. Knowing the importance that coaches place on the kicking game, it is only reasonable to allow a fair portion of time in a practice time schedule to that phase of the game. A time study chart for analyzing the kicking game appears. See Illustration 134.

Number of minutes for each drill

	1st week				2nd week				3rd week				TOTAL
DATE													
THE PUNT													
THE QUICK-KICK													
THE FIELD GOAL													
THE KICK-OFF													
THE PUNT RETURN													
THE KICK-OFF RETURN													
THE REVERSE DRILL													

Illus. 134

1. HOW TO DRILL FOR THE STANCE AND STEPS

The golfer, the baseball batter and other athletes pay strict attention to the placement of their feet before they start swinging. They have practiced a predetermined position which has been chosen, in each case, because it has proved more efficient. This setting of the feet is commonly referred to as "stance."

INSTRUCTIONS:

(1) The first job is to set the stance, to discover how the feet should be placed at the beginning of a kick. Before making any kind of punt, the kicker should stand with the kicking foot forward. Thus, most kickers will find they need take but one step with the non-kicking foot before they kick with the other. This eliminates the unnecessary extra step most untrained kickers take.

(2) Have the kicker take his stance until he feels both comfortable and solidly set, and while in this position push him forward, back, left, and right. If his feet are poorly placed the player will easily be pushed off balance. Balance is an integral part of each good, accurate kick.

(3) After the kicker has found his correct stance, have him practice taking his kicking steps and go through the motions of kicking the football. No ball is needed in this drill for steps. He is just trying to get the "feel" of the act.

(4) Sometimes it helps to outline the position of the feet both before and at the end of a simulated kick. Outlines may be marked on a large piece of cardboard. In this way the kicker can check the placement of his feet each time he reports for practice, until that placement has become second nature.

2. HOW TO DRILL FOR FOOT POSITION

The purpose of this drill is to teach punters the correct foot position when punting.

INSTRUCTIONS:

(1) Have the punters take 10 to 15 short jab steps each day, being sure the toes are pointed properly. They can do this in their rooms or elsewhere off the field.

(2) Stress the importance of the toes being depressed and the foot rigid at the moment of hitting the ball.

3. HOW TO DRILL FOR KICKING WITHOUT A CENTER

The purpose of this drill is to develop the technique of kicking when a center is not available. This is especially true during the summer vacation months when a kicker often must drill alone.

INSTRUCTIONS:

(1) When the ball strikes the hands, an important part of the kicking performance is the quick manipulation of the ball in the hands. This is necessary to bring the laces up and to extend the ball ready to place it on the foot.

(2) An excellent drill for this is obtained by tossing the ball a few inches into the air, quickly adjusting it the moment it strikes the hands. Then go through all the motions of kicking the football.

(3) See Illustration 135.

Illus. 135

4. HOW TO DRILL FOR PLACING THE BALL ON THE FOOT

The purpose of this drill is to teach the punters the correct ball position on the foot for the spiral punt.

INSTRUCTIONS:

(1) Have the kicker mark the middle seam on the underside of the ball with soft white chalk before he kicks the ball.

(2) After the kicker has completed his follow-through, observe the line made by the chalked middle seam on the instep. If that line is as stated in (3), you should have obtained a good spiral punt.

(3) Before actually kicking the ball in this drill, have the punter go through the motions of placing the ball on the foot. Always stress that the ball should lie across the instep with the nose slightly toward the inside of the front of the kicking shoe. The seam on the underside of the ball crosses the instep about halfway up the lacing. The rear of the ball lies just to the outside of the top of the kicking shoe.

5. HOW TO DRILL FOR FORM AND ACCURACY

The purpose of this drill is to enable punters to develop proper kicking form and at the same time to develop accuracy in punting.

INSTRUCTIONS:

(1) Distance is not a concern in this drill. Make sure the kicker understands that. This is a short kicking drill at a set target.

(2) Have the kicker work with another player about 10 yards apart. The kicker just meets the ball and practices until he gets it to the other man. The receiving player should hold his hands up as a target.

(3) The kicker should always check his stance, see that his running foot and the nose of the ball are pointed in the direction of the target. Always see that the ball is held properly.

Then practice the "line drive" with the nose of the ball down or up depending upon the target.

(4) Gradually lengthen the distance in this drill after the punter has mastered the fundamentals.

(5) This is also a good warm-up drill for all kickers.

6. HOW TO DRILL FOR SPEEDING THE RHYTHM OF THE KICKER

Many times a kick will be blocked because the kicker is taking too much time in his punting action. The aim of this drill is to accelerate the kicker's rhythm and coordinate the action with the center.

INSTRUCTIONS:

(1) The action of the kicker can be timed quite accurately by a stop watch. First, indicate the time the center pass takes to reach the kicker's hands.

(2) Second, and very important (this phase of the action is difficult to time because it happens so fast), judge the time the kicker has possession of the ball *before* it is kicked.

(3) Third, note the time it takes the kicker to receive the ball and get off the kick.

(4) In this manner you can determine just where the kicking action is being delayed. Perhaps it is the center's fault.

(5) During games the entire action, from the time the ball leaves the center's hands until it leaves the kicker's foot, may be timed accurately with a stopwatch.

(6) See Illustration 136.

Illus. 136

7. HOW TO DRILL FOR PUNTING UNDER PRESSURE

While in practice, many punters can kick a football well, but under game conditions they are not consistent. Therefore the wise coach will provide his punters with kicking experience under pressure.

This is also an excellent drill to teach linemen how to block a kick. Blocking punts is an art and must be practiced by drill. In addition, this drill will improve the ability of the centers in snapping the ball back to the kickers.

INSTRUCTIONS:

(1) Use a kicker, a center and two guards, tackles or ends. Line up the kicker the desired distance (10 yards unless kicking from spread formation) from the center. Then have the center snap the ball back to the kicker. The linemen rush two at a time and attempt to block the punt. Sometimes it is desirable to first rush only one man.

(2) The punter should attempt to get his kick off with regular rhythm to a safety man downfield. Many times he should try to kick the ball into the blocker's abdomen.

(3) The blocker drives in with both hands across his face for protection from possible injury to that area. He should make every effort to get the midsection of his body over the kicker's foot. He *must* go for the kicker's *foot*, never the kicker.

(4) This should be a must drill early in the season for the linemen and all kickers.

(5) See Illustration 137.

8. HOW TO DRILL FOR OVERCOMING MENTAL HAZARDS IN PUNTING

Mental hazards often cause the kicker to fail. The object of this drill is to overcome these mental factors in kicking.

INSTRUCTIONS:

(1) Have another ball passed to your kicker while he is about ready to kick the one he has already received from the center. This tends to either draw him off balance or draw his eye off the ball, or both.

(2) Cross in front of the kicker while he is about to kick.

(3) Have the line and the ends run in on him without opposition at the instant he receives the ball.

(4) Have a wet ball unexpectedly passed to him by the center, instead of the usual dry one he expected.

(5) Have him kick from the middle of a crowd with only one opening toward the goal to kick through. Use the chalk test on the kicking foot and the ball.

(6) Some of these tests will at first bother the kicker, but they can be applied to benefit him tremendously.

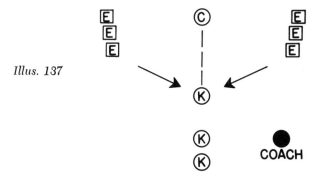

Illus. 137

9. HOW TO DRILL FOR RECEIVING BAD PASSES FROM CENTER

The center and the kicker are a team within a team. In this two-man team lies the responsibility for success or failure of every kicking play. The purpose of this drill is to provide the kicker with practice in fielding bad passes from center.

INSTRUCTIONS:

(1) Place the kicker in the shadows of his own goal post. Station a complete defensive line of six or seven men against the offensive team. Use a complete offensive team of 11 men. The kicker should attempt to punt the ball out of the end zone each time.

(2) The defensive players are to rush the kicker, but should not block the kick if they penetrate the offensive line.

(3) Instruct the center to snap his passes deliberately high, low, left, and right. The passes should not be wild, but off just enough to bother the kicker.

(4) Station three defensive halfbacks to practice receiving punts and returning them for 20 yards. They are not to be tackled, since there is to be no contact after the ball is kicked.

(5) This drill will be of tremendous value to the kickers. It should be practiced on other areas of the field.

(6) By drilling the men on the unexpected you are preparing them to play a better game.

(7) This drill is recommended during early season preparation.

(8) See Illustration 138.

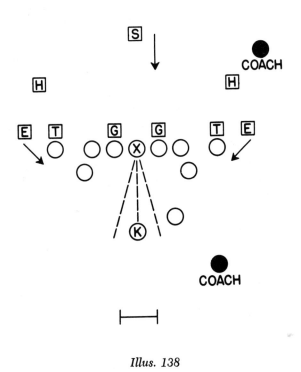

Illus. 138

10. HOW TO DRILL FOR THE KICKER'S AND CENTER'S TIMING

The center and kicker are the starting half of the little team within the team. While every man in the team is vital to the kick's success, the greatest coordination is required of these two. The purpose of this drill is to improve that coordination.

INSTRUCTIONS:

(1) Some centers can spin the ball a definite number of revolutions every time they spiral it back to the kicker. If a center will drill himself on this, the kicker is given an added advantage with very little extra work. When the ball is made to spin a certain number of revolutions over a set distance, the center can work out the position of the ball in the ground (when he is about to pass it back) so as to put it in the kicker's hand with the lacing up. This eliminates the necessity for the kicker to turn the ball in order to get the lace on top. The fraction of a second that a well-centered ball will save can mean the outcome of the game.

(2) The center must know just where the kicker prefers to receive the ball. He must know how fast a pass the kicker prefers and be able to gauge his actions so that a perfect timing in reception of the pass may be achieved.

(3) When a kicker is kicking slowly, the best thing for the coach to do is merely to say, "Kick faster." When the kicker goes too far forward, the best thing for the coach to do is to make a mark on the ground and tell the kicker to kick from behind the mark.

(4) The necessary coordination between the center and the kicker can only be accomplished by constant drilling together, day after day, until their timing is perfect.

11. HOW TO DRILL FOR KICKING OUT OF BOUNDS

The object of this drill is to practice for accuracy in kicking and to provide training in kicking out of bounds.

INSTRUCTIONS:

(1) Have the kickers forget about distance. Reemphasize that a short, accurate kick is worth much more than a long, inaccurate one.

(2) Start this drill about 15 yards back and 17 yards in from the sidelines. Use flags to mark the goal line, the five- and the ten-yard lines. Have different colored flags on each line. Use red on the goal, white on the five and yellow on the 10, with the punter using the white flag as his target.

(3) As the punter achieves control in this drill, have him move back an additional 15 yards on the same angle. The first kicking location would be on the 15, the second on the 30, and the third on the 45-yard line.

(4) Before the kickers move back, make sure they are fairly accurate at the shorter distances.

(5) See Illustration 139.

Illus. 139

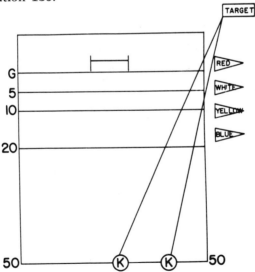

12. HOW TO DRILL FOR ACCURACY IN PUNTING

The major purpose of this drill is to develop accuracy on the part of punters. In addition, the drill will provide punt receivers with practice in catching punts and running them back.

INSTRUCTIONS:

(1) Line up the kicker on the 50-yard line and the center on the 40-yard line to snap the ball. Have a minimum of five or six footballs and one manager to assist the center when the balls are returned.

(2) Divide the linemen into two groups on the outside of the sideline strip, half on one side and half on the other. The linemen are covering the sideline area.

(3) The halfbacks and safety men work in pairs on the goal line or about the five-yard line.

(4) The intended receiver stands with his hands held high in the air. His signal is somewhat similar to a "fair catch."

(5) The kicker attempts to kick the ball to the man with the outstretched hands.

(6) The receiver catches the ball and comes up the sideline, cuts back, then passes to one of his linemen.

(7) The linemen have gone downfield to cover the kick. The lineman who receives the ball from the back returns it to the center.

(8) The kicker can alternate this drill, first to the right and then to the left.

(9) See Illustration 140.

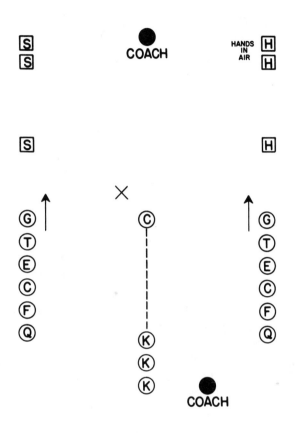

Illus. 140

13.   HOW TO DRILL FOR THE CONTACT POINT IN PLACE-KICKS

The purpose of this drill is to locate the bull's eye—you must hit the toe to place-kick the ball accurately.

INSTRUCTIONS:

(1) In practice the ball should be marked with an inverted pyramid centered on the seam in the lower half of the ball. The bottom point is placed on the rear middle seam, just three inches up from the bottom end of the ball. The top line is three inches higher (six inches up from the bottom end of the ball) and is three inches long. It is drawn at right angles to the middle seam, extending out one and one half inches on each side of it. Mark it with dark-colored chalk.

(2) In practice make a chalk dot on the front of the kicking toe. The white dot will show up on the ball when it is kicked.

(3) After each kick, note carefully just where the foot hit the ball. Having determined this, wipe the area within the triangle clean for the next kick. Be sure not to erase the triangle or the line on the rear seam of the ball because they may give additional information as to just how the kicker is contacting the ball by lines they leave on the kicking foot.

(4) The exact spot on which the place-kicker's toe should hit the ball is about five inches up from the bottom tip of the ball and directly on the rear middle seam.

(5) This same drill may be used in drop-kicking.

(6) See Illustration 141.

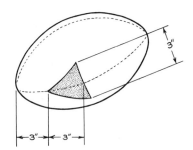

Illus. 141

14. HOW TO DRILL FOR CONVERSIONS

The purpose of this drill is to improve footwork on approaching the ball when kicking conversions.

INSTRUCTIONS:

(1) In place kicking, the kicker is approaching a fixed object, the ball. The kicker must have his steps down so pat that every time he makes an approach his feet will fall in exactly the same pattern and have precisely the same spacing. He can't expect to accomplish this by guesswork. He must mark his steps.

(2) To mark his steps, stand, as shown, with the kicking foot as it would contact the ball when the kick is made. Put a marker (piece of canvas or white cardboard) under the non-kicking foot. Then take a long step backwards to measure the distance covered by the hop forward. Bring the feet together so that the marker may be put underneath the kicking foot.

(3) Take another (but shorter) step backward with the non-kicking foot.

(4) Next bring the kicking foot alongside of it, and the kicker should be in starting position.

(5) Now the kicker should be ready to kick.

15. HOW TO DRILL FOR TOWEL KICKING

The purpose of this drill is to present another method to train the kickers for accuracy.

INSTRUCTIONS:

(1) Station the center on the 30-yard line.

(2) Place two towels on either side of the field on the 10-yard line and two more on the goal line.

(3) Allow each punter to kick three balls and then rotate to the next punter.

(4) Move back to the 40- or 50-yard line after warming up well.

(5) Punt to both sides of the field.

(6) Move the ball from hash-mark to hash-mark.

(7) Place safety men between the towels to practice catching the ball.

(8) Have them run the ball back to the center and return to the line for their next turn.

(9) See Illustration 142.

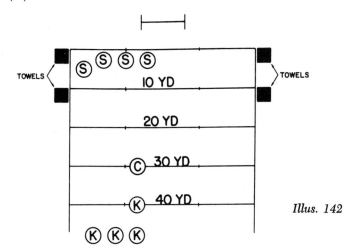

Illus. 142

16. HOW TO DRILL FOR CONVERSIONS WITH THE HOLDER

The purpose of this drill is to accustom the holder and the place kicker to pressure. This drill should help their timing and speed up the actions to simulate game conditions.

INSTRUCTIONS:

(1) A skeleton unit composed of a center, holder, place kicker and two rushers execute this drill. Substitutes may be used as rushers.

(2) The rushers start from a distance of five yards back of the defensive end positions. They should start charging at the snap of the ball.

(3) It is more efficient if only one player rushes at a time. This will help to avoid collisions.

(4) The holder and kicker work on their forms and attempt to speed up their elapsed kicking time.

(5) Have at least five balls and a manager to retrieve the kicked balls. The extra player not rushing can catch the returned balls from the manager.

(6) With one holder and one kicker, five minutes is sufficient time for this drill.

(7) See Illustration 143.

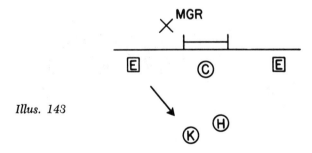

Illus. 143

17. HOW TO DRILL FOR BLOCKING A CONVERSION

The objective in this drill is to present a method of blocking conversions. All the drills suggested for blocking punts may be used against a conversion attempt.

INSTRUCTIONS:

(1) Use two full teams in this drill.

(2) Always rush the conversion kicker with *at least* nine men.

(3) Place two halfbacks at a depth of three yards in the end zone.

(4) Another plan, and an effective one, is to rush the conversion kicker with 11 men.

(5) Plan on a conversion attempt, but don't be surprised by a pass. Have the linebackers delay the offensive ends.

(6) These stunts must be practiced for proper execution the same as drilling on blocking punts.

(7) These two drills provide valuable practice for the players of the offensive team as well.

(8) See Illustration 144.

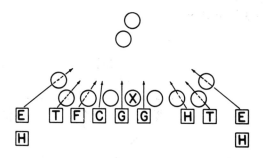

Illus. 144

18. HOW TO DRILL FOR FIELD GOALS

The purpose of this drill is to familiarize the center, the holder and the place-kicker with pressure, and to coordinate their actions so that they are letter-perfect together.

INSTRUCTIONS:

(1) A skeleton unit composed of a center, holder, place-kicker, two ends, and one rusher execute this drill.

(2) The rusher starts from five yards back of the defensive end position at the snap of the ball. He should vary his defensive alignment so as not to always rush from the same area. One rusher is more efficient than two. Collisions are frequent with two rushers. Consequently, neither should rush in pell-mell.

(3) The offensive ends get practice in covering each kick. This is most important work for an end. This drill is a good conditioner for the ends. Two sets of ends may be used.

(4) The holder and kicker work on their form and timing. The holder always marks the spot (small piece of white paper) where he will place the ball.

(5) It is desirable to begin this drill from the huddle. This allows the offense to practice their timing and simulates game conditions.

(6) A stop watch is recommended for the coach in all kicking drills.

(7) See Illustration 145.

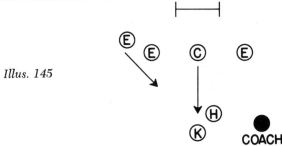

Illus. 145

19. HOW TO DRILL FOR MULTIPLE FIELD GOALS

The object of this drill is to provide practice for the three best centers, kickers and holders in field goal kicking. The drill is designed to save time, since most kicking drills are rather lengthy.

INSTRUCTIONS:

(1) Line up three sets of centers, kickers, and holders to work together in groups as a team on field goal kicking.

(2) Place the groups in various positions on the field.

(3) Each group should get practice kicking from various angles.

(4) A stopwatch should be used to determine the length of time used to get kicks away.

(5) Three to four seconds should be acceptable.

(6) Several managers are needed to return the kicked footballs.

(7) See Illustration 146.

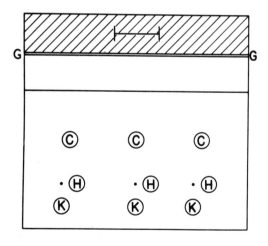

Illus. 146

20. HOW TO DRILL FOR THE KICK-OFF

The purpose of this drill is to practice kick-offs. In addition, this drill is arranged so that it will not interfere with other groups working and does not monopolize the field.

INSTRUCTIONS:

(1) This drill takes place inside of the hashmarks near the sideline.

(2) Every team should have at least two men who can kick off. Two kick-off tees are needed in this drill. Two footballs are required for each kicker.

(3) One kicker tees his ball on the 40-yard line. The other player waits to receive the ball near the goal line. In the meantime he has already teed his ball on the 10-yard line. He will kick it after the other player has completed his try. A manager is helpful in fielding stray kicks.

(4) In this kick-off drill no time is lost because each player always has a ball on the tee ready to return.

(5) Six or eight kicks each day are enough. The kick-off should be high in order to get all men down under the kick.

(6) Actually this drill should be done before or after regular practice.

(7) See Illustration 147.

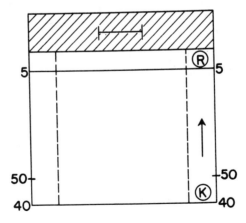

Illus. 147

21. HOW TO DRILL FOR COVERAGE OF KICKS WITH THE INTERIOR LINE

The purpose of the drill is to give the tackles, guards and center practice in covering kicks. This is a combination drill in that your punter, receivers, passers and pass receivers also get essential work.

INSTRUCTIONS:

(1) The kickers line up single file. Place the lead man 10 yards behind the center.

(2) The tackles and guards line up single file, right and left, in their customary punt-formation positions. The centers do the same.

(3) In order to get proper sequence of the covering groups, a coach stationed downfield should yell "On balance!" as the linemen approach the receiver. This is to make the linemen conscious of balance and position before attempting to make the tackle.

(4) Safetymen and halfbacks are downfield and alternate in receiving punts. The ends are 10 yards in from each sideline with the receiving units. They wait until the punt has been received and break back up-field to take a forward pass from the pass receiver. Tackles or guards may be substituted for ends in this drill. They line up as though receiving passes and will cover punts with more enthusiasm with this method.

(5) If you wish, the ends may go downfield with the line and cover the kick rather than wait with the receivers. They then wait until another punt has been received and break back up-field to take a forward pass.

(6) Defensive ends may be placed across the line of scrimmage to rush the punters. Only one end should rush the

punter at a time so as to avoid collisions and possible injury.

(7) The defensive ends should start from a position approximately five yards back of the line of scrimmage, since the punter has no protective blockers.

(8) When going down under a punt the ends and one lineman should go with the snap of the ball. The remaining linemen might hold for their counts.

(9) See Illustration 148.

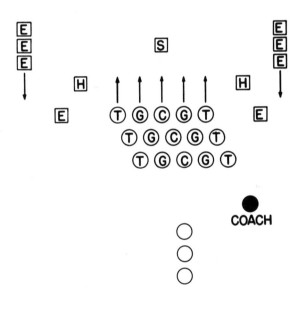

Illus. 148

22.   HOW TO DRILL BACKFIELD MEN ON RECEIV-
ING PUNTS

The purpose of this drill is to teach the punt receivers to keep their eyes on the ball, to catch and field punts.

INSTRUCTIONS:

(1) Much backfield work on the receiving end of the kick is essential.   Receivers should have daily practice of some type to keep in good form.

(2) Linemen may be used on two lines flanking the centers. To start the drill it is better to eliminate all coverage and concentrate on reception of the ball.

(3) The punters line up in their regular positions for punt formation.

(4) The punt receivers station themselves in pairs, one for interference and the other to receive the ball.   They should be downfield about 40 yards.

(5) *Every punt must be caught or fielded.*   All bounces should be played as if a game were being played.   Valuable training on fielding rolling and bouncing kicks is experienced in this drill.

(6) Have the punters kick very high as these are the most difficult to catch.

(7) As the receiver catches the ball he attempts to return up-field for at least 15 yards.   If linemen are covering the kick, he attempts to dodge a tag below the waist.

(8) The center may also be released to cover the kick if more than two are available.

(9) Men coming downfield should be encouraged to yell and otherwise try to get the receiver to take his eye off the ball.

(10) See Illustration 149.

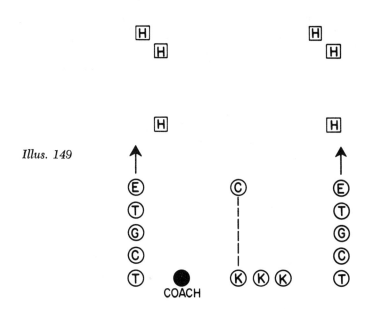

Illus. 149

COACH

23. HOW TO DRILL FOR COVERAGE OF KICKS WITH THE ENDS

One of the most important elements of the kicking game is the coverage of the kick. The purpose of this drill is to coordinate the kicker and the ends in proper coverage of a kick. This drill also provides practice for your center and punt receiver.

INSTRUCTIONS:

(1) The kicking group should consist of the center and two ends. The opposing unit should consist of two ends, two halfbacks and the safety man.

(2) Game conditions should be simulated. The kickers should kick and the ends go down on the receivers without tackling. Have the ends merely tag the receiver of the punt. This will give the back practice in side-stepping in order to

avoid being tagged. The ends will receive practice in how to come in properly from the side on the receiver.

(3) The defensive halfbacks should bother the ends all the way down field, but should not block them. Without trying to block the kick, the opposing ends should walk through or line up five yards back and rush. Substitutes may be used in this work.

(4) It is desirable from time to time to put the receivers under pressure by yelling at them as they catch the ball.

(5) It is absolutely vital that a stop watch be used to time the kicker during this drill. The kicker must always kick in less than two seconds from the time the ball goes in play.

(6) See Illustration 150.

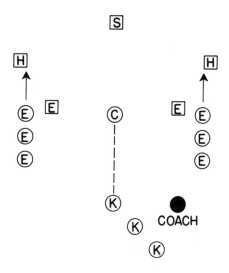

Illus. 150

24. HOW TO DRILL FOR KICK-OFF RETURNS WITH-OUT A KICKER

The purpose of this drill is to practice kick-off returns and not waste valuable time.

INSTRUCTIONS:

(1) Place the receiving team in its normal position to accept the kick-off. Select a player who can throw a long pass and substitute him for the kicker.

(2) Have the kick-off team line up on the 35-yard line. Have the passer run up to the 40 and throw the ball.

(3) The receiving team then practices its kick-off return. Few players in high school and college can kick off accurately each time. With this method each try can be meaningful. More men can alternate on the receiving team in much less time.

(4) If desired, this drill can also provide practice on covering the kick-off.

25. HOW TO DRILL FOR KICK-OFF RETURNS

The purpose of this drill is to practice kick-off returns according to a prearranged plan. Coverage of the kick-off may be stressed in this drill. There are many return plays and the plan of action depends upon the coach.

INSTRUCTIONS:

(1) In receiving a kick-off, the ball carrier should go straight up the middle two times out of three. He may try for the side-lines the third time just to cross up the opponents and keep them spread as they come down the field.

(2) Begin with dummy blocking until individual assignments are learned. If desired, return a few times under game conditions.

(3) Line up two complete teams to practice returning kick-

offs.   Locate better blockers where one return is to be made.

(4) If the return is to be made up the middle, send down *only* the key men to be blocked.   With this method you can concentrate on the technique of important blockers.

(5) After the return has been practiced several times, drill against the complete team.

(6) See Illustration 151.

26. HOW TO DRILL FOR KICK-OFF COVERAGE

The aim of this drill is to practice coverage of kick-offs so that each man will understand his assignment.   Often this is a neglected phase of the game.   It is also a good drill for conditioning all players on the team.

INSTRUCTIONS:

(1) Line up the kicking team in alignment with the ball. It is probably better to use a kicking tee to hold the ball so that you have one more man to cover the kick.

(2) Take either a charging or standing position.

(3) The fast boys and good tacklers should line up on the side you are kicking to.

(4) Generally the first wave includes everyone but the kicker and two or three interior linemen.   The second wave includes the remaining interior linemen.   The third wave is the kicker and a safety valve.

(5) To begin this drill place only one opponent on the receiving side.   Attempt to kick the ball high and get 10 men downfield.   Try for a semi-circular position around the receiver, so encircling him that it would be almost impossible for him to get away.

(6) Insist ends stay close to the sidelines and force the runner to the inside.

(7) Use a whistle to stop men in desired coverage positions. This is the result that should be aimed at.

(8) See Illustration 152.

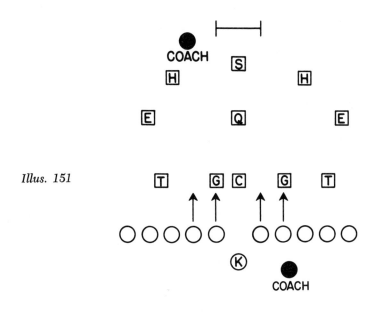

Illus. 151

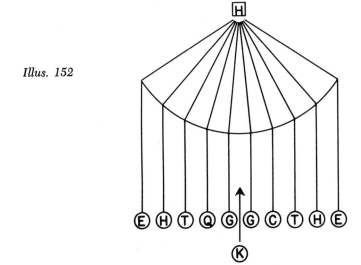

Illus. 152

27. HOW TO PRACTICE PUNT PROTECTION AND COVERAGE IN SIGNAL PRACTICE

The purpose of this drill is to practice punt formation and coverage in signal practice. It also provides players with plenty of running.

INSTRUCTIONS:

(1) Line up complete team or teams for signal practice.

(2) Practice punt formation protection and correct coverage in the signal drill. Linemen dummy-block for two counts.

(3) Assign a coach to each team. If a coach is not available, place the quarterback in charge.

(4) This drill may be used in line scrimmage also.

28. HOW TO DRILL FOR PUNT PROTECTION

The purpose of this drill is to practice punt protection without the ends.

INSTRUCTIONS:

(1) Place the five middle linemen on offense.

(2) Station three players on defense and allow them to align themselves in any position.

(3) Begin the drill by dummy blocking to teach the five middle linemen proper organization in executing their duties.

(4) Practice line blocking protection at top speed.

(5) Locate an extra player in the backfield to represent a kicker. This gives the center practice in snapping the ball at a target.

(6) See Illustration 153.

29. HOW TO DRILL FOR THE PUNT REVERSE

An important backfield maneuver which can be used on both the punt return and the kick-off return is the reverse hand-off play. The object of this drill is to provide practice for the backs in exchanging and faking the ball.

INSTRUCTIONS:

(1) Station two rows of backs approximately 17 yards apart.

(2) A coach is located behind the area of the hand-off or fake.

(3) The coach throws the ball to first one side and then the other.

(4) The back who receives the ball runs toward the opposite sideline and either hands the ball to his team mate coming in the opposite direction, or fakes a hand-off to him.

(5) The man with the ball must *always* go to the *inside.*

(6) See Illustration 154.

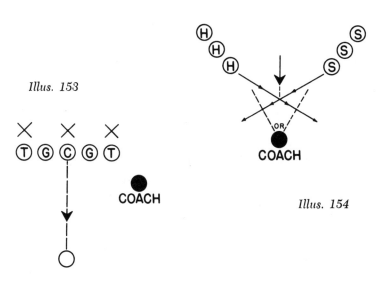

Illus. 153

Illus. 154

30. HOW TO DRILL FOR PUNTING PRACTICE WITH CHANGING TEAMS

The object of this drill is to provide kicking practice and punt protection for two teams without wasting time.

INSTRUCTIONS:

(1) Station a complete kicking team on the 50-yard line.

(2) Locate a defensive team of 11 men across the line to rush the kicker. Explain the objectives of the drill to the defensive team.

(3) The ball changes hands each time.

(4) This drill may be used in dummy and line scrimmage.

31. HOW TO DRILL FOR PUNT RETURNS

The objective in this drill is to practice punt returns without subjecting players to possible injury. This drill will also help the defensive team on proper deployment of men in blocking.

INSTRUCTIONS:

(1) This is a dummy scrimmage drill to return the punt by means of a planned course. This drill can be set up to either sideline or up the middle, or a reverse hand-off can be executed.

(2) The complete offensive team is used in this drill except it does not go downfield.

(3) Place eight dummies in specified positions downfield. Inform the defensive men which dummy they are to block, since each man has a definite blocking assignment.

(4) Carry out blocking assignments by having the men stay with their dummy until the whistle blows.

(5) This practice simplifies the player's blocking assignments and is much better than having 22 players running willy-nilly over the field.

(6) See Illustration 155.

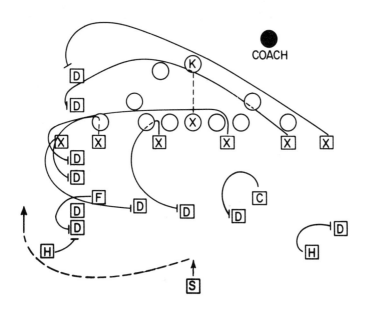

Illus. 155

32. HOW TO DRILL FOR BLOCKING PUNTS THROUGH THE MIDDLE

The objective in this drill is to execute a blocking stunt through the middle of the line. The offensive team should be getting just as much practice from this drill as the defensive team.

INSTRUCTIONS:

(1) Locate ends outside the offensive ends. Drive straight for the punter while watching the outside territory.

(2) Tackles take position outside the offensive tackles, driv-

ing off the outside of the front backs in order to draw them out.

(3) Guards execute a double pull on center and guard to strongside to pull them forward.

(4) Center stations himself about two yards behind the right defensive guard and times execution of the double guard pull in order to be in the hole when the ball is still in the air, or just received by the punter.

(5) Fullback drops back about five yards and protects his territory against kicks, runs and passes.

(6) Practice blocking punts or conversions as a team drill rather than as a group drill.   Begin at half speed and build up to full speed.

(7) See Illustration 156.

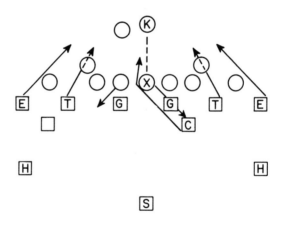

Illus. 156

33. HOW TO DRILL FOR BLOCKING PUNTS ON THE SHORT SIDE

The purpose of this drill is to execute a blocking stunt with the tackle and short side end criss-crossing.

INSTRUCTIONS:

(1) The right tackle positions himself on the outside shoulder of the offensive tackle. He must drive hard and work to the outside of the front back. He attempts to pull him along as he is being blocked.

(2) The right end lines up close to his tackle. He must charge off the heels of his tackle into the kicking area. He has no outside responsibility. His job is to rush the kicker and attempt to block the punt.

(3) The right guard stations himself in the seam between the offensive tackler and guard. He should pull the offensive tackle inward.

(4) Alternate several sets of linemen on this stunt.

(5) See Illustration 157.

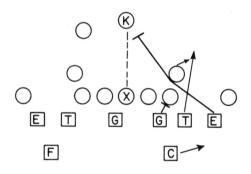

Illus. 157

34. HOW TO DRILL FOR BLOCKING PUNTS BY OVERLOADING

The purpose of this drill is to execute a blocking stunt by overloading one side of the line. This method is to be used in fourth-down situations where the opponents have three or more yards to go for a first down.

INSTRUCTIONS:

(1) The center, fullback, tackle and end overload the strong side. All four men rush the kicker.

(2) The defensive end aims for the second back and to his outside.

(3) The fullback drives straight through the area occupied by the second back. If the blocker is there, he blasts into him.

(4) The center rushes into the front back and attempts to overpower him straight backward.

(5) The tackle positions himself on the outside shoulder of the offensive tackle. He must drive inside the front back and attempt to slip into the kicking area. His path will never be clear, but if he rushes hard he will force himself through.

(6) See Illustration 158.

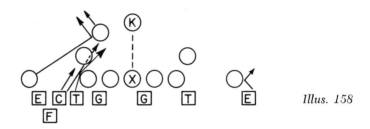

Illus. 158

35. HOW TO DRILL FOR BLOCKING PUNTS THROUGH CENTER

The purpose of this drill is to practice a plan of blocking center punts through center. There are many ways of attempting to block a kick, but any team possessing a strong pair of guards may well try this method.

INSTRUCTIONS:

(1) The guards play closer to the center than usual and the other linemen close in a little. As the ball is snapped the ends go in fast and hard but make no attempt to reach the kicker. Their sole duty is to keep the protecting backs thoroughly occupied.

(2) The guards, acting together, pull the opposing center forward on his face, while the tackles shoot across and pull down the guards, or at least pull them away from the opening.

(3) The center who has the shortest distance to go to the kicker shoots through the opening in front of the kicker.

(4) This is an effective method when well executed, but it needs two strong guards.

(5) See Illustration 159.

Illus. 159

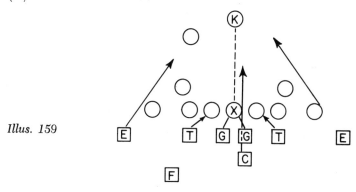

36. HOW TO DRILL FOR CHANGING TEAMS IN KICKING

The purpose of this drill is to provide variation in kicking practice and allow changing of linemen and backfield.

INSTRUCTIONS:

(1) Have the first-team line (seven men) work with the second-team backfield.

(2) Then have the second-team line (seven men) work with the first-team backfield.

(3) This drill may be used either dummy or live.

(4) It is a good competitive drill and provides motivation.

(5) See Illustration 160.

37. HOW TO DRILL IN KICKING FOR DISTANCE

The primary object of this drill is to kick for distance. All linemen are used and it provides practice in developing stance, starting speed, and coverage.

INSTRUCTIONS:

(1) The linemen (including ends) are divided equally so that four lines can be used with four men going down on each kick.

(2) The man who retrieves the ball returns it to the center.

(3) No safety men are employed in this drill.

(4) Rotate punters every four kicks.

(5) Rotate centers every four passes.

(6) See Illustration 161.

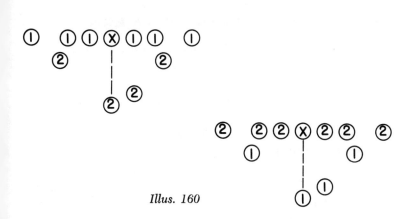

Illus. 160

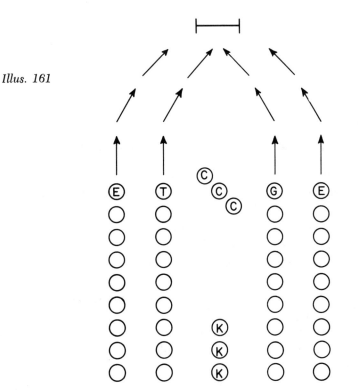

Illus. 161

38. HOW TO DRILL FOR THE QUICK KICK

The object of this drill is to practice quick kicking under game conditions.

INSTRUCTIONS:

(1) The player who quick kicks must develop his technique in separate drills.

(2) Line up a complete offensive team for scrimmage.

(3) Station a full team on defense.

(4) Instruct the quarterback to call successive quick kicks in actual scrimmage with an occasional running play to keep the defense alert.

(5) The various team units can be used by setting up a team rotation plan.

39. HOW TO DRILL FOR BLOCKING PUNTS

The purpose of this drill is to practice blocking a kick so that the lineman will gain confidence along with the proper technique.

INSTRUCTIONS:

(1) Place one kicker on offense with a center.

(2) Station one lineman on defense five yards from the kicker.

(3) Do not have the lineman move forward. He watches the kicker's foot and can move laterally only.

(4) After practicing this drill, have the kicker move back to his normal distance and let the blocker move on the center's snap.

(5) See Illustration 162.

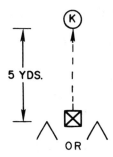

Illus. 162

40. HOW TO DRILL FOR SKELETAL PUNT PROTECTION

The purpose of this drill is to practice punt protection without having the entire squad present. This eliminates confusion and saves time.

INSTRUCTIONS:

(1) Line up a center, two guards and two tackles on offense as the kicking team.

(2) Station any four men on defense to rush the imaginary kicker.

(3) Offense line hits and holds until coach gives command and then charges downfield to cover kick.

(4) See Illustration 163.

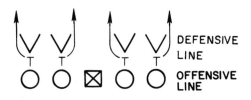

Illus. 163

41. HOW TO DRILL FOR STEPS

The purpose of this drill is to teach the kicker the necessary steps for getting the ball away without it being blocked.

INSTRUCTIONS:

(1) Two tall heavy dummies are placed eight inches apart, about three yards or one and one-half steps in front of the kicker.

(2) There is just enough space between them for the center to pass the football.

(3) The dummies should be tall enough to simulate a defensive player.

(4) This is an early-season drill to help the punter learn to take the proper steps.

(5) It is also a good drill to break a kicker of the habit of taking too many steps.

(6) See Illustration 164.

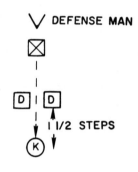

Illus. 164

6

THE PASSING GAME

The forward pass has become the dominating football weapon.
—Glenn S. "Pop" Warner

THE MOST INTERESTING ELEMENT OF THE ATTACK IN MODERN football is the forward pass. The spectator enjoys this play more than any other. It gives the players and coach a splendid method with which to advance the ball. Were it not for the forward pass, the game of football would be more or less a mathematical proposition. With the forward pass, the element of chance and speculation is tremendously increased.

Through the study of 25 football games played in various parts of the country during the year 1947, the following facts were revealed by Jeff Cravath:

1. Seventy-three per cent of the games played were won as a result of passing. The plays either set up a touchdown or directly made a touchdown.

2. Eighteen per cent of the games played were won as a result of kicking. This could have been by a field goal, blocked kick, or fumbled kick.

3. Six per cent of the games played were won by flukes.

4. Three per cent of the games played were won as a result of the running game.[1]

According to the figures mentioned, it appears that considerable time should be allotted to the passing drills, both on offense and defense.

In this chapter, individual and group passing drills will be discussed from both the offensive and defensive viewpoint.

A time study chart will be useful to a football coach in making a study of how much time was devoted to the passing game. See Illustration 165.

Number of minutes for each drill

	1st week				2nd week				3rd week				TOTAL
DATE													
PASS OFFENSE													
INDIVIDUAL PASSING DRILLS													
TEAM PASSING DRILLS													
STUNTS													
PASS DEFENSE													
INDIVIDUAL DEFENSIVE DRILLS													
TEAM DEFENSIVE DRILLS													
FOOTWORK													

Illus. 165

[1] California Association for Athletic Coaches of Secondary Schools, First Annual Coaches Clinic, University of Southern California, 1946.

1. HOW TO DRILL PASSER IN HOLDING THE BALL

The objective of this drill is to teach the passer the proper technique of holding the ball. It also emphasizes form and body balance in throwing.

INSTRUCTIONS:

(1) Two quarterbacks work this drill together, but on their own.

(2) A center is not necessary in this drill.

(3) Place the ball on the ground in the position as if the quarterback was receiving it from the center. Place the ball directly in front of him, but at an angle.

(4) At first, arrange the laces upward so that they are visible.

(5) Have him pick the ball up with his fingertips over the laces. Bring the ball up and back to right ear with *both* hands.

(6) Throw the ball and let arm follow through naturally.

(7) Two quarterbacks or tailbacks start this drill five yards apart and gradually widen this distance.

(8) After they have perfected their passing and their grasp feels comfortable, bring a center into the picture.

2. HOW TO DRILL FOR PASSING FORM

The object of this drill is to develop passing form and accuracy.

INSTRUCTIONS:

(1) Station the backs in a line across from each other. Have them practice passing form. Insist that they always concentrate on a definite aiming point. The receivers should provide a target for each throw.

(2) Instruct the passers to throw a hard, "bullet" pass, sometimes called a "loaded" ball.

(3) Also, have them practice throwing the soft lob or floating type of pass, the type of pass you can "hang on a hook."

3. HOW TO DRILL FOR ACCURACY

The object of this drill is to provide the passer with practice in developing accuracy in throwing at a stationary or moving target.

INSTRUCTIONS:

(1) Hang an automobile tire from the goal post. The tire should be about head-height from the ground.

(2) Begin by having the passer throw at the tire from a distance of five yards.

(3) Gradually move back as the passer improves his accuracy.

(4) Swing the tire back and forth to represent a moving target.

(5) Practice first at close range and then at long.

(6) Assign a manager to assist passers in retrieving balls.

(7) Five or six footballs are needed.

(8) See Illustration 166.

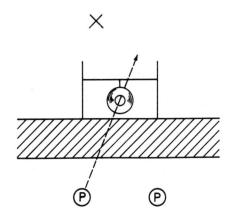

Illus. 166

4. HOW TO DRILL FOR ANTICIPATION

The object of this drill is to train the passer in anticipation. It also provides the receiver and one defender with valuable practice.

INSTRUCTIONS:

(1) Anticipation in throwing is one of the greatest assets any passer can possess. Perhaps it is the most difficult phase of the passing game to teach and to learn. Anticipation does not come naturally.

(2) The passer must anticipate when the receiver is going to break loose from the defender. He must release the ball just as the receiver breaks loose from the coverage.

(3) Use one set of ends at a time, first on the right side and then on the left. Have the ends practice their pivots, cuts, and breaks with the passer.

(4) A center is needed in this particular drill.

(5) Place one defensive man in the zone normally occupied by a halfback.

(6) Emphasize to the passer the importance of starting his release when the receiver makes his cut, *not* after the receiver is open.

(7) This is a must drill for every passer to become proficient.

5. HOW TO DRILL FOR THE LEAD PASS

This is an early season drill to familiarize the passer with his receivers so that he can adjust his throws to their speed. The basic idea of this drill is to give the passer practice in throwing ahead of his receivers, to enable them to catch the ball without slowing down. Too, it will provide the receivers with plenty of exercise by running.

INSTRUCTIONS:

(1) Have two sets of receivers on either side of the center. Each receiver runs downfield at least eight yards and breaks toward the sideline. Receivers alternate going out for the passes.

(2) Passers will strive to coordinate good passing habits as they pass to receivers breaking down and out. Give each receiver a substantial lead and let him run under the ball.

(3) Ultimately use game pass patterns in this drill. Eventually this drill can be practiced by utilizing defensive backs, thus simultaneously practicing pass offense and defense.

(4) See Illustration 167.

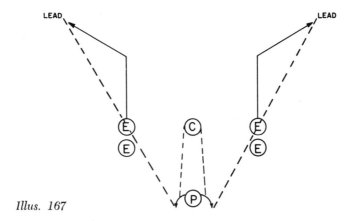

Illus. 167

6. HOW TO DRILL FOR SPLIT ATTENTION

The purpose of this drill is to teach the passers (regardless of formation) to develop split attention in passing. This drill also provides receiving practice for the ends.

INSTRUCTIONS:

(1) Have the passer look straight downfield for the two ends. He must select one, fake to him, and then throw to the other receiver.

(2) He must always focus his attention in the zone where his receivers are located.

(3) Place one defender to represent a halfback. Have the receivers break to the outside each time.

(4) Alternate passers every five minutes in this drill.

7. HOW TO DRILL FOR ARM FAKING

Arm faking is a much neglected technique in football. When a passer can be shown how easy it is to acquire this skill and how effective it is in fooling the opposing team, he will be glad to spend enough time on it to acquire proficiency. This drill is designed to improve the deception of the passer.

INSTRUCTIONS:

(1) This is a self-improvement drill to be developed in the passer's *free* time once he has been given instruction by the coach.

(2) Assume the passing position with both hands on the ball. The ball should be cocked behind the ear.

(3) Then go through the actual passing motion right down to the final movement, following through by spanking the ball into the palm of the open hand.   It is necessary to follow clear through.

(4) A good fake will momentarily freeze the defense and provide the receiver an opportunity to get away.

(5) A 10-minute rehearsal each day will be invaluable.

8. HOW TO DRILL FOR PERIPHERAL VISION

The idea behind this drill is to improve the passer's ability to select receivers downfield.

INSTRUCTIONS:

(1) When a passer starts to gauge his receiver for leading purposes, he must first set up an imaginary target. He arrives at this point by estimating the receiver's speed and the pattern of maneuvering he must negotiate before arriving at the same point as the ball. Then the passer directs his pass to this spot.

(2) A good method of developing peripheral vision in pre-practice warm-up or in group work is to form two lines of receivers extending about 10 yards from each side of the center.

(3) Then have the receivers (ends and backs) break downfield two at a time and cross in front of the passer. The receivers should run at top speed.

(4) Locate two defensive men in the position of halfbacks. Have these men cover the receivers, but not closely.

(5) While the ends are crossing, have the passer look at one man and attempt to throw to the other without swinging his glance to the second man.

(6) At first, it may take some time for the passer to analyze his receivers, but after sufficient practice, it will become much easier.

(7) See Illustration 168.

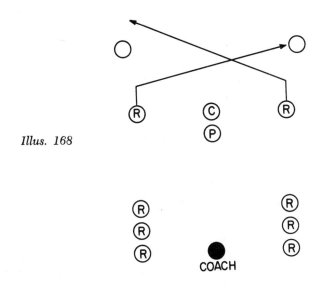

Illus. 168

9. HOW TO DRILL FOR PROTECTION AFTER PASSING

The aim of this drill is to teach the passer how to protect himself after he releases the ball. When a passer lets loose the ball he is unprotected. His arms are raised and his midsection is unguarded.

INSTRUCTIONS:

(1) Place a center, one receiver (end) and the passer on offense. Locate one defender to represent a defensive end.

(2) The passer must complete each throw before defending against the tackler.

(3) Have the passer take *one step backward* when he is about to be tackled. This will cushion the impact of the blow.

(4) Have the passer attempt to stay on his feet and tighten his abdominal muscles.

(5) After the one backward step have him roll with the

tackle. This motion will become automatic through practice.

(6) The step backward takes place *after* delivery of the ball.

(7) This is a must drill if the passer intends to throw often and stay healthy.

10. HOW TO DRILL FOR EATING THE BALL

Every passer must resign himself to the fact that he is going to get hit, and get hit hard, almost everytime he throws. The purpose of this drill is to prepare the passer for the inevitable.

INSTRUCTIONS:

(1) It is impossible for a passer to concentrate on his receivers and still worry about rushing linemen. Every good passer must sell himself to the idea that the throw must be gotten away as accurately as his ability permits, regardless of the physical consequences. No coach wants a passer to get rid of the ball to prevent himself from being hit. The passer must learn to "eat" the ball.

(2) In this drill, a center, one receiver, and the passer are necessary.

(3) Locate an end on defense to rush the passer. Have the end hold for one count before rushing, since he will not meet resistance.

(4) Each pass thrown should be from a distance of 10 yards or more. This will allow the rusher to be close to the passer on every throw.

(5) Occasionally have the receiver go downfield and drop to the ground, as if he were knocked down by a defender. Then the passer must accept the impact of the charging end and eat the ball.

(6) A stop watch may be used in the drill. The drill should consume five minutes with each passer.

11. HOW TO DRILL FOR SELECTING RECEIVERS

The objective in this drill is to teach the passer to survey the field and to throw to the open receiver. The drill also provides training in receiving for ends and backs. In addition, it offers work in defensive fundamentals for one halfback at a time.

INSTRUCTIONS:

(1) Place a player on defense to represent the defensive left half. Send two receivers downfield. One receiver breaks shallow and the other rather deep. The distance between the receiver is just enough so that the defensive man cannot cover both men.

(2) Have the passer look downfield for the two receivers. Have him select the free player and throw the ball.

(3) A stop watch should be used by the coach in this drill. Get the passer to release the ball within *two seconds*.

(4) Alternate passers and defensive halfbacks in this procedure.

(5) See Illustration 169.

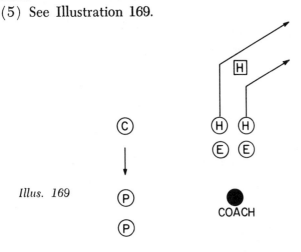

Illus. 169

12. HOW TO DRILL FOR PASSERS TIMING WITH ENDS

This drill is designed to give both passers and receivers practice in working together. The ends are the only receivers in this plan. The drill provides valuable training for the passers in throwing and the ends in maneuvering in their patterns.

INSTRUCTIONS:

(1) Station all the left ends together with one passer. Line up all the right ends with another passer. Locate the ends approximately 10 yards from each center. Two centers are required in this drill.

(2) The passer calls the pass pattern in which a particular end receives the ball in a regular pass play. The end breaks on the signal and employs all his established fakes to free himself from an imaginary defender.

(3) Shift the passers to different groups of ends. This will allow each passer to become accustomed to the center and the passer can practice his throwing to every end on the squad.

(4) To be effective, this drill should consume about 20 minutes of practice time.

(5) See Illustration 170.

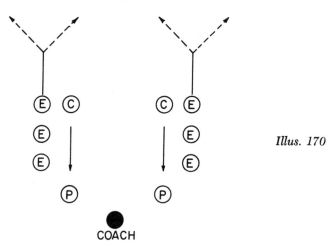

Illus. 170

13. HOW TO DRILL STEPPING INTO THE CUP

The objective in this drill is to train the passer in stepping up into the protection cup.   The passing protection is constructed to aid the passer, but only if he steps forward.

INSTRUCTIONS:

(1) Outline the area of passing protection for the passer.

(2) Place a complete team of 11 men on offense.

(3) Line up six linemen on defense to rush the passer.

(4) The five center offensive linemen will shield the passer with running shoulder blocks.

(5) Spread an old jersey on the ground to represent the cup area.   At the base of the cup outline in triangular form five dummies.   The dummies are placed closely together.

(6) With this arrangement the passer cannot go backward because he will collide with the dummies.   He will be forced to stay where he is or move forward.

(7) The coach should encourage him to step up each time a pass is called.

(8) See Illustration 171.

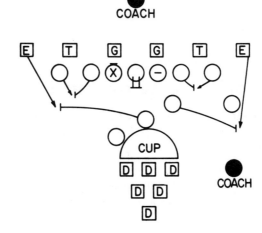

Illus. 171

14. HOW TO DRILL FOR BLINDING THE PASSER

This is a simple little drill that can be very effective. The idea of this drill is to screen the passer's vision when he is attempting to throw.

INSTRUCTIONS:

(1) The drill is designed primarily for ends, but may be used with any of the linemen.

(2) No tackling is allowed in this drill.

(3) Select the four best ends on the team. Line up one left and one right end in their respective defensive positions.

(4) Place the two offensive ends on the scrimmage line with a center to snap the ball.

(5) Place the two top passers approximately seven yards deep.

(6) The ends rush the passer as the ball is snapped. Their arms must be extended high above their heads to obstruct the passer's view or to deflect the ball.

(7) Alternate each passer after every five throws.

(8) Ends alternate from offensive to defensive each time the ball is passed.

(9) The offensive ends hook at seven yards. They do not go deep.

15. HOW TO DRILL FOR THE RUNNING PASS

The intention of this drill is to train the passer in throwing the running pass. The drill also provides defensive practice for two halfbacks.

INSTRUCTIONS:

(1) This is one of the most difficult plays in football to develop. It requires much work on the part of the passer to be successful.

(2) A skeleton offense of a center, two ends and the passer is required.

(3) Station two players on defense to represent halfbacks. Always have different colored shirts on the defenders.

(4) Instruct the defender to attempt to recognize the play as a pass or run.

(5) The passer should watch the defender. The action of the defense will determine his course. If the defender comes forward, he must throw. If the defender retreats, he should run. The defensive man's efforts can help this drill. Since this is a passing drill, throw much more than you run.

(6) Designate the number of steps that the passer should take on each particular pass. This helps the other members of the team, because they know exactly where to protect and cover.

(7) See Illustration 172.

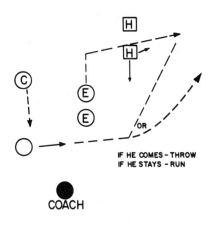

IF HE COMES – THROW
IF HE STAYS – RUN

COACH

Illus. 172

16. HOW TO DRILL FOR SELECTING THE ZONE

This drill is designed to teach the quarterback (passer) which pass patterns are most effective against specific defensive alignments.

INSTRUCTIONS:

(1) Place colored jerseys on the ground to spot the positions of defensive players.

(2) This passing drill is conducted with a skeleton unit composed of a center, ends, and backs.

(3) By way of illustration, against a 6-2-2-1 defense the quarterback will be instructed to send receivers into the following zones: right or left flat, in the middle in front of the safety, deep behind the halfbacks.

(4) The markers on the ground will serve to define these zones.   Change these zones frequently by moving the jerseys.

(5) See Illustration 173.

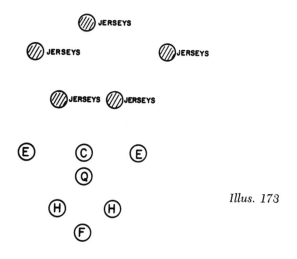

Illus. 173

17. HOW TO DRILL FOR THE FAKE PASS AND RUN

The purpose of this drill is to give the passer and one back timing practice in using the fake pass and run play. The drill also eliminates unnecessary bruises for both offense and defense.

INSTRUCTIONS:

(1) Locate on offense the one key blocker necessary to make the fake pass and run successful. In this drill he is the fullback.

(2) A center is needed to snap the ball.

(3) Place a right end on defense. This man holds a blocking dummy.

(4) As the ball is snapped, the right end moves the dummy into a spot where it would be if he were crashing. The fullback applies his block on the end dummy.

(5) When the passer senses that the fullback has position on the defender, he swings around his blocker and runs downfield. Without this key block the play would be worthless.

(6) This technique must be practiced many times. After the timing is smooth, place a live end on defense.

(7) See Illustration 174.

Illus. 174

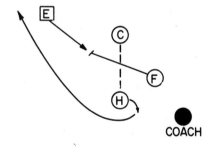

18. HOW TO DRILL SKELETAL PASS OFFENSE

The aim of this drill is to teach the offensive players most of the skills of pass offense. Furthermore, the drill provides the pass defenders with excellent practice. It is a good drill for inspiring the spirit of competition.

INSTRUCTIONS:

(1) A skeleton unit of a center, two ends and a complete backfield are employed on offense.

(2) The defense is represented by two ends, two halfbacks, safetyman, center, and fullback. Each side has a total of seven players.

(3) Place the first-string passing combination in unit *A*. Station the second string in unit *B*. The same may be done with the third and fourth strings.

(4) Unit *A* takes the ball as follows:

(a) If a short pass is completed, count 1 point.

(b) A pass longer than 15 yards counts 2 points.

(c) A pass with a lateral counts 1 point.

(d) If team *B* intercepts, it receives 1 point and possession of the ball.

(e) The ball is awarded to the opponent if a pass is incomplete.

(f) The unit that first scores 20 points wins.

(5) This drill should be supervised by one or two coaches. Suggestions should be made about certain habits that need correction.

(6) This drill may take place before practice begins. It is also a good late-season drill and a good morale exercise after a loss.

(7) See Illustration 175.

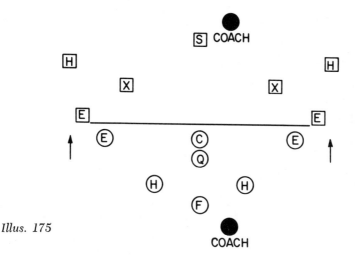

Illus. 175

19. HOW TO DRILL FOR COVERAGE OF PASSES

The purpose of this drill is to provide practice for the passer and the entire team in the coverage of passes.

INSTRUCTIONS:

(1) Select two full teams for pass scrimmage. This drill may be used either dummy or against live opposition.

(2) Run several pass patterns and then throw a deliberate interception. Throw deliberate interceptions on two out of every five passes. Make the passer captain of the coverage team. Have him yell "Cover!" after every throw.

(3) Have the passer throw interceptions in all zones of the defense, both long and short.

(4) If the drill is live, use a quick whistle to prevent injuries.

(5) After the offensive is conscious of coverage, throw one interception out of every ten passes.

(6) Don't drill on one side or one end of the field; move all over.

20. HOW TO DRILL FOR COMBINED PASSING AND DEFENSE

The object of this drill is to give the passers and receivers practice in pass offense. At the same time it provides the defenders with practice in pass defense.

INSTRUCTIONS:

(1) The right side linebackers and right halfbacks form one unit on defense. They line up in single-file order.

(2) The left side linebackers and left halfbacks form another unit.

(3) The offensive left and right ends line up in single-file lines in their respective positions. They face the defensive files, with about five yards separating the two units.

(4) The two groups should wear different colored jerseys or the defense may slip scrimmage vests of a varying color over their practice jerseys.

(5) The lead receiver will indicate by hand signal to the passer what maneuver he will make.

(6) The lead defender in front of him will attempt to cover.

(7) These men will then go to the end of their respective files.

(8) Passers will rotate, throwing alternately to the left and right.

(9) See Illustration 176.

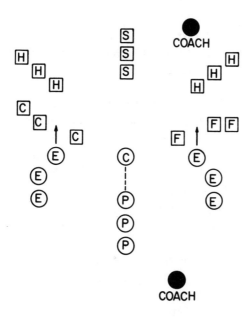

Illus. 176

21. HOW TO DRILL FOR THE FORWARD-BACK-WARD PASS

The objectives of this drill are to give passers practice in throwing accurately and to give receivers practice in throwing a lateral pass to a trailing player.

INSTRUCTIONS:

(1) The pass receivers are divided into two equal groups. One lines up single file at the left end position and the other at the right.

(2) Passers are in single file order behind the center.

(3) To start, the lead man of the right file goes down for a pass, executing fakes of his choice.

(4) The second man in the same file trails him for a lateral.

(5) Then the first two men in the left file perform similarly, and so on.

(6) Passers take five throws before moving to the rear of their file. Have managers keep record of completions and interceptions of each passer.

(7) Receivers alternate between the right and left files and between receiving forwards and laterals.

(8) This may develop into a good competitive drill.

(9) See Illustration 177.

22. HOW TO DRILL FOR PASS PROTECTION

The aim of this drill is to teach the linemen how to protect the passer without subjecting them to the unnecessary bruises involved in line contact.

INSTRUCTIONS:

(1) Station dummies in a defensive position to simulate a five-, six- or seven-man line.

(2) The players on the defensive team bring the dummies across the line of scrimmage. The offensive men protect the passer according to the play pattern.

(3) This drill will eliminate many unnecessary bruises.

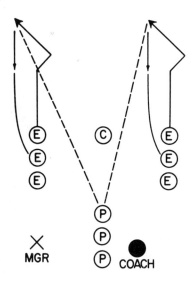

Illus. 177

23. HOW TO DRILL FOR INDIVIDUAL PASS
PROTECTION

The idea of this drill is to train the individual linemen in
the techniques of pass protection.

INSTRUCTIONS:

(1) Count off by threes and take the offensive stance. Station linemen on a straight line.

(2) As the ball is snapped, each No. 1 man pulls back deep
and actually blocks a player. The player can be a charging
end or any lineman.

(3) No. 2 and No. 3 check-block in the line. The use of
an even number of players eliminates one man losing a turn.

(4) This maneuver should be repeated the same way on the
opposite side.

(5) See Illustration 178.

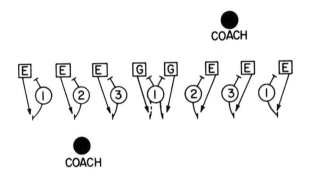

Illus. 178

24. HOW TO DRILL FOR PULL-OUT PASS PROTECTION

The aim of this drill is to provide the linemen with practice in dropping out of the line and protecting the passer.

INSTRUCTIONS:

(1) This drill is used in warming up before the actual practice begins. Body position and form are essential in this drill.

(2) The players are lined up and count off by three. Then they assume their offensive stances. At a signal from the coach, the No. 1 men drop out. They protect the passer against imaginary rushers from the left side.

(3) The No. 2 and No. 3 men check-block in the line. The No. 2 and No. 3 men perform the drop-out maneuver when their turn arrives.

(4) This routine is repeated to the right side. Any order the coach desires may be used.

(5) See Illustration 179.

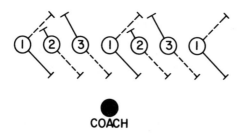

COACH

Illus. 179

25. HOW TO PROTECT THE PASSER IN SCRIMMAGE

This drill is designed to give the linemen live practice in pass-protection blocking.

INSTRUCTIONS:

(1) Run the pass patterns in a dummy scrimmage. The defense should come at the passer at one-quarter speed to begin with and later at one-half speed.

(2) Practice either with individual blocking where individual opponents are assigned, or cup-blocking where all players come together and let no one go through.

(3) The backfield men also get blocking practice when they are not receivers.

(4) Run the pass patterns against live opposition in the secondary under scrimmage conditions.

(5) The entire drill may be accelerated to top speed once the techniques are mastered.

26. HOW TO DRILL FOR TARGET PASSING

The object of this drill is to improve the accuracy of the passer as well as to increase the strength of his wrist and arm.

INSTRUCTIONS:

(1) Fasten a rope from the goal post for three targets.

(2) All the targets should represent the approximate width of a receiver's shoulders.

(3) Station a passer on the 10-yard line and then on the 20-yard line with several footballs. Have him throw for both accuracy and distance. Move him back as he improves.

(4) This is a good early-season passing drill.

(5) See Illustration 180.

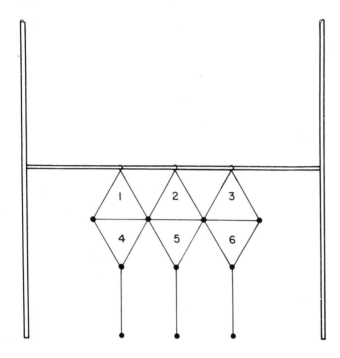

Illus. 180

27. HOW TO DRILL FOR STRING PASSING

The purpose of this drill is to train the passers in proper fundamental throwing.

INSTRUCTIONS:

(1) Place the right handed passer on his right knee.

(2) Tie a strong string between two high-jumping standards. The distance between the standards should be ten feet.

(3) Secure the string at a height of four feet.

(4) Locate three receivers in positions illustrated. The passer points his left foot at the receivers and throws over the string at the receivers to his left, right, and straight ahead.

(5) Start with a short distance to warm up and then gradually lengthen the distances.

(6) See Illustration 181.

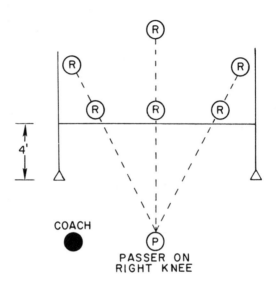

Illus. 181

28. HOW TO DRILL FOR POWER-ARM PASSING

The purpose of this drill is to increase the strength of the wrist, arm, and shoulder in passing. It is a before- and after-practice drill for the passers to warm up with the new weighted Power-Arm football. It is a fine early-season passing drill and is a valuable drill during the summer months to strengthen and improve the passer's arm. It is also an excellent drill for centers.

INSTRUCTIONS:

(1) Have all passers begin warming up with the power-arm football at a distance of four yards apart. Power-Arm footballs are readily discernible from the regulation balls.

(2) Have two quarterbacks passing the ball so that both are warming up at the same time.

(3) Gradually increase the distance between the passers as their arms become warm and limber.

(4) After a sufficient warm-up period, substitute a regular weight football and notice the psychological effect it has on the passer.

(5) This is also an excellent drill for the centers to improve wrist snap when passing the ball from spread punt formation.

(6) The Power-Arm ball is good for receivers because it makes them squeeze the ball when receiving it. Otherwise, it might slip through their fingers.

(7) See Illustration 182.

Illus. 182

29. HOW TO DRILL FOR ONE-RUSH PASSING

The purpose of this drill is to improve timing and practice pass offense and pass defense.

INSTRUCTIONS:

(1) Place two ends, a center, and a quarterback on offense.

(2) Station two defensive men over the offensive ends to delay their release. These men then rush the passer from the outside.

(3) Have one defensive lineman rush the passer from the interior line. Defenders must allow the passer to throw each time and not contact the passer.

(4) Locate two pass defenders on defense to break up the play.

(5) The offensive ends run their routes and the quarterback attempts to complete the pass. Time the quarterback with a stopwatch.

(6) See Illustration 183.

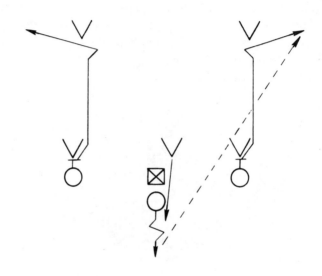

Illus. 183

30. HOW TO DRILL FOR THE HOOK PASS

The purpose of this drill is to provide practice for the line-backers in defending against the hook pass, and for the passers in throwing the hook.

INSTRUCTIONS:

(1) Place a center and quarterback on offense.

(2) Station two linebackers on defense.

(3) Locate two bell-bottom dummies ten yards deep in the hooking zone.

(4) When the quarterback drops back to throw, the line-backers must hustle to the area of the dummies.

(5) They should assume a balanced position facing the quarterback as soon as possible. They work at an angle of 90° to the quarterback.

(6) Later on, add ends to the offense and this becomes a fine hook pass drill for the passers.

(7) See Illustration 184.

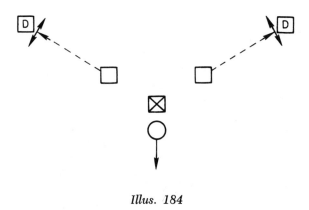

Illus. 184

31. HOW TO DRILL FOR PASSING IN CIRCLES

The purpose of this drill is to improve the quarterback's ability to throw the running pass.

INSTRUCTIONS:

(1) Use one passer and one receiver.

(2) Have them run in a circle 20 yards apart.

(3) Increase the distance to 30 yards and finally 40 yards.

(4) Have the quarterback run to the left and throw.

(5) Have the quarterback run to the right and throw.

(6) Gradually increase the diameter of the circle.

(7) This drill will help the quarterback throw on the run.

(8) See Illustration 185.

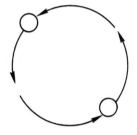

Illus. 185

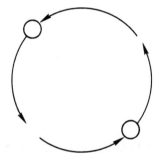

32. HOW TO DRILL FOR THE PASS GAME

The purpose of this drill is to practice pass offense and pass defense at the same time. It is also a fine competitive and morale drill.

INSTRUCTIONS:

(1) This is a drill Bob Blackman uses at Dartmouth.

(2) Place an offensive team minus the guards and tackles on offense.

(3) Station a defensive team consisting of the secondary, linebackers and ends on defense.

(4) Switch offensive and defensive ends every four plays so that the offensive ends will not become fatigued.

(5) The drill can be dummy or live.

(6) Allow the passer three seconds to release the ball. If he cannot find an open receiver, score two points for the defense.

(7) If the quarterback throws a bad pass, or the receiver drops the ball, score two points for the defense.

(8) Match the first and second teams against each other, and the third and fourth teams. Later in the week, match your first and second teams against the junior varsity or freshmen using opponents' pass patterns.

(9) Have all four units operating at the same time at opposite ends of the field.

(10) Assign a manager to keep score.

(11) See Illustration 186.

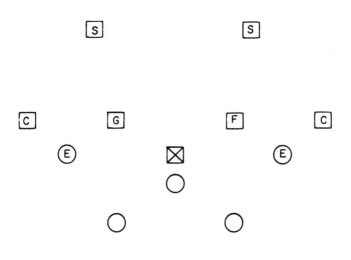

Illus. 186

THE PASSING GAME

OFFENSIVE SCORING

1 point for each yard gained on a completed pass.

50 points gained for a touchdown pass.

DEFENSIVE SCORING

5 points for every pass knocked down.

2 points for every incomplete pass not touched by the defense.

2 points if the offense can't throw in three seconds.

50 points for interception returned for a touchdown.

25 points for every interception.

33. HOW TO DRILL ON QUICK DELIVERY

The purpose of this drill is to develop a short snapping motion of the wrist when delivering the football.

INSTRUCTIONS:

(1) Place two passers, or a passer and a receiver, five yards apart.

(2) Have them play catch with emphasis on a quick delivery of the ball.

(3) Gradually lengthen the distance to ten yards apart.

(4) Next, have the passer run right and throw, then have him run left and throw.

(5) See Illustration 187.

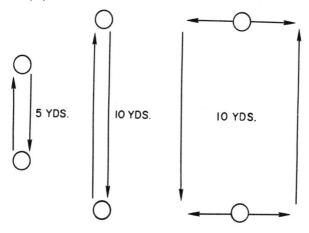

5 YDS.   10 YDS.   10 YDS.

Illus. 187

34. HOW TO DRILL FOR THE CUP

The purpose of this drill is to teach the quarterback to stay in the cup and not get too deep.

INSTRUCTIONS:

(1) Place a quarterback and center on offense.

(2) Mark off two lines, one eight yards and the other six yards behind the center.

(3) Have the quarterback retreat to a depth of eight yards and then step forward to the six-yard marker.

(4) He does not throw until his left foot hits the six-yard marker.

(5) See Illustration 188.

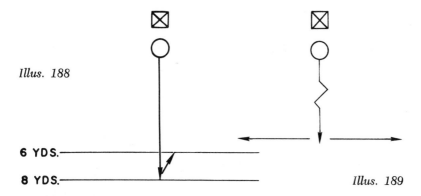

Illus. 188

6 YDS.

8 YDS.

Illus. 189

35. HOW TO DRILL FOR PASSING AGAINST RED-DOG DEFENSE

The purpose of this drill is to give the quarterback training in meeting the red-dog defense.

INSTRUCTIONS:

(1) Place a center and quarterback on offense.

(2) At the snap of the ball imagine a rush right or a rush left.

(3) Have the quarterback run off and avoid the red dog.

(4) See Illustration 189.

36. HOW TO DRILL FOR LOOKING OFF

The purpose of this drill is to provide training for the quarter-back in looking off linebackers.

INSTRUCTIONS:

(1) Place a center and quarterback on offense with two ends.

(2) Station one or two linebackers on defense. This is also a good drill for the linebackers.

(3) The quarterback receives the snap from center and hustles back, looking off the linebacker.

(4) See Illustration 190.

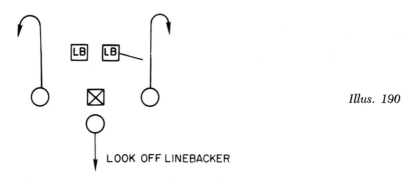

Illus. 190

LOOK OFF LINEBACKER

37. HOW TO DRILL FOR MULTIPLE PASSING

The purpose of this drill is to keep a large group of backs and ends moving.

INSTRUCTIONS:

(1) This is a good early-season drill with a large squad.

(2) Place three centers, three passers, and three receivers on offense.

(3) All the centers pass the ball at the same time and the receivers follow the same patterns they would in the game.

(4) P1 passes to the left end, P2 passes to the wing back, and P3 passes to the right end.

(5) Have your best passer throwing to the best receiver.

(6) See Illustration 191.

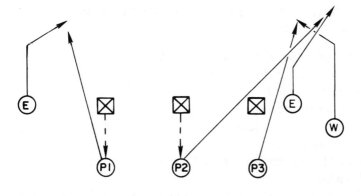

Illus. 191

38. HOW TO DRILL FOR THE SIDELINE PASS

The purpose of this drill is to emphasize the sideline pass so that the passers get the exact timing with their receivers.

INSTRUCTIONS:

(1) Have a passer, a receiver, and a center on offense.

(2) The quarterback takes the ball from the center, drops back, and throws the sideline pass to one end going out.

(3) The next quarterback will come up and take his turn. Alternate two men.

(4) The passer and one end are the only players concerned.

(5) Place a defensive man over the center in order to give the center practice in snapping the ball while he is being charged by an opponent.

(6) This drill will also help teach the quarterback to receive the ball properly on pass plays.

(7) See Illustration 192.

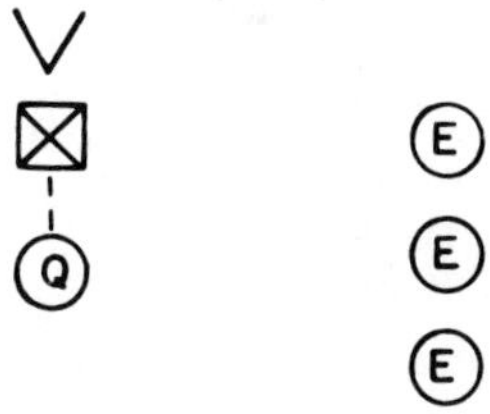

Illus. 192

39. HOW TO DRILL WITH SURPLUS BACKS AND ENDS

The purpose of this drill is to keep as many men busy as possible. The drill is designed for a large number of backs and ends on the squad.

INSTRUCTIONS:

(1) Have three lanes 10 yards wide with a defensive halfback in each lane.

(2) Have a passer for each lane throwing to ends or extra halfbacks.

(3) The defensive halfback has more of a chance to defend because of the 10 yard confinement.

(4) Alternate halfbacks every four passes.

(5) See Illustration 193.

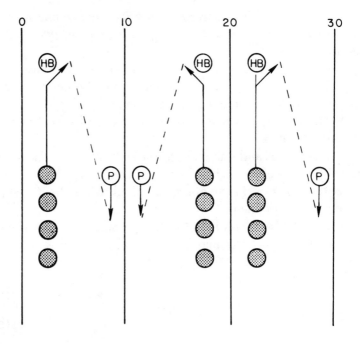

Illus. 193

7

THE RECEIVING GAME

Always look the ball into your hands.
—H. O. "Fritz" Crisler

A COACH SHOULD NEVER LOSE SIGHT OF THE FACT THAT EVERY passer is only as good as his receivers. Consequently, at least half of the success of a pass is dependent upon the man who catches the ball.

Every receiver will have his favorite method of maneuvering through the defense. Some men are good on hook passes. Others are at their best catching a ball in full stride, while still others can handle a ball chest-high, but are lost when a pass sails above their heads.

A receiver may be comparatively weak in receiving on his left side but strong in taking the ball over his right shoulder. He should, therefore, be drilled to correct his weakness.

It is the coach's job to analyze his receivers and learn what they can do best. After a certain amount of drill their outstanding individual characteristics will become somewhat apparent to the coach.   More slowly, perhaps, but most importantly, to the passers themselves.

In the drills that follow, the purpose of the author is to acquaint the receivers with all the necessary fundamentals.

1. HOW TO DRILL FOR PITCH AND CATCH

The purpose of this drill is to teach the pass receivers to keep their eyes on the ball; to catch and retain the ball.

INSTRUCTIONS:

(1) Station two pass receivers about five yards apart.

(2) Use as many units of two as possible.

(3) Each pair must have one football.

(4) No. 1 passes the ball over the head of No. 2 who leaps into the air in an attempt to catch it.

(5) Have receivers throw right, left, high and low.

(6) Increase the distance between receivers to 10 or 15 yards.

(7) This is an excellent warmup drill for all ends as they report on the field.

(8) See Illustration 194.

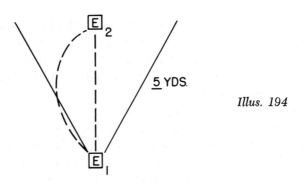

Illus. 194

2. HOW TO DRILL FOR STARTS

Except on delayed passes, it is necessary for the end to get away to a fast start. The purpose of the drill is to develop a quick break right as the ball is snapped, just as a sprinter in track develops a start that comes as close to shading the starter's gun.

INSTRUCTIONS:

(1) Line up all the ends in their offensive stances.

(2) Have the coach, on one knee, face the ends with his hands over a football to represent the center.

(3) As the ball is snapped the ends make a short *fast* run of five yards with a quick *stop*.

(4) The practice in stopping quickly will develop maneuverability in receiving passes.

(5) The receiver should be warm before this drill is attempted.

(6) If performed daily, two minutes drilling on the technique is adequate.

(7) See Illustration 195.

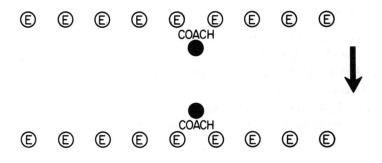

Illus. 195

3. HOW TO DRILL FOR METHODS OF HOLDING HANDS

The object of this drill is to teach the ends the correct methods of holding their hands when receiving passes. It should also teach them to relax when they are running for a pass.

INSTRUCTIONS:

(1) Have the ends run with their hands and arms high above their heads.

(2) They are simulating the position they would assume when catching a pass.

(3) This drill seems awkward, but it will help the ends to keep their hands high when running for a pass.

(4) This is a very beneficial drill for inexperienced ends.

4. HOW TO DRILL FOR KEEPING EYES ON THE BALL

The object of this drill is to teach offensive ends to keep their eyes on the ball while receiving. Failure to keep their eyes on the ball is the No. 1 error of all receivers.

INSTRUCTIONS:

(1) Have the ends practice receiving passes with one hand.

(2) Eyes *must* be focused on the ball to accomplish this.

5. HOW TO DRILL FOR QUICK REACTION

The purpose of this drill is to teach ends to be quick in reacting to a thrown ball.   It will help teach ends to receive passes.

INSTRUCTIONS:

(1) Line up all the ends in single file.

(2) Stand to the right or left with the ball ready to pass.

(3) Say "Ready, hike!"

(4) An end takes off, goes straight downfield.

(5) As he takes his second step he looks to receive the ball. It may be over his head, to his right, to his left.   The pass may be soft, too long, or too short.

(6) If the ball is thrown too short, the receiver should come back for it.   This is important.

(7) Receivers must react as quickly as possible to accept the ball.

(8) See Illustration 196.

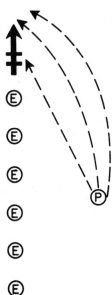

Illus. 196

6. HOW TO DRILL FOR RECEIVING IN PAIRS

The object of this drill is to practice the special offensive fundamentals used in receiving.

INSTRUCTIONS:

(1) The ends line up in two parrallel lines with a center between them.

(2) Keep plenty of distance (8–10 yards) between the center and ends so the passer can view his receivers.

(3) Allow the passer to call the pass pattern to be run.

(4) The ends should then execute their fakes as the called play directs.

(5) After the ends have had considerable practice in catching without opposition, a pair of defensive halfbacks and a safety man should be used to give the receivers practice under truer conditions.

(6) See Illustration 197.

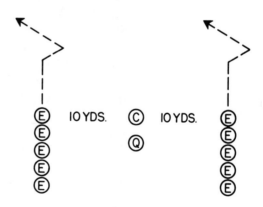

Illus. 197

7. HOW TO DRILL FOR RECEIVING BY NUMBERS

This is a simple drill but a very fundamental one for all receivers whether ends or backs. Many passes are dropped because the receiver takes his eyes off the flight of the ball. The purpose of this drill is to help eliminate dropping forward passes. This drill will almost force the receiver to keep his eye on the ball.

INSTRUCTIONS:

(1) A number two inches high is painted on each quadrant of the football.

(2) Use the same number on each quadrant of the ball.

(3) Have four or five footballs for this drill, all with different numbers painted on them. Omit No. 1 since it is too easy to recognize.

(4) Have each receiver call the number as the ball reaches his hand.

(5) These same balls may be used in backfield drills (see Drill 41, Chapter 5, p. 65).

(6) See Illustration 198.

Illus. 198

8. HOW TO DRILL FOR MULTIPLE RECEIVING

The purpose of this drill is to develop pass-catching ability of the ends and backs and to learn and perfect pass patterns.

INSTRUCTIONS:

(1) Have three centers line up adjacent to each other.

(2) Have three passers (quarterbacks or tailbacks) line up in their proper positions relative to the centers.

(3) Have the ends and backs in the end positions so that they can run the pass patterns.

(4) Have each pass pattern designated. The pattern may be called by one of the passers.

(5) If one passer calls the pattern, all three throwers run that particular course. Alternate having the passers call the plays.

(6) Have each passer throw in such a way that every receiver gets a chance to receive a pass.

(7) In the event that there are four men involved in the pattern, station a fourth passer to one side with a ball to throw. If a fourth center is available, he should be with the passer.

(8) It is important that each receiver get the opportunity to receive.

(9) If each man is to be a receiver, he will run hard. This eliminates loafing for players who know that they *are not* to receive the ball.

(10) See Illustration 199.

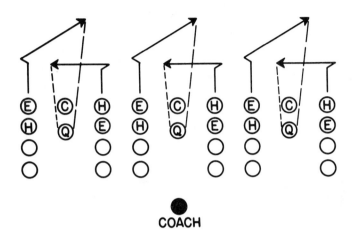

COACH

Illus. 199

9. HOW TO DRILL FOR SERIES BALL HANDLING

The purpose of this drill is to provide the ends with practice in receiving and passing. There is also center practice in snapping the ball to a passer.

INSTRUCTIONS:

(1) Locate a formation of ends in one line on either side of a passer.

(2) The passer throws to No. 3 who drives for 10 yards after receiving the pass.

(3) No. 3 then passes to No. 4, who in turn tosses the ball to the assistant center.

(4) Line rotation is as follows: No. 4 takes the place of No.

1 and passes the ball to the next man. After passing he goes
to the No. 2 position. Everybody moves up on each change.
(5) All men receive and all men pass in this drill.
(6) See Illustration 200.

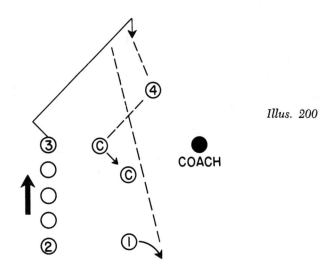

Illus. 200

10. HOW TO DRILL FOR A FORWARD LATERAL

*The purpose of this drill is to teach receivers how to relax
when catching the ball. This method is called a forward lateral drill.*

INSTRUCTIONS:
(1) Station the left ends 10 yards to the left of the center.
(2) Locate the right ends 10 yards to the right of the center.
(3) The left end proceeds first in this drill. Have a passer
throw him a pass. After he catches the ball he laterals to the
right end cutting behind him.

(4) The end receiving the lateral must delay slightly.
(5) The lines alternate in receiving the pass.
(6) All members of the squad can participate in this drill.
(7) A group can be used with each coach.
(8) See Illustration 201.

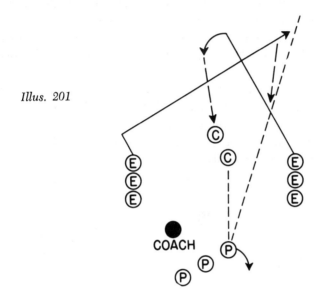

Illus. 201

11. HOW TO DRILL FOR ROUND-ROBIN PASSING AND RECEIVING

The purpose of this drill is to create a competitive passing scrimmage involving a large number of men.

INSTRUCTIONS:

(1) Two complete teams are lined up on offense and defense.

(2) Defensive players tag instead of tackling.

(3) Defensive linemen stop after crossing the line of scrimmage and protect their territory.

(4) The coach should call "time" on the passer if he holds the ball too long.

(5) A run of five yards before the ball carrier is tagged counts as a completed pass. This option keeps the defense alerted for a fake pass and run.

(6) A change will be made every 10 minutes until each team has had an equal number of offensive and defensive opportunities.

(7) The manager keeps tab on the passes completed by and against each unit. At the close of the drill, the offensive and defensive winners are announced.

(8) This competitive passing drill is excellent for morale.

(9) See Illustration 202.

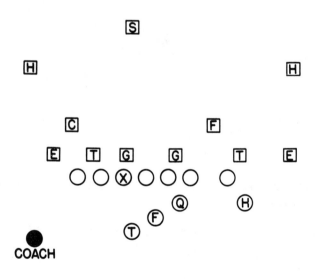

Illus. 202

12. HOW TO DRILL FOR THE MACHINE GUN

If the coach desires especially to improve the receiving technique of his ends, this drill of "machine-gunning" the receiver is recommended. The purpose of this drill is to develop competition among the ends and aid in developing peripheral perception as well as unerring coordination.

INSTRUCTIONS:

(1) Place four offensive men in half-moon formation. Any one of the four will hold a football.

(2) The end who will receive the machine-gunning stands five yards away and faces the other four men. He is also given a football.

(3) As the coach commands "Go!" the lone player snaps the ball to any one of the four men facing him.

(4) Simultaneously, any one of the other players fires the other ball to the lone player.

(5) A rapid combat of machine-gunning with the footballs ensues.

(6) The lone gunner must receive without fumbling and must pass the other ball while the second ball is on its way.

(7) The instant that he fumbles a pass, he is out and another man from the half-moon formation takes his place.

(8) The highest score is determined after all five men have had a chance at receiving.

(9) See Illustration 203.

Illus. 203

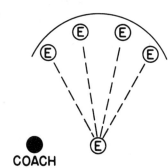

COACH

13. HOW TO DRILL FOR CUTTING

The object of this drill is to improve the cutting ability of the ends. Very few receivers can really cut sharply.

INSTRUCTIONS:

(1) Station an end on the line of scrimmage in his offensive stance.

(2) No passer or center is used in this drill.

(3) Place a dummy on defense to represent the defensive halfback.

(4) Have the ends practice cutting inside and outside.

(5) The secret in executing a sharp cut is *not to run at top speed.* When the time comes for the cut, the end can make a better angle if he is running at half speed.

(6) Pick up full speed *after* the cut.

(7) See Illustration 204.

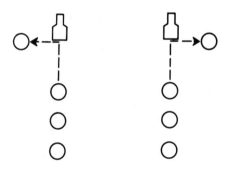

Illus. 204

14. HOW TO DRILL FOR LEARNING PASS PATTERNS

The purpose of this drill is to provide ends with practice in learning their pass routes. The backfield also gets work in ball handling.

INSTRUCTIONS:

(1) This is an early season drill.

(2) The defensive group is composed of two linebackers, two halfbacks, two ends, and the safety man. The ends are optional in this drill.

(3) Line up two ends, a complete backfield, and a center on offense.

(4) Have the extra ends and backfield men behind the offense waiting their turn.

(5) Run all pass plays and rotate ends every play.

(6) Rotate backfields every five plays.

(7) See Illustration 205.

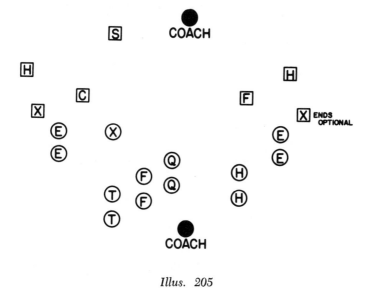

Illus. 205

15. HOW TO DRILL FOR THE SIDELINE PASS

The purpose of this drill is to provide practice for the ends in running the sideline pattern.   The drill allows the passer to improve upon his accuracy in throwing.

INSTRUCTIONS:

(1) Line up all the right ends approximately 17 yards in from the near sideline.   Use the hash-marks as a marker.

(2) Have the center from six to eight yards inside of the right ends.   Station a manager to help the center on return passes from the ends.

(3) Place a dummy on defense at a distance of six or seven yards to represent the halfback.

(4) A passer is located under the center or at a distance of five yards, depending upon the formation.

(5) Have the receiver and passer work on exact timing to complete the pass just before the end goes out of bounds.

(6) Use the same procedure for the left ends, but on the other side of the field.

(7) Have the idle ends play pitch and catch while awaiting their turn.

(8) See Illustration 207.

16. HOW TO DRILL FOR THE BUTTON HOOK

The purpose of this drill is to provide practice for ends in executing a hook technique.   Passers also benefit.

INSTRUCTIONS:

(1) Line up two centers and two passers.   The centers are stationed 10 yards apart.

(2) Place all the left ends and all the right ends on their respective sides of the field.

(3) Have the ends practice nothing but hooks for 10 minutes.

(4) The lines alternate in going downfield for the pass.   In this way the coach can watch each group and offer suggestions. No time is wasted.

(5) After the ends become proficient in this technique they may drill on the hook-and-go maneuver.

(6) See Illustration 206.

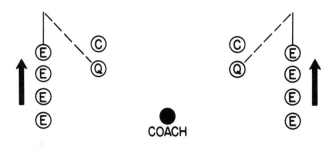

Illus. 206

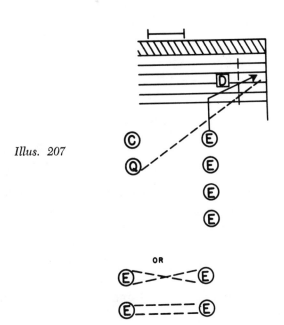

Illus. 207

17. HOW TO DRILL FOR EVASIVE ACTION

The aim of this drill is to teach offensive ends the various maneuvers used in evading the defensive halfbacks.

INSTRUCTIONS:

(1) This drill begins without a ball or a center.

(2) The ends should line up in their normal offensive end positions and follow the leader in executing fakes.

(3) After the maneuvers have been mastered, the ends should practice receiving passes while executing these same techniques.

(4) See Illustration 208.

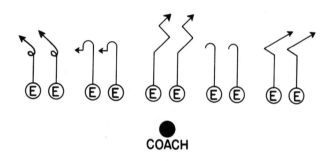

Illus. 208

18. HOW TO DRILL ENDS TO FIGHT FOR THE BALL

The purpose of this drill is to teach offensive ends to fight for the ball when its possession is contested, which is the case when a defensive back attempts to intercept.

INSTRUCTIONS:

(1) The ends are arranged in the formation of a loose huddle.   All men in the huddle are receivers.

(2) The coach stands at some distance to throw the pass. He should be in position to observe the action.

(3) The players contest each other for possession of the ball.
(4) As many huddles like this as feasible may be used.
(5) See Illustrations 209a and 209b.

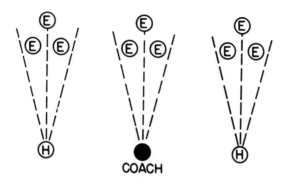

Illus. 209a

Illus. 209b

19. HOW TO DRILL FOR ADJUSTMENTS

The purpose of this drill is to provide training for the receiver in poorly-thrown passes.

INSTRUCTIONS:

(1) Locate a center on offense with either the right or left end.

(2) The end is in his normal offensive stance at a distance of about eight yards from the center.

(3) Select a passer and position him according to the offensive formation.

(4) Have the end break downfield for a pass. He should look for the ball at five or six yards.

(5) The passer throws the ball behind the end or throws a short pass which he must come back to receive.

(6) The receiver attempts to adjust himself to make the catch.

20. HOW TO DRILL FOR GETTING FREE BY THE FAKE AND SLIDE

The purpose of this drill is to teach the ends to avoid getting held up on the line of scrimmage.

INSTRUCTIONS:

(1) Have the end take a three-point stance on the line.

(2) Station a defensive tackle in front of him and a linebacker in his proper position.

(3) The end fakes a shoulder block on the tackle and slides outside.

(4) Next the end steps into the linebacker, pivots, and steps away from him.

(5) He should throw his buttocks into the backer and then release.

21. HOW TO DRILL FOR GETTING FREE BY THE SUBMARINE

An end must be drilled to release himself when he is being held up on passes. He will not become confused if he knows several techniques to break clear. The purpose of this drill is to provide the ends with a method of getting free when a pass is called.

INSTRUCTIONS:

(1) This drill should be practiced daily when the ends combine with the backs.

(2) Station an offensive end on the line of scrimmage in a three-point stance.

(3) Place a defensive tackle directly in front of him.

(4) First have the end make an upward head fake.

(5) Next have him drop low and forward to the ground on all fours. He should crawl for two steps.

(6) With the same momentum he comes up on his feet and releases himself.

(7) After getting free he must run under control until he makes his fakes and cuts.

(8) Never allow an end to go out unmolested. Prepare him for game conditions.

22.   HOW TO DRILL FOR GETTING FREE BY THE PIVOT

The purpose of this drill is to teach the ends to avoid getting held up on the line of scrimmage when a pass is called.

INSTRUCTIONS:

(1) Place the offensive end on the line of scrimmage in a three-point stance.

(2) Assign a tackle to play directly over the end.   Instruct the tackle to delay the end.

(3) Have the end pivot on his inside foot and whirl to the outside.   He is simply pivoting and rolling out of the hands of the defender.   Plenty of arm motion is needed in the pivot.

(4) After getting free he should run with his hands approximately chest-high.

(5) This technique will become automatic if practiced daily.

23.   HOW TO DRILL FOR GETTING FREE BY ATTENTION

The object of this drill is to provide practice getting free by the "attention" method.

INSTRUCTIONS:

(1) Locate the offense end on the line of scrimmage in his normal stance.

(2) Station a defensive tackle over the end or on his outside shoulder.

(3) Instruct the tackle to deliberately hold the end from releasing downfield.

(4) The offensive end must yell "Holding!" as loudly as he can to attract attention.   He should wave his arm and do anything to make the officials conscious of what is occurring.

(5) Have the defensive tackle hold the end in scrimmage to watch his reactions.

24. HOW TO DRILL FOR GETTING FREE BY FLANKING

This drill is designed to give the ends training in breaking clear when being held on the line of scrimmage.

INSTRUCTIONS:

(1) Locate the end on offense with his customary three-point stance.

(2) Station a tackle on his outside shoulder and a linebacker directly over him.

(3) Instruct the defense to knock the end down.

(4) Have the end widen five yards and go out for the pass.

(5) If the defensive moves out, have the end widen another five yards.

(6) This is a good method of getting free when you are sure the defense is planning to gang you.

25. HOW TO DRILL FOR NUMBERS

The purpose of this drill is to teach quick reaction to pass defenders.

INSTRUCTIONS:

(1) Have four backs line up horizontally on the 20-yard line.

(2) Number each back from one through four.

(3) Place a passer on the 30-yard line and have him pass to either sideline.

(4) The coach calls any number through four and the defensive back whose number is called attempts to intercept the football.

(5) See Illustration 210.

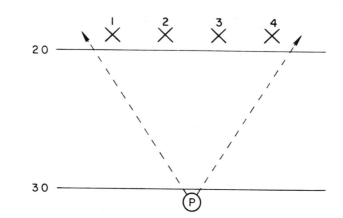

Illus. 210

26. HOW TO DRILL FOR NUMBERED RUNNING

The idea behind this drill is to provide forward pass practice for passer and receiver. This might be of value for teams that use a zone numbering method of pass offense.

INSTRUCTIONS:

(1) Place a center, a passer, and a receiver on offense.

(2) The coach calls the zone route to the receiver.

(3) This is a good method to check receivers in early pre-season drills.

(4) See Illustration 211.

Illus. 211

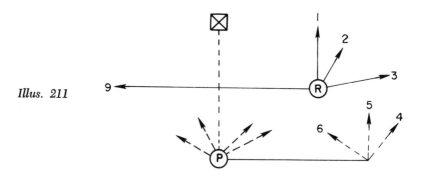

27. HOW TO DRILL FOR CUTTING TOWARD GOAL LINE

The object of this drill is to provide the ends with practice catching passes and cutting immediately toward the goal line.

INSTRUCTIONS:

(1) Many ends have a tendency to drift several yards after catching a pass without realizing that they should be touchdown bound.

(2) Have the end run a pattern parallel to the line of scrimmage.

(3) Place two bell-bottom dummies five yards apart.

(4) Assign a coach or passer to throw passes to the end in the area between the two dummies.

(5) Stress pivoting sharply between the two dummies and starting at once toward the goal line.

(6) Emphasize that yardage is measured in only *one* way.

(7) See Illustration 212.

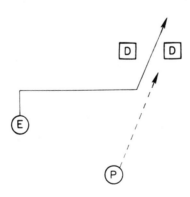

Illus. 212

28. HOW TO DRILL FOR THE DOUBLE HOOK

The purpose of this drill is to provide practice for the ends in hooking against resistance.

INSTRUCTIONS:

(1) Place two ends, a center, and a quarterback on offense.

(2) Station two linebackers on defense to defend against the hook pass.

(3) Use extra linebackers and extra ends to delay the receivers.

(4) This is a good drill for the linebackers as well as for the offensive ends.

(5) See Illustration 213.

Illus. 213

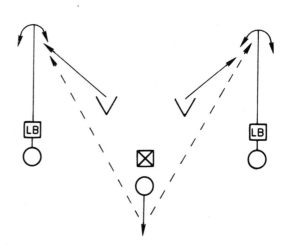

8

THE CENTERING GAME

*The most important lineman, regardless
of the formation.*
—Frank Leahy

THE CENTER'S POSITION ON OFFENSE INVOLVES MORE RESPON-
sibility and is the most difficult to play of any position on the
line. His principal duty is passing the ball to the backfield
men, so that it can be handled safely on all types of plays,
regardless of the formation.

The first item of importance in the play of the center is the
stance. He must assume his position so that it will be comfortable, solid and afford him freedom of movement of the
arms when passing the ball between his legs. There are three
types of stances used today, (a) with the feet even, (b) with
the left foot forward, and (c) with the right foot in advance
of the left, provided the center is right-handed. We definitely
favor the latter stance and the drills we describe are confined
to that stance.

In passing the ball, the spiral pass is the fastest and is almost universally used.

287

The blocking of the center is confined almost entirely to check blocking in the line and good drills of this type are invaluable. However, there are times when he is called upon to cooperate with a teammate in cross-blocking and double-teaming. In some cases, he is relieved of his blocking assignments in the line, and sent downfield to block.

The center is usually depended upon to spark the team, and he should show plenty of enthusiasm for his job. His attitude either way is contagious. If he is full of life and snap, these qualities will be reflected in the work of his teammates: they will play harder and with more spirit.

There is a scarcity of good drills involving the fundamentals of center play, and more are needed. Drills for stance, passing, and blocking will be discussed in the order named.

1. HOW TO DRILL FOR STANCE

The purpose of this drill is to teach the center a correct stance.

INSTRUCTIONS:

(1) Have the center assume his natural stance. Insist that the stance be comfortable.

(2) Teach the stance to the center by having him react to shoves and pushes from various directions until a comfortable, workable position is obtained.

(3) Assist the center in improving his stance by resorting to the mirror technique.

2. HOW TO DRILL FOR STANCE EXERCISE

The object of this drill is to provide the center with a warm-up drill.

INSTRUCTIONS:

(1) Have the center assume as wide a base as possible.

(2) This loosens and strengthens the crotch, knee joints, hamstring and quadricep muscles by alternately twisting the torso left and right.

(3) See Illustrations 214a and 214b.

Illus. 214a

Illus. 214b

3. HOW TO DRILL FOR CENTER'S TIMING

The purpose of this drill is to improve the center's timing.
INSTRUCTIONS:

(1) Improve the centering speed by timing the difference in time between the center snap and the center's contacting his opponent.

(2) If there is an appreciable lag, the player is not centering and blocking with the same motion.

(3) This is definitely needed and must be practiced daily.

4. HOW TO DRILL FOR THE *T* PASS

The object of this drill is to teach the center to make the T *pass.*
INSTRUCTIONS:

(1) Teach the center to make the *T* pass by telling him that the sound of the ball striking the quarterback's hand must be heard all over the field. (Frank Leahy offers a new suit to the center who draws blood from the quarterback's hand.)

(2) Have the center hold his head so far that he will have sore neck muscles.

(3) Teach the center to grip the ball as hard as possible by asking him to make a game by trying to squeeze some pig juice out of it.

5. HOW TO DRILL FOR BLOCKING

The object of this drill is to provide blocking practice for two or three centers.

INSTRUCTIONS:

(1) Have the center assume his normal position over the ball.

(2) Place another center holding a blocking dummy to his right side. After several blocks, the dummy is held to the left side.

(3) If a third center is available, he awaits his turn and observes the techniques of the other two players. He may become a quarterback to receive the ball.

(4) The reason for having two or three centers together is that any corrections in one's blocking will be heard by the others. This system prevents needless repetition by the coach.

(5) See Illustration 215.

Illus. 215

6. HOW TO DRILL FOR GETTING DOWNFIELD

The object of this drill is to make the center conscious of downfield blocking.

INSTRUCTIONS:

(1) Emphasize the importance of downfield blocking to the center by suddenly leaving an empty space before him in dummy drill.

(2) Point out that he is not helping the team by standing there.

(3) Centers habitually consider it an injustice that they should be given any duties beyond the primary one of snapping the ball.

7. HOW TO DRILL FOR PASS PROTECTION

The object of this drill is to train the center and two guards in pass protection.

INSTRUCTIONS:

(1) Line up a center and two guards on offense.

(2) Place two guards and a linebacker (B4) on defense.

(3) Have an extra lineman act as a back to receive the ball.

(4) Time the offense to see how long they can hold the fort.

(5) See Illustration 216.

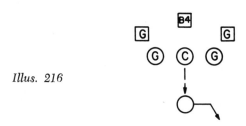

Illus. 216

8. HOW TO DRILL FOR QUICKNESS IN HEAD SNAP

The object of this drill is to provide practice for the center in lifting his head after snapping the ball.

INSTRUCTIONS:

(1) Have the center assume his normal stance.

(2) Place a backfield man four yards away from the center.

(3) After snapping the ball to the backfield, the center should immediately lift his head and elbows to insure good blocking.

(4) Use a stop watch to time his reactions in head snap.

(5) Keep moving the backfield closer to the center and time the head snap. As the ball is released, the center's head should be snapped up before the ball reaches the backfield.

(6) See Illustration 217: In the upper picture he has kept his head down too long and is in poor position to block because he cannot see his opponent.

(7) In the lower picture, the head has been snapped up before the ball reached its destination and he is set to block.

WRONG

RIGHT

Illus. 217

9. HOW TO DRILL FOR ACCURACY WITH CANVAS

This drill is designed to aid the offensive center, especially if he is training for a single wing offense. The drill will help him to become accurate with his passes.

INSTRUCTIONS:

(1) A piece of canvas two feet square can be rigged with four holes. The holes should be large enough for a football to pass through.

(2) The canvas may be hung from the goal post or any similar structure.

(3) Have the center place himself five yards from the mounted canvas.

(4) The numbered holes provide him approximate targets.

(5) Hole no. 1—Right knee of spinning fullback
   Hole no. 2—Left knee of spinning fullback
   Hole no. 3—Middle of abdomen
   Hole no. 4—Direct to the tail back

(6) This drill may be used before daily practice. After a week's practice, all the centers can be graded by a coach on their accuracy.

(7) See Illustration 218.

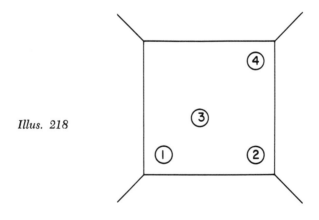

Illus. 218

10. HOW TO DRILL FOR CHECK-BLOCKING

The object of this drill is to provide practice for the center in check-blocking. This is primarily for single wing drill.

INSTRUCTIONS:

(1) Place a center on offense with two guards and a left end.

(2) Station two active linemen on defense, one a guard, and the other a tackle.

(3) Position one man in the backfield to receive the ball.

(4) First have D pull left and the center must check-block to his right. A and B use a lead post block on the tackle.

(5) Next have both B and D pull right with A releasing downfield. The center uses a left shoulder check-block.

(6) This situation is difficult for any center. Have B and D pull right with the guard directly over the center. A checks momentarily, and releases downfield. The center uses a left shoulder block to check the guard's progress.

(7) This same situation and others may be developed by having B block out at the hole and D pulling through the hole. A head-fakes, and releases downfield.

(8) See Illustrations 219a and 219b.

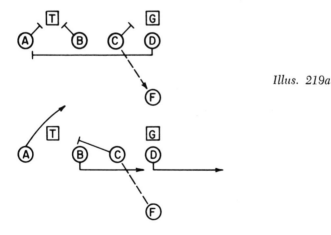

Illus. 219a

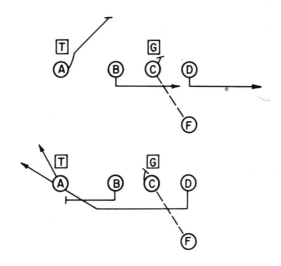

Illus. 219a (cont'd)

Illus. 219b

11. HOW TO DRILL FOR GRIP

The drill is designed to teach the center how to grip the ball.
INSTRUCTIONS:

(1) Have the center grip the ball lightly with the laces down (if single wing center). The thumbs are almost touching with fingers well spread.

(2) If the grip seems awkward, have the center take the ball as if he were going to throw a forward pass and place the ball on the ground.

(3) Emphasize little weight over the arms and on the ball. The weight should be over the ball of the feet.

12. HOW TO DRILL FOR THE LIFE-PRESERVER

The object of this drill is to provide practice for the center in blocking an opponent in every conceivable situation.
INSTRUCTIONS:

(1) Place a center on offense with a football. Assign a backfield man, whether *T* or single-wing, to receive the snap. A center should never practice blocking without passing the football to another player.

(2) Locate an aggressive guard to play directly over the center to begin the drill. Gradually proceed, being careful not to destroy the center's confidence.

(3) Have the guard vary his charge and position frequently. In this manner the center will be prepared to block his opponent in every possible situation.

(4) This is a "must" drill for every center and because of the importance of this position, we refer to the drill as the "life-preserver."

(5) See Illustration 220.

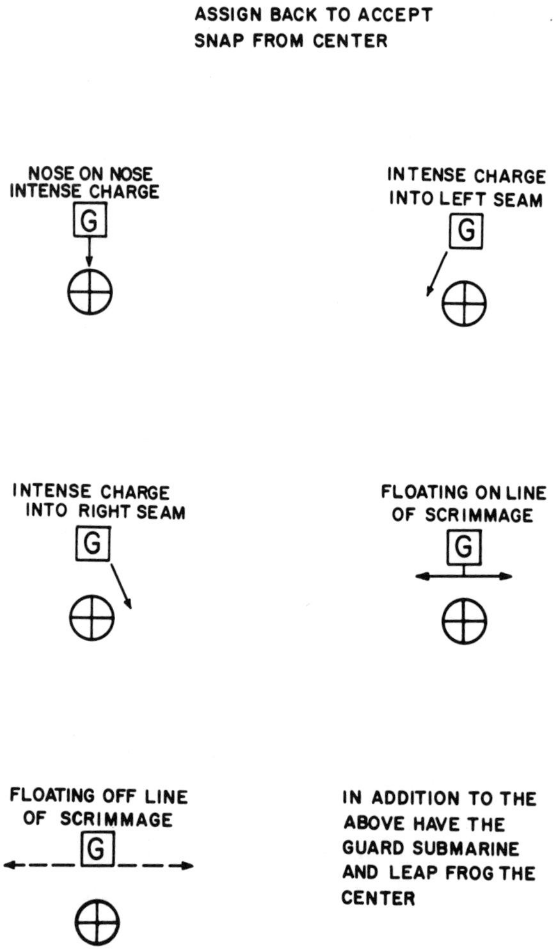

ASSIGN BACK TO ACCEPT
SNAP FROM CENTER

NOSE ON NOSE
INTENSE CHARGE

INTENSE CHARGE
INTO LEFT SEAM

INTENSE CHARGE
INTO RIGHT SEAM

FLOATING ON LINE
OF SCRIMMAGE

FLOATING OFF LINE
OF SCRIMMAGE

IN ADDITION TO THE
ABOVE HAVE THE
GUARD SUBMARINE
AND LEAP FROG THE
CENTER

Illus. 220

13. HOW TO DRILL FOR POWER-WRIST CENTERING

The purpose of this drill is to strengthen the wrist of the center. This drill may be a pre- or post-practice drill for the center to warm up with the new weighted Power-Wrist football. This is a special weighted ball for centers. It is an excellent early-season drill and is a valuable drill during the summer months to improve the center's snap from spread or punt formation.

INSTRUCTIONS:

(1) Have all centers drop to one knee. Let them warm up with the Power-Wrist football at a distance of five yards. Have them throw the ball overhead with wrist snap only. Gradually lengthen the distance as the centers' arms and wrists become warm and limber.

(2) After a warm-up period of five minutes, substitute a regulation ball.

(3) You will be pleased with the results of this drill, because your centers' passing ability will be greatly improved.

(4) See Illustration 221.

Illus. 221

14. HOW TO DRILL CENTER FOR BLOCKING ON PUNTS

This drill is designed to give the center some individual attention on making his block after snapping the ball.

INSTRUCTIONS:

(1) A center and kicker are positioned on offense.

(2) One or two defensive men alternate rushing the kicker.

(3) This is also a useful drill for blocking punts.

(4) See Illustration 222.

Illus. 222

9

QUARTERBACK GAME

*A sound understanding of offensive football is the basic require-
ment of a good quarterback. He must be able to play the position
physically and mentally.*

—Bud Wilkinson

It has been our belief that only a few coaches know how
to train a quarterback. These drills will prove an excellent
guide for obtaining a standard performance from quarterbacks. The drills within this chapter are not complicated nor
do they require a great deal of time. They should be so handled
that they will occupy only that period allotted to group work
in the early part of the season. Considerable stress should be
laid upon getting the quarterback ready to handle his attack
for the first game.

Overcoaching

Great care should be exercised to avoid overcoaching. At
every stage of the game the quarterback should be encouraged
to make his own decisions. Everything possible should be done
to develop his initiative and confidence. After the season is

301

two or three weeks old the quarterback coach should retire to a position of friendly criticism and encouragement. In this manner only can the quarterback be trained to develop self-reliance and initiative.

1. VOICE AND BEARING DRILL

A good voice is an exceedingly desirable asset. In this drill the quality of the voice plus field position is stressed.

INSTRUCTIONS:

In this drill, a team or skeleton team of a backfield and center is assembled either from substitutes or quarterbacks, and the quarterback candidates are required to call formation and signals. A candidate may shift the team and change his field position slightly between each play. The coach, by example or by constructive criticism, shows the quarterback what he actually wants called. In this drill, the quality of the voice tone should be brought out. The quarterback is like an officer in command of troops, and he must be able to get his commands across in the proper manner.

2. IRREGULAR ALIGNMENT DRILL

The purpose of this drill is to provide training for one quarterback in analyzing irregular spacing in defensive alignment.

INSTRUCTIONS:

Another quarterback drill is handled as follows: two complete teams, either first and second, or, if more convenient, third and fourth, are assembled. The quarterback is required to use flankers on every play and call the signal for the most advantageous play resulting from defensive players being out of position. The coach should require the defensive players to take improper distances and intervals in order to develop the quarterback's judgment. For instance, a guard at times should leave an excessive gap between himself and the tackle, or a corner back should move up close to the line. The quarterback should be required to call the play immediately. After the quarterback has developed a few days under this training, he should be required to pick flaws where he can find them by close analysis of the defense.

3. SCORING DRILL

The purpose of this drill is to provide the quarterback training in calling plays within the 10-yard line.

INSTRUCTIONS:

The quarterback should have a daily drill at scoring touchdowns. This scoring drill is handled by requiring the quarterback to take positions in the opponent's territory while at either group or individual drill, and then to call the proper plays for scoring. The coach may call the down and distance. After the quarterback has developed, however, he will make his own decisions.

4. PAPER-AND-PENCIL DRILL

The object of this drill is to provide training for the quarterbacks in the off-season.

INSTRUCTIONS:

Quarterbacks should be worked during the off-season of the year off the field of play with a blackboard or pencil and paper. The coach should draw a miniature field of play, locate the ball thereon, assume the down and distance, and require the quarterback to call the formation and signal. In this manner the quarterback can be trained and ready for spring practice or fall competition.

5. VOICE DRILL

The purpose of this drill is to provide practice for all three quarterbacks in voice inflection.

INSTRUCTIONS:

A clever quarterback can produce determined, concentrated play by inserting those qualities into his voice. He can also produce fire and dash from certain manners of command. Unhappily, he can, by an unfortunate use of his voice, also bring about nervousness and start his men before the ball is in play. This drill may be practiced with only four men—three quarterbacks and a center. One candidate should play the quarterback position, the other two candidates play right and left halfbacks.

6. NEW PLAY DRILL

The purpose of this drill is to acquaint the quarterback and the squad with details when a new play is presented.

INSTRUCTIONS:

Whenever the squad is given a new play, the coach should first explain its execution, going over the assignment of each man, the purpose of the play, and the circumstances under which is can best be used. The last item should be stressed first with all the quarterbacks and then with the team, either on the blackboard or on the field.

7. TALKING-IN-THE-HUDDLE DRILL

The purpose of a drill of this type is to enforce complete attention and silence when the quarterback enters the huddle.
INSTRUCTIONS:
Upon entering the huddle, if the quarterback hears any talking he does not call the play. He waits until there is absolute silence before making his call, even if it results in a penalty for taking too much time. There may be better drills to discipline a squad of Mexican generals, but this one has proven effective.

8. SELF-DEFENSIVE DRILL

The purpose of this drill is to give the quarterback a chance to study defensive alignments.
INSTRUCTIONS:
A serious fault of most quarterbacks is calling signals with heads "buried" and seldom studying the defensive alignment of the opposition. Many times in practice not all of the quarterbacks are occupied. Occasionally have one of these quarterbacks attend the practice sessions of the defensive line. In this way, the signal caller can secure valuable insight into defensive strategies.

9. DEFENSIVE STRATEGY MAP

The purpose of this drill is to provide defensive training for the quarterback so that he can call plays intelligently.
INSTRUCTIONS:
Many coaches begin teaching strategy to their quarterback with a discussion of offensive. Actually, offensive football is meaningless unless the field general understands the basic

alignments of defense. Make a strategy map of defenses that might be encountered in various zones of the field. This is a fine drill. The quarterback must understand what he is attacking.

10. PASSING CHART DRILL

The purpose of this drill is to test the quarterback on his passing offense.

INSTRUCTIONS:

(1) Use an 8½ x 11 sheet or card as illustrated.

(2) It is good practice to have the field general put down the play numbers in the zone where he thinks passes might be completed.

(3) See Illustration 223.

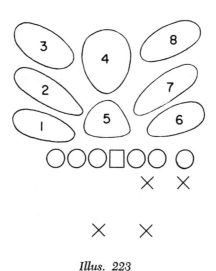

Illus. 223

11. POST-PRACTICE DRILL

The purpose of this drill is to train the quarterback in re-sourcefulness, initiative, confidence, and imagination.
INSTRUCTIONS:
Much strategy may be taught in odd hours. This may be done after practice by eating with the quarterback at the training table, by walking with the quarterback from the locker room to dinner, by walking or riding with the quarterback to his rooming house. On trips, the coach and the quarterback may ride together. This keeps the quarterback constantly thinking football and permits the coach to offer constructive criticism.

12. GAME CHART DRILL

This is a post game summary to analyze the tactics employed.
INSTRUCTIONS:
Some type of a chart should be kept of each scrimmage and each game. It should contain most everything, including:
A. Play used.
B. Ball carrier.
C. Field positions.
D. Yards gained or lost.
E. First downs.
F. Penalties
G. Fumbles.
H. Passes attempted and completed.
I. Yards gained passing.
J. Punts: number, distance, and average.
By studying this chart, the mistakes of the scrimmage or the previous game can be noted and possibly avoided in the future. If film is not available, this chart can be substituted.

13. DEFENSE DRILL

The object of this drill is to provide written homework for the quarterback.

INSTRUCTIONS:

Give the quarterback one examination each week. Outline five or six defenses against your offense and the quarterback will be required to take these diagrams home, study them, and choose the plays of your own system that could possibly gain ground against these various defenses.

14. PLAY ASSIGNMENT DRILL

The purpose of this drill is to test the quarterbacks in offensive assignments.

INSTRUCTIONS:

The quarterbacks are required to diagram the duties of every man on every play. This will help when a man in the line reports some peculiarity in alignment of an opposing player. It will simplify play selection for the quarterback. Mimeographed assignment sheets are helpful.

15. CHART DRILL

The purpose of this drill is to replay and analyze the previous game played.

INSTRUCTIONS:

Have quarterbacks draw charts of the games played and go back over them studying what was done and what should have been done.

16. NEWSPAPER DRILL

The purpose of this drill is to make the quarterback alert by studying newspaper accounts of the games.

INSTRUCTIONS:

By careful study of the newspapers a quarterback can often familiarize himself with many of the characteristics and weaknesses of players and of future opposing teams.

17. RATING PLAYS

The object of this drill is to provide training for the quarterback in evaluating the offense.

INSTRUCTIONS:

Have the quarterback list all of his plays. This list should be revised from time to time, eliminating weaker plays and the plays not used. At the end of the season put on a smaller card a short list of successful plays and the game in which they were used.

18. STRATEGY CHART

The object of this drill is to offer assistance to an inexperienced quarterback.

INSTRUCTIONS:

In this drill, the coach maps out a chart and requires the signal caller to memorize it. He is to call only those signals which are placed in a corresponding zone of play on the field.

When this plan is followed, all initiative is taken from the quarterback and he becomes a mechanical signal caller who completely disregards the play situation and calls his signals regardless of the defense. It just isn't reasonable to follow any set rules or system of generalship, no matter how green the quarterback may be. The only reasonable way to advance the ball is through the weakness of the opposition. Plays that were highly successful last week may not work at all in this week's game. It isn't always possible to determine in advance what will be the weak spots in the opponent's defense. Therefore the strategy chart should not be used unless absolutely necessary.

19. RECOGNITION DRILL

The object of this drill is to give the quarterback training in offense and defense recognition.

INSTRUCTIONS:

Show previous-game movies to the quarterback and make him call the defense, the play, the yardage, the down, and the tackler as quickly as possible. Tell the quarterback not to make a conscious effort to see individual items, but rather to scan rapidly the objects under observation. He should try to make this scanning automatic. The quarterback should take this recognition drill as soon as the game movies are available. The information received from showing of the movies is charted and serves as an inventory of the previous game.

20. TWO-MINUTE DRILL

The purpose of this drill is to provide the team scrimmage practice against the clock.

INSTRUCTIONS:

Place an offensive team 10 or 15 yards from the goal line and tell them that there are one or two minutes remaining in the half or until the end of the game. They cannot stop the clock.

It is good practice for them to think and act quickly in getting in and out of the huddle and in trying to score before the time is up. It is wise to do this often in scrimmages.

21. CHECKER DRILL

The idea behind this drill is to get the quarterback thinking ahead by use of objects.

INSTRUCTIONS:

It is possible to teach generalship on a table with checkers.

22. AFTER-DINNER DRILL

The purpose of this drill is to teach generalship where it should be taught.

INSTRUCTIONS:

My personal preference has always been strongly in favor of teaching generalship on the field itself. Take an odd half-hour in the evening or at any other convenient time to meet quarterback candidates on the field. Begin with a broad theory. Divide the field into three zones, called for convenience defensive zone, neutral zone, and enemy zone. Defensive territory lies between our own goal and 35-yard line. Neutral grounds runs from there to the enemy 35-yard line.

23. OBSERVATION DRILL

The purpose of this drill is to make the quarterback alert in scrimmage.

INSTRUCTIONS:

When your quarterback is not in the practice scrimmage, have him stand by and study his teammates. By doing this, he may notice, for example, that the right tackle has exceptional ability when blocking to his right but is a little weak when operating to his left. Some time in a game when things are mighty tough it might pay touchdown dividends to have such information at his finger tips. At every opportunity have him think in terms of what he would do under various game conditions. Who is the best pass receiver? Who is the fastest-starting back? Who runs the hardest? All of these little things will help the quarterback immeasurably if he has them in a notebook before the first game of the season. A coach can teach for hour after hour, but once the 11 men go on the field, their success lies completely in the hands of the man calling the plays.

24. SCOUT DRILL

The purpose of this drill is to provide the quarterback with detailed scout information.

INSTRUCTIONS:

Prior to any game the quarterback should meet and inquire from the scout as to the defensive merits of the opponents. Every bit of information he obtains should be carefully digested and catalogued for future reference. Any little tips that the quarterback can get before entering a contest should be thought over thoroughly and tested fairly early in the game.

25. VOICE DRILL

This drill provides the quarterback with extra work to improve his voice.

INSTRUCTIONS:

Much can be done by ambitious candidates to improve the quality of the voice and the manner of calling the signals. As in most things, practice is the best teacher. Quarterbacks should drill themselves in calling signals aloud when away from the field. Drill at home in front of a mirror. They should work for clearness and avoid slurring. Each syllable should be bitten off so that it stands out sharply. Cultivation of a definite rhythm is helpful. Above all, the field general must give the signal as if he meant it.

26. STRATEGY-SESSION DRILL

The idea behind this drill is to allow all the quarterbacks to meet and analyze various tactical situations.

INSTRUCTIONS:

There should be special meetings of the quarterbacks and the coach, in which the coach sets up various tactical situations and asks for the best play for the occasion. Frequently there are several suggestions. All should be listed, and then followed by a frank and open discussion of the merits of each suggestion. This not only serves to associate the correct play with the given situation but furnishes an excellent analysis of each play. It should prove helpful to the coach as well as to the quarterbacks if the players are led to express themselves frankly and fully.

27. SIGNAL DRILL

The purpose of this drill is to provide tactical training for the quarterback and one team when running signals.

INSTRUCTIONS:

One thing all quarterbacks can do is always to play the field during signal drill; i.e., whenever the team runs signals, the quarterback can suit the play to the position on the field in which he finds himself; or better still, maneuver the team to the spot from which he wishes to call a certain play. This practice can be made even more valuable, and more fun for the quarterback, if he uses his imagination to picture all sorts of situations and calls his plays accordingly.

28. PROBABLE-DEFENSE DRILL

This drill is to provide the quarterback practice in running plays against probable defenses.

INSTRUCTIONS:

Have the quarterback on Monday or Tuesday diagram defensive alignments expected from opponents to determine which plays should be most effective against them. After deciding which plays would be best, he should then work these plays into a series. This series would then be stressed during the practices preceding the game.

29. CHART AND DIAGRAM DRILL

The purpose of this drill is to allow the quarterbacks to get strategy more firmly in mind.

INSTRUCTIONS:

Use charts and diagrams to clear up hazy points. Have a

special room or bulletin board for quarterbacks only. Put diagrams on a blackboard and let the boys who are interested view them.

30. SPECIAL PLAY DRILL

The purpose of this drill is to associate the quarterback with certain plays to be used in various areas of the field.

INSTRUCTIONS:

Quarterbacks must learn to associate certain plays with certain spots on the field. This is particularly true of special plays and fancy plays, and to a lesser extent of all plays. To help form these associations, the quarterbacks should be given charts of the field and asked to write the signal for each play upon the spot from which it should normally be expected to work best.

31. WALKING DRILL

The purpose of this fine drill is for the coach and the quarterbacks to walk and talk strategy.

INSTRUCTIONS:

The best place to teach generalship is on the practice field. The coach should make it a practice to walk over the playing field with the quarterbacks, stopping at various places, and saying something like this: "It is the middle of the second quarter; score, nothing to nothing; weather conditions just as they are now; we get the ball here first and ten. What would you call?" If the quarterback answers the right play, then go on to something else. If he calls the wrong play, stay right on that same spot until the situation is clear in his mind. This is an excellent drill.

32. METRONOME DRILL

The purpose of this drill is to develop uniform rhythmic cadence among the quarterbacks.

INSTRUCTIONS:

This drill should be practiced with all the quarterbacks, first one at a time and then all together. Use a metronome as a measuring instrument for each candidate's voice. Set the metronome for the tempo you desire. In this drill insist on quality of voice tones, and sharpness should be brought out. See Illustration 224.

Illus. 224

33. TOUCHDOWN SEQUENCE DRILL

The purpose of this drill is to prepare for the inevitable and help build morale.

INSTRUCTIONS:

(1) Place the football anywhere on the field and inform your captain and quarterback that they have 30 seconds to score. They are behind by six points.

(2) Call out the time, yards, distance, etc. It is good practice for both offense and defense.

34. SCORING ZONE DRILL

The purpose of this drill is to simulate game conditions and prove to the team that 30 seconds is sufficient time to score.

INSTRUCTIONS:

(1) Place the football on 20-yard line in the scoring zone and inform the quarterback that he has 30 seconds to score.

(2) Another method is to place the ball on the five-yard line in scoring territory and order the offensive team to see how many times it can score in 30 seconds.

(3) Still another method is to place the ball on the five-yard line and inform the offensive team that it has 15 seconds to score.

(4) Again, place the ball on the 25-yard line and inform the offensive team it is behind 7-6 with 15 seconds to play. This provides good field goal practice under game conditions.

35. CONCLUDING THE SIGNAL DRILL

The purpose of this drill is to make time a factor so that the final part of the signal drill can be a training period for the quarterback.

INSTRUCTIONS:

(1) When concluding the signal drill, place a time limit on the quarterback.

(2) Inform the quarterback he is behind by four points with two minutes remaining. He can *not* call time out.

(3) He may employ his touchdown sequence in this situation.

36. QUARTERBACK TESTING DRILL

The object of this drill is to test the quarterback's knowledge of his team's offensive assignments against both odd and even defenses.

INSTRUCTIONS:

(1) Use an 8½ x 11 examination sheet or card as illustrated.

(2) The sheet is divided into thirds, listing the anticipated defenses of your next opponent.

(3) The quarterback can pencil in the offensive assignments of all eleven men against the expected defense.

(4) See Illustration 225.

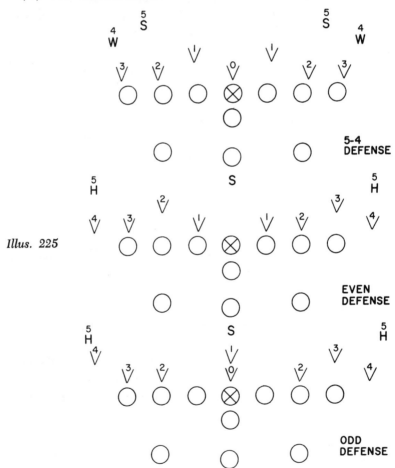

Illus. 225

5-4 DEFENSE

EVEN DEFENSE

ODD DEFENSE

37. BLACKBOARD DRILL

This is a foundation drill in generalship. The object is to train the new quarterbacks in calling plays against segments of a specific defense.

INSTRUCTIONS:

(1) Start to train the quarterback at the blackboard by using only the interior linemen on defense.

(2) Place two guards on defense, simulating a six-man spacing.

(3) Have the quarterback select plays that hit over the offensive center's area.

(4) Have him select plays that will go directly outside of these men in the event they are pinching or stunting to protect this area.

(5) Next, place a defensive man over the center and a linebacker behind him in the 5-3 defense.

(6) Again, have him select plays that go to either side of these men. If they are stunting, forming a six-man defense, indicate the plays he should call.

(7) Then add a third defensive man, simulating a 5-4 defense, and have the quarterback select the correct plays when they are playing straight and when stunting.

(8) Add two more defensive men and repeat the same procedure.

(9) Next, have the quarterback select plays using only one-half of his offensive line.

(10) Then add the other half of the line and repeat the procedure.

(11) This drill should give the inexperienced quarterback a clear picture of basic generalship against standard odd and even defenses.

38. DANGER-ZONE DRILL

The object of this drill is to provide practice in generalship in getting out of the hole.

INSTRUCTIONS:

(1) This should be a must drill once a week, because a mistake in this zone can mean a touchdown.

(2) Place the offensive team on its own five-yard line with a first and ten situation and the score tied.

(3) Have the quarterback review his generalship to get out of this zone.

(4) This is a very important drill.

39. SCORING ZONE HUSTLE DRILL

The purpose of this drill is to provide running and offensive timing along with motivation. This is a good "pep" drill for morale if not overdone.

INSTRUCTIONS:

(1) Line up the entire team anywhere in the scoring zone without opposition.

(2) Have the team spring from the huddle and run the play called with everyone sprinting across the goal line.

(3) Do this for approximately 10 to 20 times and get everyone making a lot of noise—but still concentrating.

40. DEFENSIVE FILM LOOP DRILL

The purpose of this drill is to use already-prepared defensive film loops to train the quarterback.

INSTRUCTIONS:

(1) Don Canham's "Champions on Film: Set No. 1—Defensive Formations" consists of 27 different alignments in slow motion, used against all offensive formations.

(2) Each loop has a game clip to show that specific defense in action in a collegiate contest.

41. QUARTERBACK TESTING SHEET DRILL

The purpose of this drill is to test the quarterback's generalship against three anticipated defenses.

INSTRUCTIONS:

(1) Another method of testing your quarterback for a particular game is to use an 8½ x 11 examination sheet.

(2) The sheet is divided into thirds, listing the major anticipated defenses used by your next opponent.

(3) The quarterback may test himself and be tested by the coach on these cards. He simply diagrams the assignments of all eleven men against each defense on the card.

(4) The quarterback is required to list the strength and weakness of each particular defense anticipated. Each defense may be listed on a separate card or sheet for better organization.

(5) Any comments that the quarterback may want to make may be recorded at the bottom of the sheet.

(6) See Illustration 226.

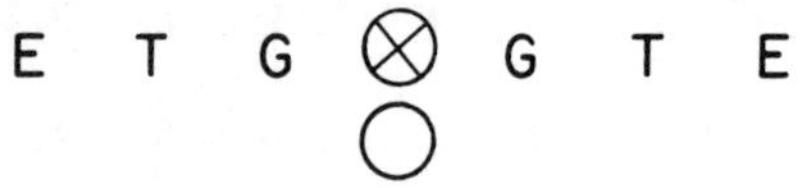

E   T   G   ⊗   G   T   E
○

Strength of particular defense:	Note variations of this defense:
Weakness of particular defense:	

Our plays that go best against this defense:

General comments relating to this defense:

Illus. 226

42. QUARTERBACK ACCUMULATIVE SHEETS

The purpose of these quarterbacks accumulative sheets is to teach recognition of all defensive alignments.

INSTRUCTIONS:

(1) Present your quarterback with a copy of the accumulative defensive sheets, after you have discussed them with him.

(2) These sheets are to be used as a constant reference throughout the season.

(3) Test him on these sheets by having him diagram all offensive assignments for a specific play.

(4) These sheets may be used for testing another player.

(5) See Illustration 227.

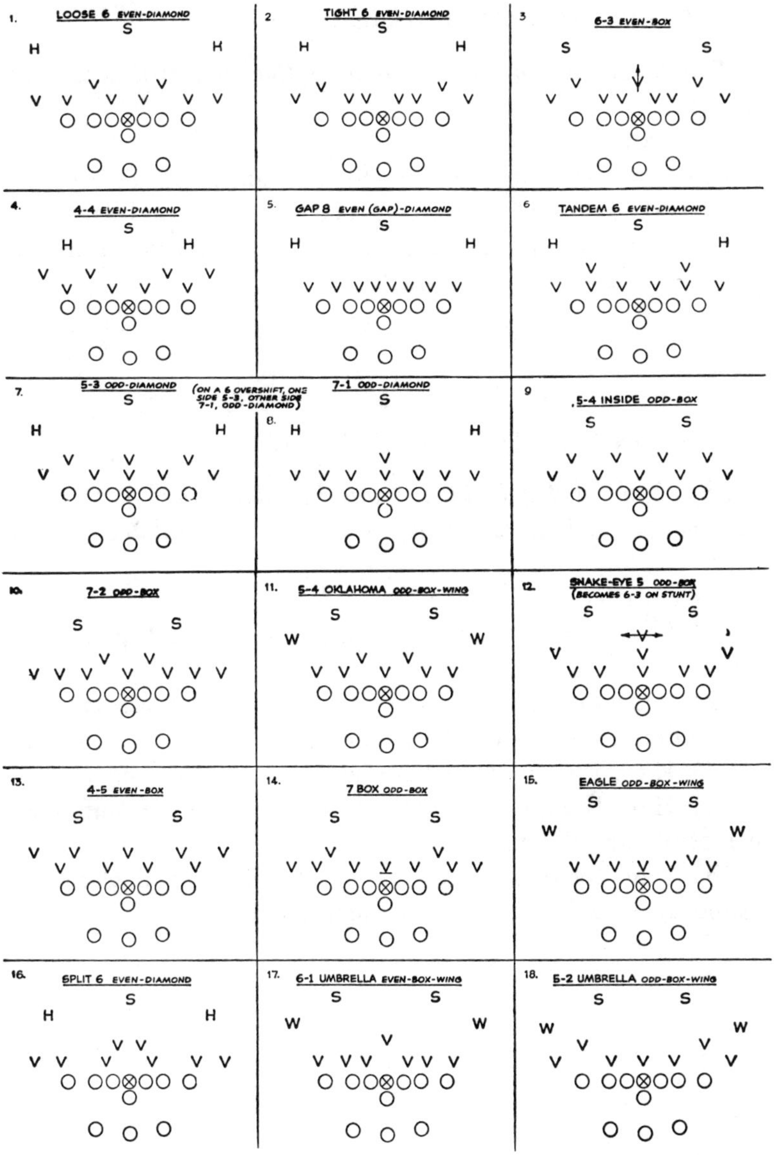

1. LOOSE 6 EVEN-DIAMOND
2. TIGHT 6 EVEN-DIAMOND
3. 6-3 EVEN-BOX
4. 4-4 EVEN-DIAMOND
5. GAP 8 EVEN (GAP)-DIAMOND
6. TANDEM 6 EVEN-DIAMOND
7. 5-3 ODD-DIAMOND (ON A 6 OVERSHIFT, ONE SIDE 5-3, OTHER SIDE 7-1, ODD-DIAMOND)
8. 7-1 ODD-DIAMOND
9. 5-4 INSIDE ODD-BOX
10. 7-2 ODD-BOX
11. 5-4 OKLAHOMA ODD-BOX-WING
12. SNAKE-EYE 5 ODD-BOX (BECOMES 6-3 ON STUNT)
13. 4-5 EVEN-BOX
14. 7 BOX ODD-BOX
15. EAGLE ODD-BOX-WING
16. SPLIT 6 EVEN-DIAMOND
17. 6-1 UMBRELLA EVEN-BOX-WING
18. 5-2 UMBRELLA ODD-BOX-WING

Illus. 227

43. TAPE RECORDER DRILL

The purpose of this drill is to allow the quarterback to check himself.

INSTRUCTIONS:

(1) Provide a tape recorder for the quarterback's use.

(2) It is an excellent device to check cadence and voice tone.

(3) Have the quarterback use the tape recorder until both cadence and voice are satisfactory.

44. MAGNETIC FOOTBALL DRILL

The object of this drill is to train the quarterback with miniature magnetic football players on a metal simulated football field.

INSTRUCTIONS:

(1) Place eleven minature magnetic football players on offense.

(2) Place eleven of the same on defense and arrange them into different defensive alignments.

(3) Have the quarterbacks identify each defense.

(4) Have the quarterbacks call out the strengths and weaknesses of each defense.

(5) Have the quarterbacks select the offensive plays that are sound against the weakness of each defense.

Part III

THE DEFENSIVE GAME

10

DRILLS FOR THE
LINEMAN

In tackling, keep your eye on the runner's belt buckle.

—A. A. Stagg

THE BASIC FUNDAMENTAL OF THIS PHASE OF THE GAME IS tackling. In the course of a game the player may be called on to make tackles on or near the line of scrimmage and in the secondary. Sometimes he will have to meet the ball carrier head on, and sometimes from the side or rear. The football coach needs certain drills to impart these techniques to the players. Many such drills are included in this chapter.

The reader will find in this chapter, although they are all not tackling drills, ones that are kindred. An example of this is the Forearm Shiver Drill. This drill is intended to teach a technique that might enable them to gain position for a tackle. Another such drill is the Spinning-Out Drill, which is designed to teach linemen the correct form for spinning-out of a block and back into the holes so as to be in position to tackle the ball carrier.

Tackling is quite a strenuous activity. Obviously a coach could not use too many drills for teaching this activity in any single practice session. Consequently, the collection of drills herein should afford a coach a varied assortment of proper drills that will not only create interest on the parts of the players, but will also offer the coach a repertoire from which to choose.

It takes considerable time to develop all defensive skills, and an accurate record of the actual time spent on each phase of the defensive game will help considerably in developing a successful football machine. A record of the time spent on each drill should be kept on a practice time chart. See Illustration 228.

1. HOW TO DRILL FOR WARM-UP TACKLING

The object of this drill is to provide the tacklers with a warm-up before actual contact is made. The tacklers gain confidence when they do not work against live competition all the time.

INSTRUCTIONS:

(1) Players pair off, one man holding the bag on the ground and the other lined up in front of it.

(2) The coach can line up as many bags as he can handle.

(3) Start the boys one yard away from the bags then gradually move them back to five and ten yards.

(4) Players rotate after each tackle.

(5) Spirit is a dominating factor in this drill, and if the

Number of minutes for each drill

	1st week					2nd week					3rd week					TOTAL
DATE																
CHARGING																
HEAD-ON TACKLING																
SIDE TACKLING																
STUNTS																
OPEN FIELD																
LOOPING																
CROSS CHARGING																
HIT AND REACT																
FOREARM SHIVER																
TRAP REACTION																
HAND FIGHTING FOR ENDS																
CRASHING FOR ENDS																
RUSHING PASSES																

Illus. 228

coach keeps the players hustling they will pick up the tempo themselves and make the drill a success.

(6) This drill is best when it is used as a group drill, and a good stopping point is when the players are "ready" both mentally and physically.

2. HOW TO DRILL FOR CORRECT FORM

The object of this drill is to teach the players the correct form for the head-on tackle.

INSTRUCTIONS:

(1) This drill is used at half speed first, then at full blast later.

(2) The players are lined up in two lines facing each other.

(3) First one line and then the other performs a head-on tackle upon the signal from the coach.

(4) Then the entire procedure is reversed.

(5) The coaches move up and down the line watching the players tackle.

3. HOW TO DRILL FOR CHARGING

This drill is designed to develop charging power for the linemen on defense.

INSTRUCTIONS:

(1) Have six linemen take their defensive position with the correct foot back and the correct hand down.

(2) Station another set of six linemen on offense opposite the defense.

(3) Place a center on offense with a player to receive the ball as it is snapped.

(4) The defensive linemen watch the ball and charge with it from below, with the back and legs straighened on contact.

(5) Insist that the elbows are straight and locked.

(6) Have the defensive man's hands meet the shoulders of the offensive lineman. The hands should contact the shoulder area in front and below the collar bone.

(7) Have them apply power in an upward direction, thereby

forcing the offensive players into an upright position and at the same time pushing them backward.

(8) See Illustration 229a; see 229b for another charging drill.

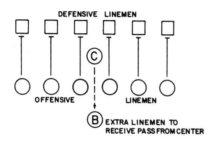

Illus. 229a

Illus. 229b. Box Charging Drill. On signal from reserve quarterback or coach, each squad charges into the opposite squad's area.

4. HOW TO DRILL FOR STAYING LOW

The purpose of this drill is to teach the players that the lowest charge usually wins.

INSTRUCTIONS:

(1) Line up the players opposite each other about two feet apart.

(2) When the ball is snapped have the players charge forward on hands and feet for five yards.

(3) Then they come up into a semi-crouch charging position for two or three yards.

(4) The players try to shove each other back using only the shoulders.

(5) The players with the lowest charge will have an advantage.

(6) Repeat the whole process over again.

5. HOW TO DRILL FOR LINE CHARGE

The main objective of this drill is to train the defensive lineman in crossing the line of scrimmage and to make contact before his opponent does.

INSTRUCTIONS:

(1) The best drill for this type of work is the one-on-one drill shown in Illustration 107.

6. HOW TO DRILL FOR CHARGING AND TACKLING

The object of the drill is to provide tackling practice on a moving target.

INSTRUCTIONS:

(1) Charge a suspended dummy held up by the coach three yards away.

(2) The coach lets the bag go and hits on the shoulder of the player as he tries to tackle or forearm shiver the bag.

(3) This drill develops the shoulders, charging technique, and tackling fundamentals.

7. HOW TO DRILL FOR THE HEAD-ON TACKLE (DUMMY)

This is a progressive type of tackling drill in which the players do not do too much rough work early in the season.   It is an excellent drill to start tackling instructions.

INSTRUCTIONS:

(1) First have the players practice tackling the hanging dummy for developing form.

(2) Line up the players in single file order about five yards away from the dummy.

(3) Have them start from a three-point stance and drive to the dummy, making the tackle with head either to the right or to the left of the dummy.

(4) Stress continuance and a driving follow-through with short, wide, choppy steps.

8. HOW TO DRILL FOR HEAD-ON TACKLE

The object of this drill is to practice the fundamentals necessary in tackling.

INSTRUCTIONS:

(1) Line up two opposing lines, one as runners, the other as tackles.

(2) The coach should stand at the line of scrimmage correcting mistakes.

(3) Practice should begin at close range and never be more than four yards.

(4) Include practice on both shoulders even though you prefer to tackle on one side only.

(5) See Illustration 230.

9. HOW TO DRILL FOR WASHBOARD TACKLING

This drill is designed to teach tackling with economy of time and effort.

INSTRUCTIONS:

(1) The players are divided into two lines of ball carriers facing two lines of tacklers.

(2) The ball carriers must run the gantlet of the tacklers.

(3) The tacklers are instructed to wait until the ball carrier is definitely past the previous tackler.

(4) The previous carrier is now in the tackler line and proceeds to tackle the oncoming ball carriers.

(5) Allow sufficient space between the lines to avoid collisions.

(6) See Illustration 231.

Illus. 230

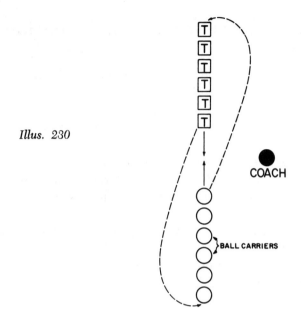

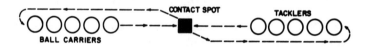

Illus. 231

10. HOW TO DRILL FOR THE SIDE SHOULDER TACKLE

The purpose of this drill is to provide practice for the players in the shortest possible time in side tackling.

INSTRUCTIONS:

(1) Divide the players into two lines facing each other five yards apart.

(2) In one line are the ball carriers, the other the tackles.

(3) The coach stands at the end of the tackling line and directs the ball carriers to run towards him as he moves his foot for the signal.

(4) The next pair then run and tackle while the preceding pair rest and review their positions for the next time around.

(5) Include practice on both shoulders.

(6) See Illustration 232.

11. HOW TO DRILL FOR THE SIDE TACKLE

This drill is designed to teach the tackler to drive his body across in front of the ball carrier.

INSTRUCTIONS:

(1) Station the ball carriers in two lines.

(2) Have an equal number of tacklers on defense in two lines.

(3) The ball carrier starts running to the side line and receives the ball from the coach in the form of a lateral pass.

(4) The ball carrier tries to elude the tackler *without* cutting back into the field of play.

(5) The tackler attempts to corner the ball carrier next to the sideline to make the tackle.

(6) See Illustration 233.

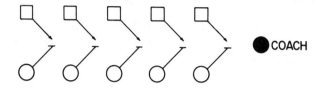

Illus. 232

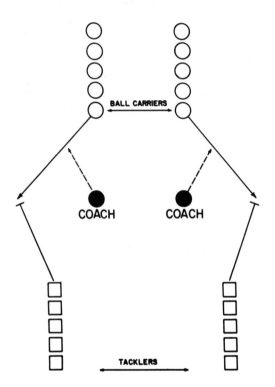

Illus. 233

12. HOW TO DRILL FOR VARIATION

The object of this drill is to teach live tackling against a ball carrier who is maneuvering, and to teach the ball carriers to evade tacklers.

INSTRUCTIONS:

(1) Place two dummies five yards apart.

(2) Line up the ball carriers on one side of the dummies and the tacklers on the other.

(3) The ball carriers and tacklers turn their backs to each other and wait for the signal from the coach.

(4) On the whistle the two players immediately spin around and move forward.

(5) The ball carriers must stay within the confines of the dummies and attempt to avoid being tackled.

(6) The tacklers attempt to bring down the ball carriers.

(7) Use as many of these units as is feasible.

13. HOW TO DRILL FOR STUNT TACKLING

This drill is designed to develop defensive fundamentals for the interior linemen.

INSTRUCTIONS:

(1) Follow the Gestalt Method of learning these skills—whole-part-whole.

(2) Begin in slow motion and advance to half speed, and then to full speed.

(3) The tackles and guards line up in single file order in front of the tackling dummy.

(4) Two linemen representing an offensive tackle and end

or tackle and guard take their position five yards in front of
the dummy.

(5) The defensive man, on the ball snap, executes any of
his stunts trying to break through the two offensive linemen.

(6) The stunts may include diving under, slicing, a forearm
shiver, and so on.

(7) After the charge, the defensive guard or tackle brings
down the dummy.

(8) See Illustration 234.

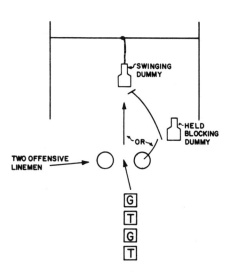

Illus. 234

14. HOW TO DRILL FOR STUNT PRACTICE

This drill is designed to practice the various stunts necessary for a lineman to know in order to play an effective game on defense.

INSTRUCTIONS:

(1) Have the players line up two against one.

(2) Alternate lines after two stunts by each defensive player.

(3) See Illustration 235.

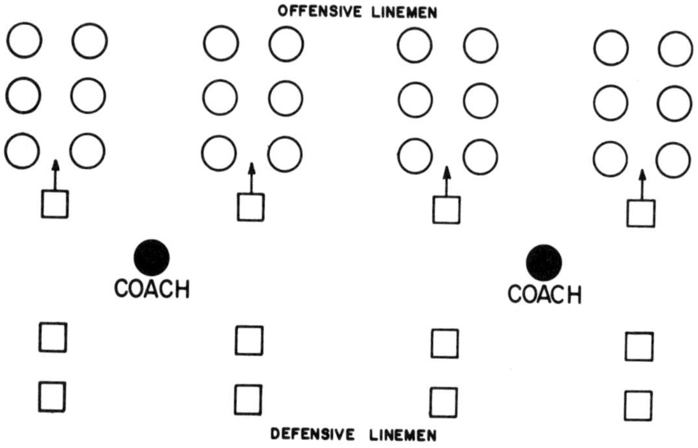

OFFENSIVE LINEMEN

COACH   COACH

DEFENSIVE LINEMEN

Illus. 235

15. HOW TO DRILL FOR ANGLE OPEN FIELD TACKLING

The purpose of this drill is to teach the squad angle tackling in open field.

INSTRUCTIONS:

(1) Line the players up and count off by threes.

(2) No. 1's step out a good yard from the group and face one end of the field at right angles to the tackler. No. 2's then step out with a long step with the foot on the side away from runner and shoot the shoulders across in front of the man representing the ball carrier.

(3) The man being tackled does not move forward, or to the side, but permits himself to be tackled.

(4) You are just trying to get the "feel" in this drill and the actual open field tackling comes later.

(5) This is a rotation drill where the lines trade off in tackling and being tackled.

(6) See Illustration 236.

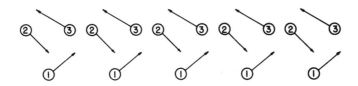

Illus. 236

16. HOW TO DRILL FOR DIVIDED SQUAD TACKLING

The purpose of this drill is to develop leg lift and drive after tackling.

INSTRUCTIONS:

(1) The squads are divided equally.   Line them up facing each other about five yards apart.

(2) Tackling is one-on-one at one-quarter speed. The tackler makes contact with his shoulder, lifts the opponent, carries him five yards and sets him down on his feet.

(3) This drill conditions the shoulders to shock and can be used every day without danger of injury.

17. HOW TO DRILL FOR THREE DUMMY TACKLING

This is a late season drill designed for rough contact work.

INSTRUCTIONS:

(1) Place three dummies with enough spacing to permit a runner to get through.

(2) Line up the players from 10 to 15 yards apart.

(3) Have both the runner and tackler start on a signal by the coach.

(4) The runner uses the dummies as interference, picking his hole at the latest possible moment to confuse and elude the tackler.

(5) Have the lines alternate.

(6) See Illustration 237.

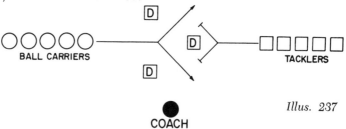

BALL CARRIERS

TACKLERS

COACH

Illus. 237

18. HOW TO DRILL FOR CHEEK-TO-CHEEK TACKLING

The purpose of this drill is to develop tackling form and reaction.

INSTRUCTIONS:

(1) Line up men back to back five yards apart.

(2) Upon a signal from the coach, the players turn and run at each other, one as a tackler and the other as a runner.

(3) Alternate men as tacklers and runners.

(4) This drill allows the players to practice tackling form.

(5) See Illustrations 238a and 238b.

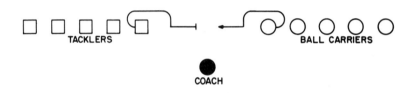

Illus. 238a

Illus. 238b

19. HOW TO DRILL FOR TACKLING

The purpose of this drill is to develop tacklers in the shortest possible time without subjecting them to injuries.

INSTRUCTIONS:

(1) Line up players in two lines facing each other about four yards apart. It is better to have men paired according to weight.

(2) Start with line A tackling with right shoulder and line B carrying the ball. Start at half speed and work up to full speed.

(3) The coach commands "Ready-charge!" and the first man on A-line tackles the first man in B-line at a point somewhere in front of the coach.

(4) When the men hit the ground, they jump up and return as quickly as possible to their respective positions.

(5) The coach may comment and then go on to the next pair and repeat the command.

(6) When the coach reaches the end of the line, he turns around and B-line becomes the tacklers and A-line the ball carriers.

(7) This is repeated until all men have tackled three times with left shoulder.

(8) A side tackle may be done in the same manner with the ball carrier running at a 30-degree angle to either side of the tackler.

(9) See Illustration 239.

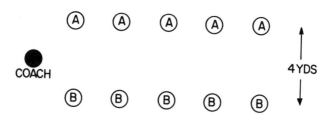

Illus. 239

20. HOW TO DRILL FOR THE SLAUGHTER BOX

This is a strenuous tackling drill under live conditions and should be used sparingly.

INSTRUCTIONS:

(1) The linemen are spread out up and down the field ten yards apart.

(2) Either backs or other linemen at one end of the field run in and out of the tacklers trying to get through them.

(3) If the runner is tackled, he must get up and continue on to the good line.

(4) The tacklers cannot cross the marked line in front of them, but they may move laterally.

(5) See Illustration 240.

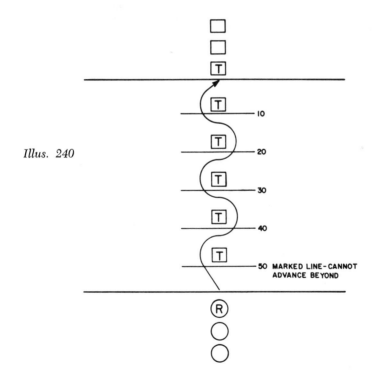

Illus. 240

21. HOW TO DRILL FOR ROTATION TACKLING

This drill is designed to provide tackling practice by a rotation plan.

INSTRUCTIONS:

(1) Divide the squad into groups of 10 men each.

(2) Squads which are not tackling can be working on other individual skills.

(3) Squad No. 1 practices tackling.   Squad No. 2 works on blocking.   Squad No. 3 does passing.   Squad No. 4 practices cadence-charging drill.

(4) Squads rotate every five minutes.

(5) See Illustration 241.

22. HOW TO DRILL FOR STUNTS IN ACTION

This drill is designed to help the players develop defensive stunts while attempting to tackle the ball carrier.   The drill provides blocking practice for ends and wingbacks.

INSTRUCTIONS:

(1) Two offensive linemen (end and wingback) station themselves opposite a defensive tackle.

(2) Place a tailback in the backfield to receive the ball from center.

(3) The coach, using hand signals, calls for a wide play, an off-tackle play, or a cutback.

(4) The end and wingback, depending upon the signal they get from the coach, may take the tackle in or out.   On a wide end run the end may take him alone.

(5) The tackle tries to use "split vision" and work defensive stunts that have been developed in practice to reach the ball carrier.

(6) A pulling guard may be added to run interference.

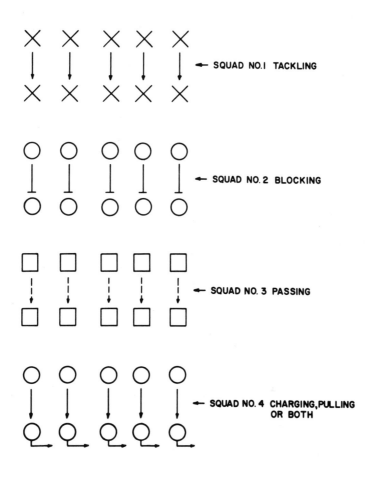

Illus. 241

23. HOW TO DRILL FOR SPINNING OUT

The purpose of this drill is to teach the linemen the correct form for spinning out of a block and back into position to tackle.

INSTRUCTIONS:

(1) Have four players lined up in defensive stances. Several short lines are best in this drill.

(2) At a signal by the coach, the players charge and block hard into the dummies, then react as if they were taken to one side or the other.

(3) Have them spin out of their block and back into position, being mindful to move laterally or backward to get in front of the ball carrier.

(4) This drill should be repeated several times daily to be effective.

(5) See Illustration 242.

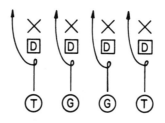

X – HOLDER
D – DUMMY

Illus. 242

24. HOW TO DRILL FOR SPLITTING THE SEAM

The purpose of this drill is to practice getting between the offensive linemen.

INSTRUCTIONS:

(1) Line two bags up next to each other to simulate offensive linemen.

(2) There are at least four ways for players to handle this situation:

(a) Concentrate on either one of the men alone and hit that man with straight shoulder charge.

(b) Use a dip charge. This is done by charging low right between two bags. The object is to knock the feet out from under both opponents at the same time.

(c) You can knife between the two, turning your body edgewise in an attempt to split the "seam" and slide through the narrow opening.

(d) You can use a double coordination movement. This is done by lining up in front of one opponent and on the first move directing your force at the other. The next step is back at the other opponent and the third step is to the ball carrier. The purpose of the move is to fight pressure.

(3) The players rotate after each drill. If a man holds the dummy once he should then take a turn practicing the maneuver.

(4) The coach can use as many groups of bags as he thinks he can handle.

25. HOW TO DRILL FOR HIT AND REACT

The purpose of this drill is to create competition among line-men in teaching the offensive charge and defensive protection of a lineman's territory.   This is one of the finest drills in foot-ball.

INSTRUCTIONS:

(1) Place two dummies five yards apart to mark the lateral limits of the contest area.   Both dummies should be held by players.

(2) A straight line between the bags is considered the line of scrimmage.

(3) One offensive and one defensive player take their positions on the line, facing each other.

(4) The coach places his hand low on one of the bags so each player can see it, then snaps it away to simulate the center pass.

(5) On the snap, the offensive player attempts to block the defensive player right or left.

(6) The defensive player attempts to protect his territory (the space between the dummies).

(7) After the first pair has contested to the best two-out-of-three "falls," another pair takes over.

(8) The next time around, the offensive and defensive assignments are reversed.

(9) A ball carrier may be included as the drill progresses.

(10) See Illustrations 243a and 243b.

26. HOW TO DRILL FOR LOOPING

This drill is designed to provide for the defensive line and linebackers in looping.

INSTRUCTIONS:

(1) Place a six-man line and two linebackers on defense.

(2) Locate seven dummies on offensive to represent the offensive line.   Each dummy is held by a player.

(3) Have the defensive jolt the dummy with a forearm charge straight ahead and then loop either to the right or left. Usually to the strong side.

(4) Practice looping in dummy scrimmage with complete offensive and defensive teams.

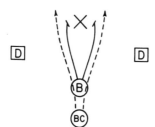

Illus. 243a

D – DUMMY
B – BLOCKER
BC – BALL CARRIER

Illus. 243b

27. HOW TO DRILL FOR THE FOREARM SHIVER

This drill is designed to practice straightening up an offensive lineman in order to gain position.

INSTRUCTIONS:

(1) Pair off the linemen in two rows, one to represent defense (holding dummies) and one to represent offense.

(2) The dummies are held waist high and parallel to the ground to simulate a lineman's shoulders.

(3) The defensive linemen jolt the dummies with *the heels* of their hands with the arms straight and stiff.

(4) They must step simultaneously with the back leg as the blow is delivered, ending in a crouched out stretched position with the head up.

(5) The object of the shiver is to keep the opponent from gaining contact.

(6) After gaining control of the opponent, throw him to either side and move quickly toward the play.

(7) See Illustration 244 for another method.

28. HOW TO DRILL FOR THE FOREARM LIFT

This drill provides the defensive linemen with another stunt to escape being blocked. This drill should be used after the basic fundamentals of line play are mastered.

INSTRUCTIONS:

(1) Pair off two men, one holding the dummy and the other lined up in front of the dummy in a defensive stance.

(2) Have the player holding the bag tilt it forward to simulate a crouched lineman.

(3) On the initial charge the defensive player should come

Illus. 244. Wheel of Fortune. This device, shown as used in a drill for the forearm shiver, can be used for many other offensive and defensive drills.

up with the forearms and the back of the hands, hitting the dummy, and straightening it up.

(4) The initial charge must be powerful enough to straighten up the blocker.

(5) Follow through with hands to get rid of the blocker and go toward the play.

(6) The defensive maneuver is to be used occasionally, but not as a regular diet.

29. HOW TO DRILL FOR PROPER USE OF HANDS

This drill is of particular value to linemen in teaching them the proper use of their hands and the proper appreciation of their power on defense.

INSTRUCTIONS:

(1) Locate six linemen on defense and place them slightly to the right of the offensive linemen.

(2) Station a center on offense and an extra lineman to receive the snap.

(3) With the snap of the ball the players on defense drive up from below with both arms straight and locked at the elbows.

(4) Have them drive both hands against the side of the opponent's neck and drive him *out* and back.

(5) Later change the defense to the left, and then straight in front of their opponents and repeat the drill.

(6) When a charging sled is not available this drill should be practiced frequently.

(7) See Illustration 245.

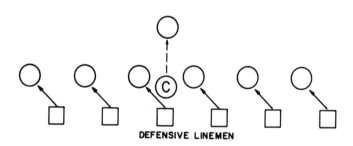

DEFENSIVE LINEMEN

Illus. 245

30. HOW TO DRILL FOR GUARDING THE LINE

The object of this drill is to teach the defensive players not to give ground.

INSTRUCTIONS:

(1) Station five dummies across a line about three yards apart.

(2) One player must hold each dummy.

(3) ○ indicates the players lined up in a three-point stance *facing* the coach.

(4) × indicates the men holding the dummies.

(5) On a signal the players pivot and pull toward the bags.

(6) Have the players hit with a driving right or left shoulder block.

(7) The object of this drill is for the men holding the dummies not to lose any ground; in other words they are "guarding the line."

(8) See Illustration **246**.

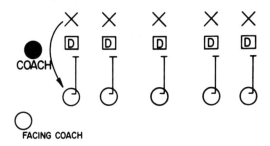

Illus. 246

31. HOW TO DRILL FOR LEFT AND RIGHT TRAP REACTION

This drill is designed to teach defensive linemen to react to a trap from either side.   It also provides the offensive linemen practice in executing a trap.

INSTRUCTIONS:

(1) The offensive players are given a number from 1 to 4.

(2) The defensive player is given the number 5.   He is placed either in front of No. 2 or 3 at his discretion.

(3) The coach stands behind the defensive player to give the signals.

(4) If "1" is given, No. 5 is trapped from that side and Nos. 2 and 3 split.

(5) If "4" is given, No. 5 is trapped from the other side.

(6) If "2" is given, No. 2 is the lead block and No. 3 is the post.

(7) If "3" is given, No. 3 is the lead and No. 2 is the post.

(8) See Illustration 247.

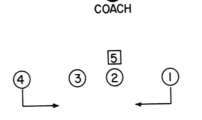

Illus. 247

32. HOW TO DRILL FOR MOUSE TRAP REACTION

The object of this drill is to develop quickness and agility in linemen when reacting to a mouse trap type of play.

INSTRUCTIONS:

(1) The players are lined up and assume their defensive stances.

(2) Several shorter rows are better than one long row.

(3) At the command of the coach, the players charge an imaginary opponent, stop on hands and feet and, as if expecting a trap block, drop low so as not to be an easy target and quickly retreat to fill the hole.

(4) Players should keep head up and eyes open.

(5) This drill should be repeated several times.

33. HOW TO DRILL FOR DEFENSIVE REACTION

The purpose of this drill is to give the linemen practice in playing a defensive position while being exposed to a number of situations.

INSTRUCTIONS:

(1) See Drill 38, in Chapter 4.

34. HOW TO DRILL FOR GUARD REACTION

*The purpose of this drill is to give the defensive guards prac-
tice in facing two blockers on the line of scrimmage, with a
wingback and blocking back or pulling linemen in position to
trap him.*

INSTRUCTIONS:

(1) Place the guard on the line in his defensive stance.

(2) Station 1 and 2 directly in front of him as offensive
linemen.

(3) Locate 3 one yard back of the line and about three yards
to the right of 1.

(4) Position 4 also one yard back and about three yards to
the left of 2.

(5) The coach stands back of the guard to give hand signals.

(6) On a signal with one finger, 1 and 2 double-team the
guard, trying to turn him right or left or straight back as the
coach designates.

(7) On a signal with two fingers, either 1 or 2 blocks individually (check block) on the guard and the other pulls out
right or left.

(8) One signal with three fingers, 1 and 2 pass up the defensive guard as he charges through without opposition. He
is now trapped by 3 or 4.

(9) See Illustration 248.

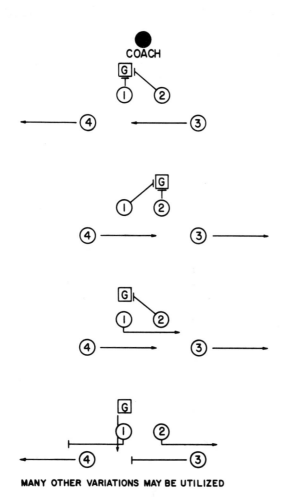

MANY OTHER VARIATIONS MAY BE UTILIZED

Illus. 248

35. HOW TO DRILL THE DEFENSIVE TACKLE

The object of this drill is to give the defensive tacklers prac-tice in playing off the outside shoulder of an offensive end with the wingback in front of him, and a pulling linemen in position to trap him.

INSTRUCTIONS:

(1) The tackle is placed on the line in his defensive stance.

(2) Station No. 1 a yard in back of the imaginary line of scrimmage and off his outside shoulder.

(3) No. 2 is on the line of scrimmage and off his inside shoulder.

(4) No. 3 is about a yard back and about three yards to the tackler's inside.

(5) The coach stands behind the defensive tackle and gives the hand signals.

(6) On a specified signal, 1 and 2 blockers double-team, blocking the tackle to the right or left.

(7) On another signal, 2 blocks the tackle in and 1 goes down for a pass.

(8) On another signal, 1 blocks the tackle in and 2 goes down for a pass.

(9) On another signal, 1 and 2 fake blocks and go out for passes; as the tackle charges through, 3 trap-blocks him.

(10) See Illustration 249.

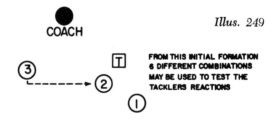

Illus. 249

FROM THIS INITIAL FORMATION
6 DIFFERENT COMBINATIONS
MAY BE USED TO TEST THE
TACKLERS REACTIONS

36.   HOW TO DRILL THE DEFENSIVE END

The purpose of this drill is to practice fundamentals neces-sary for developing a defensive end.

INSTRUCTIONS:

(1) Station the ends on defense and split them into two groups, right and left ends.

(2) One group becomes the defensive ends first, and the other group becomes the blockers.

(3) Two offensive halfbacks, a fullback and another end huddle to decide which way to block the end.

(4) The defensive end takes his initial step each time and then tries to recover to the outside.

(5) See Illustration 250.

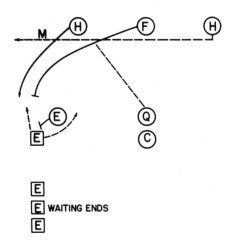

Illus. 250

37. HOW TO DRILL THE DEFENSIVE END AGAINST BACKFIELD BLOCKING

The object of this drill is to teach the ends defensive line play.   This is also a good drill for teaching backfield men the shoulder block.

INSTRUCTIONS:

(1) Line up the fullbacks and halfbacks on offense with a center.

(2) Locate two ends on defense.

(3) With the snap of the ball have the ends take two quick steps straight forward then turn in to meet the backs.

(4) The halfbacks and fullbacks also start with the ball and attempt to shoulder block the ends out.

(5) See Illustration 251.

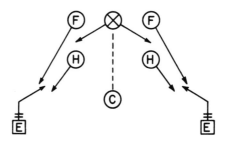

Illus. 251

38. HOW TO DRILL FOR END PLAY

The purpose of this drill is to simulate game conditions in teaching defensive end play. It also provides practice in blocking, ball carrying and tackling.

INSTRUCTIONS:

(1) Line up one end as a ball carrier and one as a defensive end, along with two optional blockers.

(2) The coach stands behind the defensive ends and, without their seeing the signal, indicates that the ball carrier should run to the inside or outside.

(3) The optional blockers block accordingly.

(4) The men rotate from one position to the other.

(5) Two groups can work this drill at the same time.

(6) See Illustration 252.

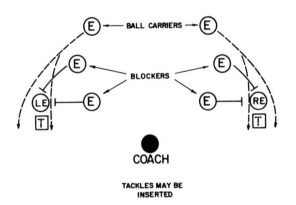

Illus. 252

39. HOW TO DRILL FOR CRASHING

The purpose of this drill is to develop a crashing-type end.
INSTRUCTIONS:

(1) A drill for this type of end play is difficult to develop because of the element of injury to the defensive men.

(2) Actual *scrimmage* conditions are desirable for teaching an end to crash effectively.

(3) Always insist that the end's charge carry *deep* in the opponent's backfield to meet the interference.

(4) If the end strips the play of its strength, he has accomplished his objective.

(5) Other drills for special situations regarding end play should also be developed and the time allotted to them on the time-study chart.   Some of these drills are blocking kicks, defense against forward passes, and how to block an end going down under kicks.

40. HOW TO DRILL FOR HAND FIGHTING

The object of this drill is to train the ends to fight off interference and turn the play to the inside.
INSTRUCTIONS:

(1) Locate the ends on defense.

(2) Station a line of offensive blockers one yard opposite.

(3) Have three blockers advance toward the end.

(4) The end hits with the hands or shoulders to ward off the first blocker, bounces, recovers, and meets the next blocker, bounces, recovers, and so on.

(5) This drill will develop speed and footwork in each play.

(6) See Illustration 253a; see 253b for another method.

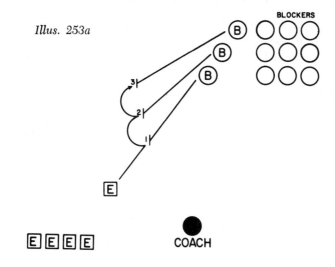

Illus. 253a

Illus. 253b. *Defensive Footwork Drill for Ends. Ends react defensively to vocal signals from coach: "Sweep!" "Off-tackle!" "Pass!" and so on. Ends should keep their feet moving continually.*

41. HOW TO DRILL FOR RUSHING THE PASSER

The purpose of this drill is to provide the practice for both rushing and protecting the passer. This is an excellent drill to develop footwork on offense and aggressiveness on defense.

INSTRUCTIONS:

(1) Line up several players on defense to rush an imaginary passer.

(2) Place another line of players on offense to block the rusher and defend the passer.

(3) The rusher may change directions at least twice in attempting to get past the blocker.

(4) Have the defender maneuver and stay in front of the rusher by gradually giving ground and fighting pressure.

(5) See Illustration 254.

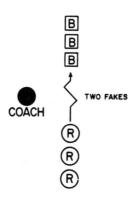

Illus. 254

42. HOW TO DRILL FOR RUSHING THE PASSER

The purpose of this drill is to allow the linemen to practice their defensive thrust and then react to rush the passer.

INSTRUCTIONS:

(1) Place a center on offense with six players to hold offensive dummies.

(2) Have these men in alignment that would normally be occupied by offensive linemen.

(3) Station two other offensive players with dummies in position where the ends would contact opposition.

(4) Have the center snap the ball to an extra lineman representing a ball carrier. Station this man at a depth of five yards.

(5) Insist that the six defensive linemen charge aggressively into the dummy representing the offensive blocker.

(6) Next have them locate the ball and quickly move toward it.

(7) The ball carrier may charge forward, run at an angle, move laterally right or left, or he may retreat as if to pass, which is the primary intention of the drill.

(8) After the defensive men contact the dummies they must react quickly and pursue the ball carrier.

(9) See Illustration 255.

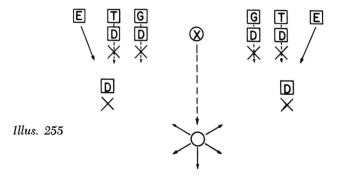

Illus. 255

43. HOW TO DRILL FOR GETTING ACROSS THE LINE

The purpose of this drill is to practice getting across an imaginary line of scrimmage.

INSTRUCTIONS:

(1) Position three complete lines on defensive, one after the other, facing a center.

(2) Have each line approach the center and concentrate on getting across the line.

(3) Emphasize ball reaction to each unit.

(4) Have the center pass the ball very early or late.

(5) Stress low body position as the linemen charge.

(6) See Illustration 256.

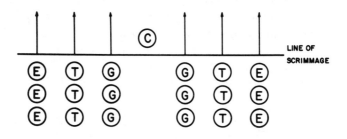

Illus. 256

44. HOW TO DRILL FOR RUSHING THE PASSER

The object of this drill is to practice and improve on methods of rushing the passer as a means of pass defense.   It also provides the offensive linemen practice in protecting the passer.
INSTRUCTIONS:

(1) Line up a complete offensive team and have them practice throwing pass patterns.

(2) Line up a complete defensive team.

(3) The offense proceeds to throw all their passes and to protect the passer.

(4) The defensive men work stunts in pairs to rush the passer.

(5) These looping defensive maneuvers can be incorporated into regular defenses against running plays.

(6) See Illustration 257.

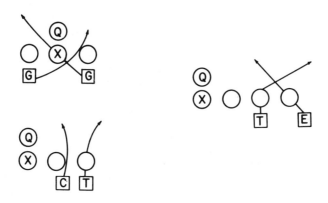

Illus. 257.   Here are several rushing stunts that may be employed.

45. HOW TO DRILL FOR AGILITY

The object of this drill is to develop agility for the linemen.
INSTRUCTIONS:

(1) Place the linemen in three rows.

(2) Have them assume their defensive stance.

(3) On a signal from the coach the head lineman from each file comes running forward.

(4) After five yards of running the coach gives the following oral signals: left, right, back, down, rip, left, right, back, and so forth. He keeps them moving quickly.

(5) Either the oral command or the signal command may be used.

(6) Always use a cross-over step. Never allow them to run in an arc.

(7) This drill may also be used for the pass defenders.

(8) See Illustration 258.

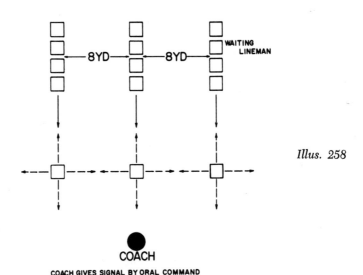

Illus. 258

COACH GIVES SIGNAL BY ORAL COMMAND

46. HOW TO DRILL FOR THE RIP-UP

The purpose of this drill is to teach the linemen who play over the offensive center the fundamentals of the rip-up.

INSTRUCTIONS:

(1) A bag is held parallel to the ground to simulate the offensive center's shoulders. The bag is held waist high, firmly against the forward leg.

(2) Place a defensive player one foot back and directly in front of the bag.

(3) On a verbal signal from the coach have the defensive man jolt the bag with the forearm and step simultaneously with the rear leg.

(4) Rotate the players after three blocks.

(5) Use as many men as is feasible.

(6) See Illustration 259.

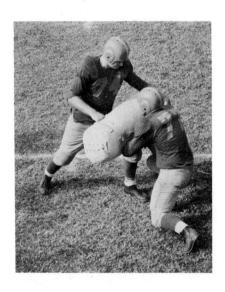

Illus. 259

47. HOW TO DRILL FOR HONEST PURSUIT

The purpose of this drill is to keep the four center linemen from pursuing too fast.

INSTRUCTIONS:

(1) Place four linemen on defense and have them take their defensive stance.

(2) The ball carrier starts out as if going around end and then reverses his field as illustrated.

(3) See Illustration 260.

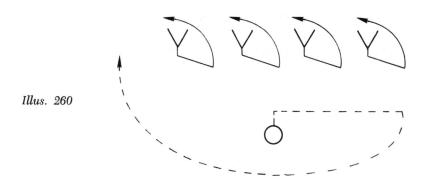

Illus. 260

48. HOW TO DRILL FOR POSITION RUSHING

The idea of this drill is to practice rushing the passer and then get in correct position to block after the rush.

INSTRUCTIONS:

(1) Place four center linemen on defense.

(2) Station a passer on offense five yards deep.

(3) On a pre-arranged signal, they rush the passer who throws to one of two standing receivers.

(4) After the ball is released, the linemen turn the corner downfield on the opposite side from which they started their rush.

(5) This drill also helps eliminate the habit of looking to see if the pass has been intercepted.

(6) Later on, use standing dummies for the rushers to pull block.

(7) See Illustration 261.

Illus. 261

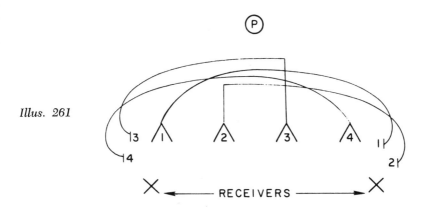

49. HOW TO DRILL FOR HANDS UP

The purpose of this drill is to provide practice for the linemen in getting their hands up and rushing the passer.

INSTRUCTIONS:

(1) Station a passer five yards deep.

(2) Locate a center on offense.

(3) Place four linemen on defense. These men take their regular defensive stance and as the ball is snapped, they bring their feet up, taking short steps, but they do *not* cross the line of scrimmage.

(4) Have the passer throw a quick pass over their heads, or between them, and try to complete it for from seven to ten yards.

(5) Ask the linemen to try and catch the ball, instead of knocking it down.

(6) Place five receivers downfield 10 yards.

(7) See Illustration 262.

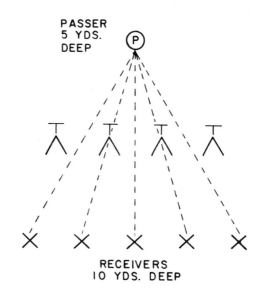

Illus. 262

50. HOW TO DRILL FOR OPEN FIELD TACKLING

The purpose of this drill is to practice open field tackling without limits.

INSTRUCTIONS:

(1) Place a back on offense who is a fairly elusive runner.

(2) Station one tackler on defense approximately five yards from the runner.

(3) The runner may cut to either side and in any direction.

(4) The tackler should attempt to get the runner chest high. Do not go for the feet.

(5) See Illustration 263.

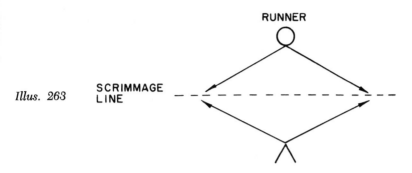

Illus. 263

51. HOW TO DRILL FOR CLOSE LINE TACKLING

The purpose of this drill is to improve close line tackling stressing head up, back firm, tail low, and feet spaced shoulder width apart for proper balance.

INSTRUCTIONS:

(1) Place two dummies approximately five yards apart.

(2) Station two tackles on defense.

(3) Use a reserve back as a ball carrier positioned four yards deep.

(4) The ball carrier runs to three different spots. He may run to the right, left, or straight ahead without any interference.

(5) Stress good tackling position in this drill.

(6) See Illustration 264.

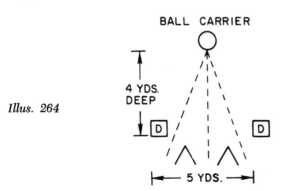

Illus. 264

52. HOW TO DRILL FOR GANG TACKLING

The purpose of this drill is to teach gang tackling and teach close line tackling position.

INSTRUCTIONS:

(1) Place two dummies approximately ten yards apart.

(2) Station four tacklers on defense.

(3) A ball carrier at a depth of six yards may run any place between the two dummies.

(4) Stress good tackling position with both feet moving by taking short choppy steps.

(5) The first man who contacts the ball carrier stops him and holds him up until all other linemen have a chance to get a shoulder on him.

(6) If a tackler fails to make a good tackle, he becomes the ball carrier.

(7) Needless to say, use a reserve back as a ball carrier.

(8) See Illustration 265.

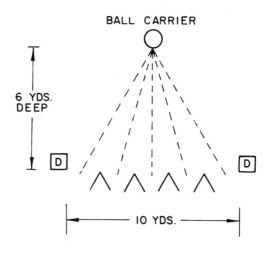

Illus. 265

53. HOW TO RUSH THE PASSER

The purpose of this drill is to practice rushing the passer.
INSTRUCTIONS:

(1) Place a center, quarterback, and two backs on offense.

(2) Station two bell-bottom dummies to resemble the offensive tackles and help the ends align properly.

(3) Line up two ends on defense to rush the passer.

(4) Have the ends rush hard outside of the blockers, drive with the shoulder and spin fast to the inside.

(5) Have them practice all techniques to rush the passer.

(6) See Illustration 266.

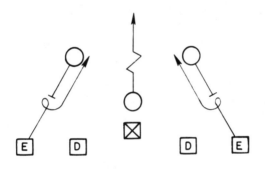

Illus. 266

54. HOW TO DRILL FOR RUSHING THE PASSER

The purpose of this drill is to give the lineman training in rushing the passer.

INSTRUCTIONS:

(1) Have five men line up on defensive alignment for a five-man line.

(2) Place a dummy over each man with the dummy lying flat (bottom pointing toward the defensive man)

(3) Use two offensive men, one to center the ball and the other standing back to imitate a passer.

(4) On the snap of the ball the defensive men hit the bags with a shoulder charge, then drive them for three or four yards.

(5) The passer either fades back or rolls out so that the defensive men obtain reaction training.

55. HOW TO DRILL FOR 10 YARD TACKLING

The purpose of this drill is to provide practice in line tackling in a restricted area.

INSTRUCTIONS:

(1) Line up two backs sidewise on the field between the 10-yard line and the goal line.

(2) The two backs should be approximately ten yards apart.

(3) Use freshmen to act as ball carriers to run through both tacklers.

(4) The first back attempts the tackle. If he is successful he may drop out, the second back moves up and another back takes his place.

(5) One solid tackle by each back is necessary.

(6) If a back misses he must take another turn until a solid tackle is made. The backs keep moving forward.

(7) Have plenty of ball carriers—at least five are necessary.

(8) See Illustration 267.

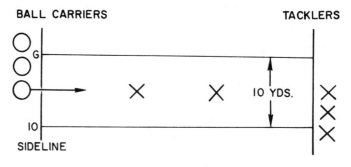

Illus. 267

56. HOW TO DRILL FOR SHOULDER TACKLING

The purpose of this drill is to practice tackling without using the arms.

INSTRUCTIONS:

(1) Place two tall dummies with holders. These dummies are approximately five feet high.

(2) Line up tacklers 10 yards from these tall dummies.

(3) Have the tacklers hit the dummies with their shoulder only—not using their arms to tackle.

(4) This is a good drill to prevent arm tackling.

(5) Alternate shoulders until their form is good before using the arms.

(6) See Illustration 268.

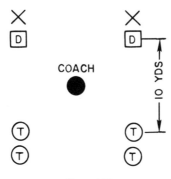

Illus. 268

57. HOW TO DRILL FOR TOUGHNESS

The purpose of this drill is to develop leg drive, staying low, and improved reactions.

INSTRUCTIONS:

(1) We call this a toughness drill because if the five men holding the dummies give the defensive lineman plenty of resistance, he won't get through the gap.

(2) The two dummies closest to the lineman are ten inches apart and held by big linemen.

(3) The defensive lineman must fight his way through the dummies. He generally is on the ground by the time he is through.

(4) The coach, who has positioned himself behind the center dummy, signals which dummy the player should tackle or block.

(5) See Illustration 269.

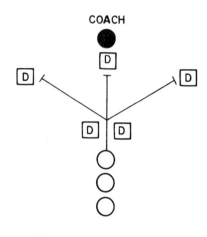

Illus. 269

58. HOW TO DRILL FOR SHIVERS

The purpose of this drill is to provide practice for the guards and tackles in using the forearm shiver.

INSTRUCTIONS:

(1) Place tackles facing tackles.

(2) Place guards facing guards.

(3) Have them practice forearm shivers on each other for three minutes.

(4) Reverse procedure.

(5) See Illustration 270.

Illus. 270

GUARDS   TACKLES

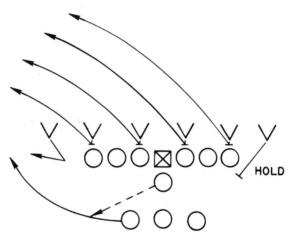

HOLD

Illus. 271

WIDE PURSUIT

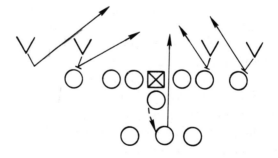

INTERIOR PURSUIT

59. HOW TO DRILL FOR PURSUIT

The purpose of this drill is to practice the proper angles of pursuit.

INSTRUCTIONS:

(1) Place a reserve unit on offense with a complete backfield.

(2) Station your first defensive team on defense minus the secondary.

(3) Have the offense run quick pitch-outs and plays up the middle. Later run a reverse.

(4) Insist on proper angle of pursuit after each man gets across the line just before pursuing.

(5) See Illustration 271.

60. HOW TO DRILL FOR THE MEAT GRINDER

The purpose of this defensive drill is to teach the importance of being low and warding off blockers.

INSTRUCTIONS:

(1) Place four dummies in the corners of a square.

(2) Put a player in the square and call him the "meat."

(3) Have some men line up single file facing the player in the square.

(4) At the signal "block," have them go for the "meat" one at a time in rapid succession.

(5) The coach positions himself beside the square and yells, "block, block, block, block," etc. The front man in the line will go when he hears the signal "block."

(6) If the player ever gets knocked out of the square, or if he ever gets knocked down, he is automatically out.

(7) See Illustration 272.

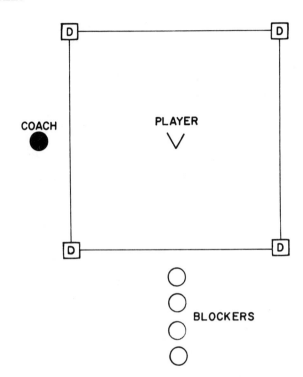

Illus. 272

61. HOW TO DRILL FOR BAG TACKLING

The purpose of this drill is to teach footwork to the defensive end plus reaction to a command.

INSTRUCTIONS:

(1) Place three dummies in a triangle five yards apart.

(2) Have one man holding the front dummy.

(3) Have a defensive left end line up with correct foot position and make contact with the front dummy.

(4) At a command of "left" the end breaks off left after warding off the dummy and tackles the bag on the left to simulate tackling a passer. If the call is "right" he tackles on the right to simulate the handoff going through the line.

(5) See Illustration 273.

Illus. 273

62. HOW TO DRILL FOR BALANCE

The purpose of this drill is to teach the importance of balance for defensive linemen.

INSTRUCTIONS:

(1) This is a good drill to liven up practice.

(2) Place a defensive player in a four point stance.

(3) The player must knock away the dummies in his path and then take jolting blows from your players who are armed with air dummies.

(4) He must then tackle a swinging dummy.

(5) Receiving numerous jolts just before making the tackle simulates game conditions.

(6) It proves to the player that he cannot charge forward without being properly balanced.

(7) See Illustration 274.

Illus. 274

63. HOW TO DRILL ENDS FOR PROTECTION OF TERRITORY

The purpose of this drill is to give the ends practice in protecting his inside and still rush the passer.

INSTRUCTIONS:

(1) Alternate ends in defense.

(2) Use extra ends as offensive ends.

(3) Have the end line up on the outside shoulder of the offensive man.

(4) The defensive end's job is to protect the area between himself and the next man to his inside which would be the tackle.

(5) See Illustration 275.

Illus. 275

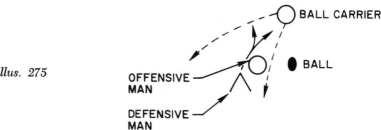

64. HOW TO DRILL FOR MEETING PULLING LINE-MAN

The object of this drill is to give the defensive ends practice in meeting the charge of pulling lineman coming close to the line of scrimmage for an inside out block.

INSTRUCTIONS:

(1) Place three dummies on offense along with two pulling guards.

(2) Ends are taught to take their positions just off the line of scrimmage, take two short diagonal steps and meet the guards charge with the inside forearm and shoulder.

(3) See Illustration 276.

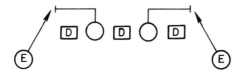

Illus. 276

65. HOW TO DRILL FOR LOW MAN

The object of this drill is to teach the defensive linemen the importance of staying low.

INSTRUCTIONS:

(1) Place two men shoulder to shoulder and on a given signal have them try to push one another backwards.

(2) This can be done in either a tripod stance or better on all fours.

(3) See Illustration 277.

LINES A&B CHARGE ON
WHISTLE OR CADENCE

Illus. 277

66. HOW TO DRILL FOR GETTING ACROSS THE LINE

This drill is designed to provide practice for two defensive linemen who are having trouble getting across the line of scrimmage and rushing the passer.

INSTRUCTIONS:

(1) Place five linemen on offense. These men could be from reserve squad.

(2) Station these two "waiting" linemen on defense.

(3) The offensive men can charge two on one, one on one, trap, and simulate pass protection. This will provide all the conditions that defensive linemen encounter.

(4) See Illustration 278.

Illus. 278

67. HOW TO DRILL FOR RECOVERING A FUMBLE

The purpose of this drill is to develop competition in recovering a loose ball.

INSTRUCTIONS:

(1) Divide the men into groups of ten. Split each group into five pairs, with men of equal speed standing together.

(2) The coach stands in front of the group and gives numbers 1 through 5.

(3) At each call the two men whose number is called try to get the ball that the coach throws on the ground.

(4) See Illustration 279.

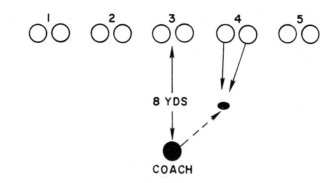

Illus. 279

8 YDS

COACH

68. HOW TO DRILL FOR PLAYING A HALFBACK'S BLOCK

The object of this drill is to provide practice for the defensive end in playing a halfback's inside out block.

INSTRUCTIONS:

(1) The procedure is the same as playing the blocks of the offensive guards.

(2) Play inside out block with the shoulder and forearm. If the halfback is trying to pull deep and take the end in on a wide play, the end plays him at arm's length, keeping the halfback from getting to his legs.

(3) See Illustration 280.

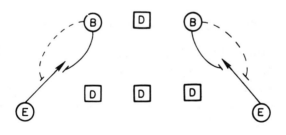

Illus. 280

69. HOW TO DRILL FOR IN AND OUT

The purpose of this drill is to give practice to the defensive end against a complete backfield running off tackle or around end.

INSTRUCTIONS:

(1) Line up a complete backfield on offense. Have them run off tackle or around end with the halfbacks taking ends either in or out.

(2) Line up a left and right end on defense and use a fullback to run an off tackle play either way. This gives one halfback a chance to rest.

(3) This is a fine drill for teaching quick reaction.

(4) See Illustration 281.

Illus. 281

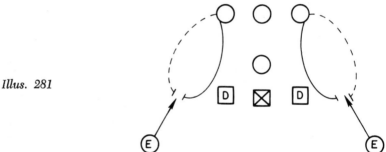

70. HOW TO DRILL FOR SPLITTING THE SEAM

The purpose of this drill is to teach the defensive man to get between and past two offensive linemen.

INSTRUCTIONS:

(1) Six offensive linemen arrange themselves in pairs, five yards separating each pair.

(2) On a snap signal the defensive man attempts to split the seam of the pair.

(3) After succeeding or failing he repeats the procedure with the second pair and then the third.

(4) By rotating in this manner both offense and defense can benefit more than if they continually work against the same men.

(5) See Illustration 282.

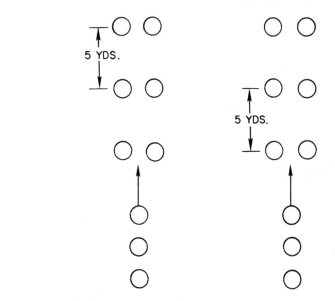

Illus. 282

71. HOW TO DRILL FOR SIDELINE TACKLING

This drill is designed to teach the sideline tackling.

INSTRUCTIONS:

(1) Station the ball carriers in two lines on the hash marks.

(2) Have an equal number of tacklers on defense on the hash marks.

(3) Place two centers and two quarterbacks on their respective hash marks.

(4) The ball carrier takes a quick toss from the quarterback and runs toward the sideline. Alternate sides.

(5) As the drill begins the ball carrier attempts to elude the tackler *without* cutting back into the field of play.

(6) The tackler attempts to corner the ball carrier by using the sidelines to make the tackle.

(7) See Illustration 283.

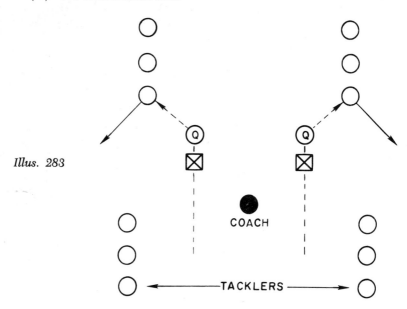

Illus. 283

72. HOW TO DRILL FOR COOPERATIVE OFFENSIVE FUNDAMENTALS

The object of this drill is to provide fundamental practice for the offensive line. This drill also offers excellent practice for six defensive players.

INSTRUCTIONS:

(1) Have a tackle-to-tackle scrimmage without the backfield men.

(2) Run against five-, six- and seven-man lines with two line backers.

(3) This drill teaches the interior linemen both fundamentals and play assignments.

(4) If desired, extra tackles and guards may run as ends.

(5) See Illustration 284.

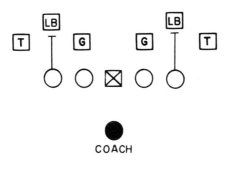

Illus. 284

73. HOW TO DRILL FOR RECOVERING FUMBLES

The object of this drill is to practice recovery of a fumbled ball with resistance.

INSTRUCTIONS:

(1) Place a blocker on offense.

(2) A coach is standing three yards behind the blocker.

(3) The defensive man takes on the blocker and then recovers fumble thrown by the coach.

(4) See Illustration 285.

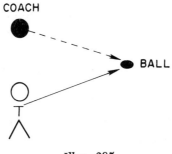

Illus. 285

74. HOW TO DRILL FOR PURSUIT

The purpose of this drill is to teach the proper pursuit angle for the interior lineman.

INSTRUCTIONS:

(1) Line up an offensive line without the ends. Position a quarterback and one other back in the backfield.

(2) Place two guards and two tacklers on defense.

(3) Use a ball carrier who is expendable. Have the offense run sweeps, slants, reverses and straight back passes.

(4) Have the defensive men hit and then react.

(5) See Illustration 286.

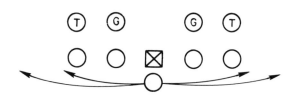

Illus. 286

75. HOW TO DRILL FOR THE BOARDS

The purpose of this drill is to develop balance along with toughness.

INSTRUCTIONS:

(1) Place a board one foot wide and 10 feet long on the ground.

(2) Start two men in the middle of the board and let them go at it. See which man can push the other backwards off the end of the board.

(3) A variation of this drill on the same board can be effective.

(4) Have a man holding a dummy on the board.

(5) Station a blocker at the end of the board. The blocker takes several shots at the bag, keeping his legs wide apart.

(6) See Illustration 287.

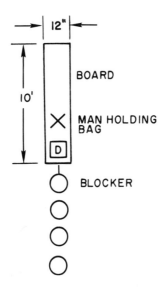

Illus. 287

76. HOW TO DRILL FOR CROSSING THE LINE

This drill is designed to give the ends practice in getting across the line of scrimmage.

INSTRUCTIONS:

(1) Place a reserve center on offense with a football.

(2) Station ten ends on defense.

(3) As the center moves the ball either early or late the end concentrates on getting across the line fast and low.

(4) See Illustration 288.

Illus. 288

77. HOW TO DRILL FOR FOOT WORK

This is an early season drill to strengthen the legs and provide excellent practice in foot work for back peddling.

INSTRUCTIONS:

(1) Have all the ends, left and right, get in a single line behind each other.

(2) Have the first man in line stand on one of the yard lines.

(3) First have them run in place, with knees as high as possible. Keep this up until they reach the next yard line, which will be five yards. They all follow the first man.

(4) The next drill is running backwards with knees as high as possible. Have the men run with knees high for two yards; then while running in place have them start doing a 360-degree turn to the left and then the right. Upon completing both turns they should sprint out at full speed for five yards.

(5) See Illustration 289.

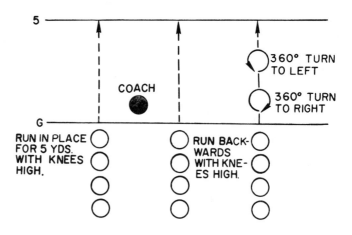

Illus. 289

78. HOW TO DRILL FOR WRESTLING

The purpose of this drill is to eliminate any delay and "wrestling" by linemen in getting across the line.

INSTRUCTIONS:

(1) Place three dummies in front of a defensive man.

(2) Station another held dummy seven to ten yards deep.

(3) The defensive man hits and scrambles over the dummies, rushes and tackles the downfield dummy within two seconds.

(4) See Illustration 290a.

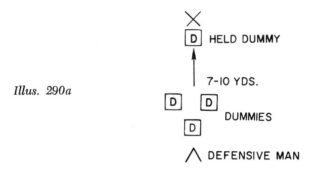

Illus. 290a

Second (more advanced). The object is to fight through men with air bags—hit and roll off first dummy—block or tackle the downfield dummy (290b).

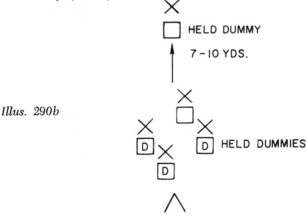

Illus. 290b

Third. The idea is to fight through men with air dummies and get by a blocker who knows which way the passer will run (right or left) and will block accordingly. Tag the man with the ball with two hands on the waist (290c).

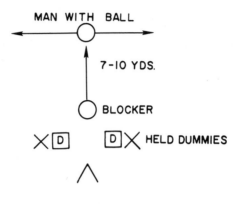

Illus. 290c

79. HOW TO DRILL FOR RUSHING THE PASSER

The purpose of this drill is to provide practice for the interior line in rushing the passer.

INSTRUCTIONS:

(1) Split linemen into offensive and defensive units.

(2) Locate a standing dummy seven yards deep to represent a passer. Place a foreign colored jersey over the dummy.

(3) Use a stop watch to time the rushing linemen. Keep a record of individual performances to instill competitive spirit.

(4) See Illustration 291.

Illus. 291

11

DRILLS FOR THE SECONDARY

Defense against a forward pass is a rushed pass.

—John "Ox" Dagrosa

THE TECHNIQUE OF PASS DEFENSE HAS BECOME A PRIMARY DEfensive skill in football. Body position, footwork, and peripheral vision are skills that must be executed every day of the season. Other skills must also be developed to acquire good defensive ability. All maneuvers discussed in this chapter appear in the time-study chart. See Illustration 292.

All skills in football are developed through constant repetition of the various maneuvers, through which habits are formed.

Doing the right thing at the right time in an emergency is a matter of habit. Well coached teams acquire the habit and, as a conse-

399

Number of minutes for each drill

	1st week				2nd week				3rd week				TOTAL
DATE													
FOOTWORK													
INDIVIDUAL PASS DEFENSE													
PLAYING THE BALL													
DEFLECTIONS													
INTERCEPTIONS													
RUNNING BACKWARDS													
ONE-ON-ONE													
OUTNUMBERED													
TACKLING													
BALL FIGHTING													
BODY POSITION													

Illus. 292

quence, are quick to take immediate advantage of the mistakes of others.[1]

The author believes that a player on defense must expect that every play is going to be a pass until the play develops. It is necessary for backs to be alert and to play the ball closely.

It matters little what type of pass defense is used or how

---

[1] John L. Griffith, *The Fundamentals of Football* (New York: Thomas E. Wilson and Company, 1923), p. 3.

effective the drills used are. The successful pass defense depends upon the individual "brains" and abilities of the men
in the secondary.

Pass defense drills are sometimes quite lengthy, and unless
well organized much time can be wasted in practice sessions.
The time-study chart is a valuable guide to a coach in determining the amount of time spent on drills for the secondary.

1. HOW TO DRILL FOR PLAYING THE BALL

*The object of this drill is to give the defensive backfield and
linebackers practice in pass defense, pass interception, and
return of intercepted passes.*

INSTRUCTIONS:

(1) Place the linebackers, halfbacks and safety man in their
normal defensive positions.

(2) The defensive quarterback calls a defense.

(3) At a voice signal from the coach, meaning that a pass
is indicated, the secondary fades quickly into its defensive
zone.

(4) The passer lined up with a center then throws the ball
to any point in the secondary he chooses.

(5) All defenders take part in the "play," those nearest the
ball going for it and the others quickly forming interference for
the return of an intercepted pass.

2.   HOW TO DRILL FOR INDIVIDUAL PASS DEFENSE

The object of this drill is to teach the individual pass de-fenders to become proficient at defending against passes.

INSTRUCTIONS:

(1) Have the center and quarterback take their normal offensive positions.

(2) Locate the offensive ends in two lines.

(3) Place the pass defenders in their normal defensive positions.

(4) On the snap signals, the pass receivers break into the secondary for a pass.

(5) They execute their own individual maneuvers in order to evade the defender.

(6) The passer attempts to complete the pass.

(7) The pass defender attempts to block or intercept the passes.

(8) See Illustration 293.

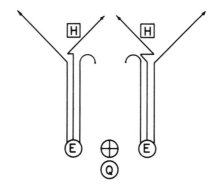

Illus. 293

3. HOW TO DRILL FOR PASS DEFENSE

The purpose of this drill is to give the defensive backs practice in defending against passes. The drill also provides practice for the ends in receiving and the quarterback in throwing.
INSTRUCTIONS:

(1) Line up the centers and passers right behind them in their regular passing positions.

(2) Station the pass receivers in their normal offensive end positions.

(3) Have the pass defenders face the receivers in their regular defensive positions, about seven yards deep.

(4) The offensive ends give the passer a signal by placing one, two, three, four, or even five fingers behind their backs, indicating whether they will eventually go to the left, right, down behind the defender, or come back on a hook.

(5) The receiver goes on the snap number called by the passer and attempts to evade the defense.

(6) The pass defender attempts to intercept the pass or at least knock it down.

(7) See Illustration 294.

4. HOW TO DRILL FOR SKELETAL PASS DEFENSE

The object of this drill is to provide the defensive backs and linebackers practice in protecting against passes. This drill also gives the players practice in learning their pass patterns and the quarterbacks practice in passing.
INSTRUCTIONS:

(1) The center, fullback, two halfbacks, and safety take their normal defensive positions for pass defense.

(2) An offensive formation of the passer and ends is utilized to run their own pass patterns, or the opponent's pass design may be employed.

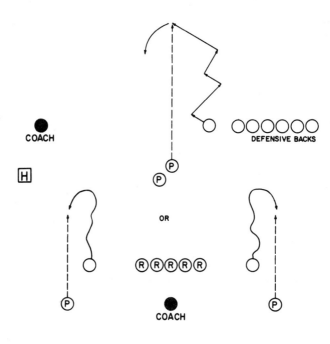

Illus. 294

(3) The pass patterns should be diagrammed on cardboard so that the backs and ends can see the pattern.

(4) On the snap number given by the quarterback, the offensive players run the pass plays and the defenders attempt to block or intercept them.

(5) Sometimes defensive ends may be used to rush the passer and make the drill more realistic.

(6) Different colored jerseys on the offensive or defensive will clarify the drill.

5. HOW TO DRILL FOR PASS INTERCEPTION

The object of this drill is to give the entire backfield practice in intercepting the ball.   It also provides a warm-up for the backs and passers before a practice session.

INSTRUCTIONS:

(1) Place the fullbacks, halfbacks, and safety in their normal defensive positions facing the passers.

(2) Leave the passers behind the center.

(3) On the snap of the ball, the defenders drop back into the position they would be in if a man came into their territory.

(4) No pass receivers are sent out in this drill.

(5) The passer takes the ball and retreats into passing position.   He attempts to throw to a spot where the defense cannot reach the ball.

(6) The defenders go after the ball at its highest point, to intercept or bat it down.

(7) Occasionally throw the ball over the safety man's head and make him run for it.

(8) The passers alternate.

6. HOW TO DRILL THE MAN-FOR-MAN PASS DEFENSE

The purpose of this drill is to provide practice for the backs in covering receivers with a man-for-man defense.

INSTRUCTIONS:

(1) Place two backs on defense for five passes each.

(2) Divide the rest of the backs into two lines and have them go down and break any direction they choose.

(3) Alternate lines to speed up drills.

(4) Insist that the defensive men catch the ball or at least knock it down or be able to tackle the receiver.   Keep weaker men on defense longer in order to correct mistakes.

7. HOW TO DRILL FOR PASS-INTERCEPTION ABILITY

The purpose of this drill is to develop ability in intercepting enemy passes.

INSTRUCTIONS:

(1) The defenders line up on the goal line, opposite the goal posts.

(2) The passers stand near the mid-field stripe.

(3) The passers throw the ball in the general direction of the coffin corner.

(4) The passer throws a high lofting pass to either corner.

(5) The players standing on the goal line attempt to intercept the pass and return up field.

(6) See Illustration 295.

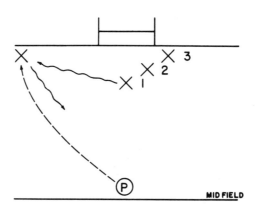

Illus. 295

8. HOW TO DRILL FOR GROUP INTERCEPTION

The purpose of this drill is to give the entire backfield and linebackers practice in defending against passes with the objective of intercepting them.

INSTRUCTIONS:

(1) Locate the passers in a line eight yards apart. Each passer should have at least three footballs.

(2) Place all the centers and fullbacks on a line about six yards deep, the halfbacks 10 yards farther back, and the safety men beyond them 15 or 20 yards back.

(3) The passers use this as a warm-up and practice trying to get the ball in between all of these men.

(4) The defensive man nearest the ball will attempt to intercept, or at least bat the ball down if he cannot intercept it.

(5) See Illustration 296.

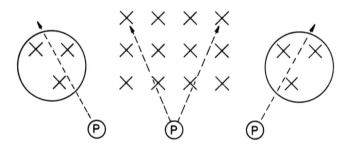

Illus. 296

9. HOW TO DRILL FOR ZONE PASS DEFENSE

The purpose of this drill is to provide practice for the secondary and tertiary when employing a zone pass defense.

INSTRUCTIONS:

(1) Place a complete backfield on defense with two lines of pass receivers.

(2) Send down two receivers to do any maneuver they wish.

(3) Insist that each man play his territory by keeping in line with his teammates.

(4) Defensive men must catch the ball, knock it down, or be able to make the tackle.

(5) This drill may also be used to learn pass patterns and provide pass practice for the quarterbacks by placing ends and complete backfield on offense.

(6) See Illustration 297.

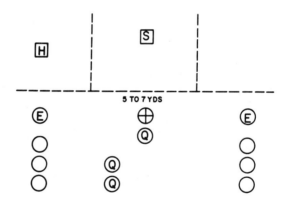

Illus. 297

10. HOW TO DRILL FOR FOOTWORK

This drill is designed to provide practice for all the backs to develop proper footwork.

INSTRUCTIONS:

(1) Position all the backfield men as linebackers or half-backs.

(2) Allow approximately five yards between each player.

(3) The coach stands in front of the group with a football.

(4) By motion of the ball, the players respond to the directions.

(5) Warn the backs never to cross their feet while defending.

(6) See Illustration 298.

Illus. 298

11. HOW TO DRILL FOR PLAYING THE BALL

This drill is designed to provide practice for the secondary in playing the ball.

INSTRUCTIONS:

(1) Place a complete secondary on defense.

(2) Line up the passers on offense to throw the ball to any open spot they can find in the defense.

(3) Station a center on offense with several footballs.

(4) If the pass is intercepted, all the other backs form interference and run the ball back to return it to the center.

(5) See Illustration 299.

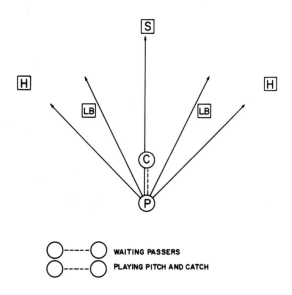

Illus. 299

12. HOW TO DRILL FOR INDIVIDUAL PASS DEFENSE

This is a combination offensive and defensive halfback drill used primarily to develop the secondary.

INSTRUCTIONS:

(1) Line up the right and left ends on offense with a center.

(2) Place two halfbacks on defense.

(3) The defensive halfbacks keep the receivers to the inside if possible, and under no circumstances do they turn their backs on the passer.

(4) Alternate lines after each play.

(5) See Illustration 300.

13. HOW TO DRILL FOR RETREATING FOOT RACE

The object of this drill is to teach footwork required for rapid retreating.

INSTRUCTIONS:

(1) Place men in pairs according to speed and give them a starting signal from the thirty yard line.

(2) Have the players retreat as rapidly as possible, facing the coach with their feet apart and the body in the boxer's position.

(3) The coach uses his arms to change their direction left or right and watches for incorrect use of the feet.

(4) The boxer's skipping step is the best for speed.

(5) This drill may be varied by using other commands such as "stop, left, right, reverse," and so forth.

(6) The first player to reach the goal line is the winner.

(7) See Illustration 301.

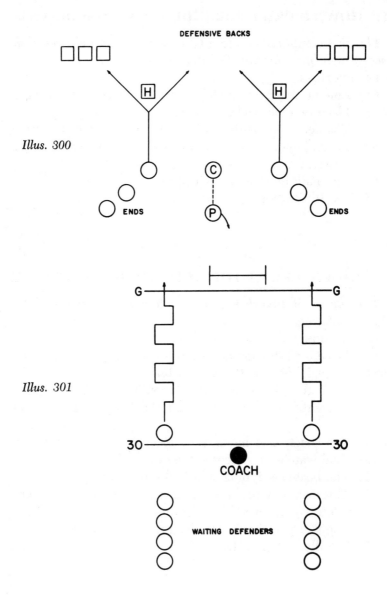

Illus. 300

Illus. 301

14. HOW TO DRILL FOR WATCHING THE END

The purpose of this drill is to improve the reactions of the defense halfbacks in determining whether the play is a pass or a run. This drill is to be used when preparing for a T formation team.

INSTRUCTIONS:

(1) Station two halfbacks on defense. Instruct them to watch the near side end and near side tackle.

(2) Place two ends and two tackles on offense.

(3) Locate one tackle on defense.

(4) Have the end on each play run into the halfbacks' territory.

(5) Have the offensive tackle either block hard or retreat slightly to protect for a forward pass.

(6) If the tackle blocks hard, the defensive halfback should come up fast. If the tackle goes through his pass protection steps the halfback should give ground.

(7) See Illustration 302.

15. HOW TO DRILL ONE-ON-ONE

The object of this drill is to teach the defensive halfbacks that good pass defense tactics are difficult to learn.

INSTRUCTIONS:

(1) Place a center, an end, and a passer on offense.

(2) Station a halfback on defense seven yards deep.

(3) Allow the end and passer to plan their pattern. This places the halfback under great handicap.

(4) This drill should make the defensive halfbacks realize that they need much training on defending against passers.

(5) See Illustration 303.

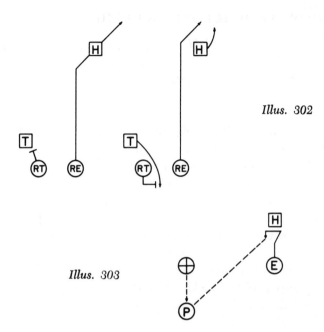

Illus. 302

Illus. 303

16. HOW TO DRILL FOR BEING OUTNUMBERED

This drill is designed to be fun while teaching footwork, agility, and reaction.

INSTRUCTIONS:

(1) A defensive player is opposed by two attacking players. The two offensive players are stationed five yards from the defender.

(2) He must guard an area outlined between two dummies stationed ten yards apart.

(3) The two offensive players try to out-maneuver the one defender by lateral passing only.

(4) The attacking players are given a time limit of 20 seconds to advance the ball for a point.

(5) A clever defender can feint and stall to defeat the offense.

(6) This is a good drill for both linebackers and secondary.

17. HOW TO DRILL FOR BACKFIELD TACKLING

The basic object of this drill is to give the backfield men practice in tackling. The drill provides blocking practice for the linemen and gives them a chance to carry the ball.

INSTRUCTIONS:

(1) Give a guard or tackle the ball and have him line up with a lineman as blocker in front of him.

(2) Place a defensive backfield down field.

(3) Prescribe boundaries to limit the drill areas.

(4) On a signal, the blocker and ball carrier take off.

(5) The defensive back attempts to tackle the runner.

(6) The blocker tries to clear the way for the ball carrier.

(7) See Illustration 304.

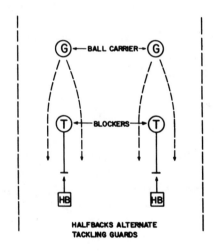

Illus. 304

18. DEFENSIVE TACKLING DRILL FOR HALFBACKS AND SAFETIES

The purpose of this drill is to train the secondary in live tackling practice under simulated game conditions.

INSTRUCTIONS:

(1) Place two halfbacks and a safety man in their respective positions.

(2) The rest of the backs then line up in a single line to carry the ball.

(3) The coach or ball handler stands on a hash mark and commands "charge," then laterals the ball to the ball carrier after he has started running.

(4) The ball carrier runs as if he were on an end run and the outside halfback and safety man proceed to tackle him as a unit.

(5) The ball handler then goes through the same routine to the opposite side.

(6) Restrict the ball carrier to approximately 15 yards of space in which to run.

(7) See Illustration 305.

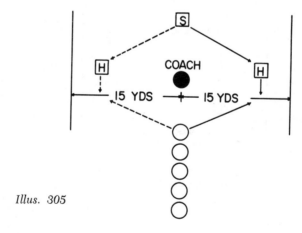

Illus. 305

19. HOW TO DRILL FOR CHANGING DIRECTION

Since football is a game of footwork, this drill is designed to train the secondary in changing direction.

INSTRUCTIONS:

(1) Two players line up five yards apart, facing a coach who is five yards away.

(2) By use of hand signals, the players move as quickly as possible in any direction indicated by the coach.

(3) Insist that the players watch the coach at all times.

(4) Five minutes are sufficient.

(5) See Illustration 306.

20. HOW TO DRILL FOR DEFLECTION

The object of this drill is to improve the reactions of the linebackers and secondary.

INSTRUCTIONS:

(1) Line up all the linebackers and secondary in two lines in single file order.

(2) Place a passer ten yards from the first player in line.

(3) Have the first player run forward as the passer sets to throw. The ball should be thrown hard at him.

(4) The receiving player does *not* try to catch the ball. He should deflect it and the second man will trail him. As the football is tipped, the second man reacts to catch the ball.

(5) Have the players attempt to fool the second man by deflecting the ball where he cannot get it.

(6) This is a good morale drill for the players.

(7) See Illustration 307.

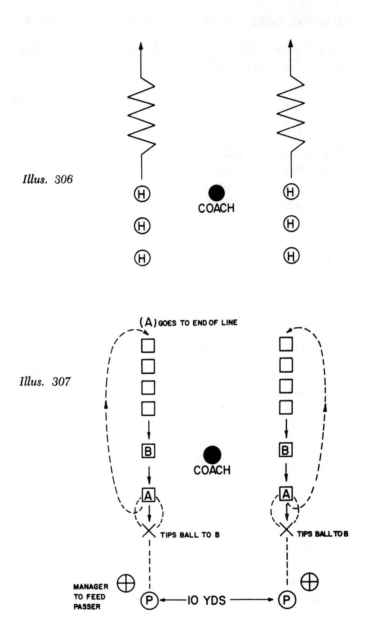

Illus. 306

Illus. 307

21. HOW TO DRILL FOR COMBINATION

The object of this drill is to combine tackling and pass defense under game conditions.

INSTRUCTIONS:

(1) Place the halfbacks on defense in their respective positions.

(2) Line up two ends, a center, a quarterback, and a fullback on offense.

(3) Place two reserve tackles in front of the offensive ends.

(4) Instruct the halfbacks to watch the end. If the end blocks, he comes forward to tackle. If the end releases, he covers the end on a pass.

(5) See Illustration 308.

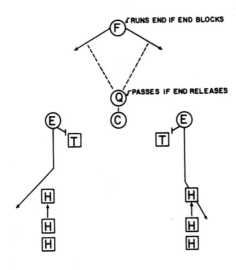

Illus. 308

22. HOW TO DRILL FOR TACKLING

*The purpose of this drill is to provide tackling practice for
the halfbacks.*

INSTRUCTIONS:

(1) Line up the defensive halfbacks in their respective
positions.

(2) Place a center on offense with a quarterback and a fullback.

(3) A coach is on the line of scrimmage to represent an end.
Next to the coach should be a standing dummy.

(4) Have the defender watch the coach. If the coach
slaps the dummy it signifies a block by the offensive end.
Then the defensive back comes up on the outside to make
the tackle.

(5) Have the halfbacks line up with outside foot back to
emphasize the outside.

(6) See Illustration 309.

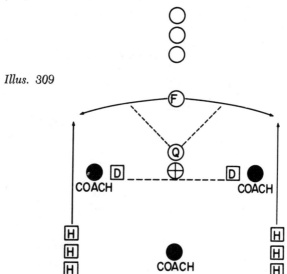

Illus. 309

23.   HOW TO DRILL FOR RUNNING BACKWARDS

This drill is designed to practice catching a thrown ball while running backwards.

INSTRUCTIONS:

(1) Have the backs line up one yard from the coach.

(2) On a signal from the coach the lead player runs laterally for three yards around a standing dummy.

(3) After reaching the dummy, have the player run backwards.

(4) The coach throws the football so each player must recover to catch the ball.

(5) Insist that the men run backwards as fast as they can.

(6) See Illustration 310.

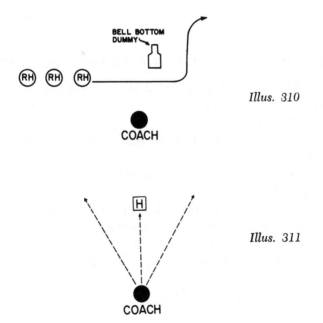

Illus. 310

Illus. 311

24. HOW TO DRILL FOR BALL FIGHTING

This drill is designed to develop ball fighting ability. A wall drill is excellent to train a defensive halfback.

INSTRUCTIONS:

(1) Place one defender facing the wall two feet away.

(2) Throw football toward wall or board.

(3) As the ball descends, have the defender jump and catch it at its highest point.

(4) Insist on reaching for the ball with two hands.

25. HOW TO DRILL FOR GOING FOR THE BALL

The object of this drill is to practice going for a ball thrown in several directions.

INSTRUCTIONS:

(1) Position one player on defense ten yards from the backfield coach.

(2) Begin the drill by throwing the ball directly at the defender.

(3) Gradually increase difficulty for the defender, i.e., fake one way and throw another; throw longer, harder, and so forth.

(4) Stress watching the passer and the ball at all times.

(5) The coach should watch the footwork of each defender very closely.

(6) See Illustration 311.

26.   HOW TO DRILL FOR MEETING THE BALL

The object of this drill is to teach the defenders how to catch the ball.

INSTRUCTIONS:

(1) Place two lines of backs ten yards apart.

(2) Have one football for each two defenders. The two lines throw the ball back and forth.

(3) Emphasize going up and out for the ball and being aggressive.

(4) Stress the importance of getting off the ground and catching the ball at the highest possible point.

(5) See Illustration 312.

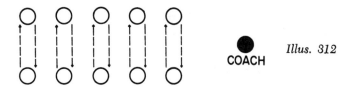

COACH

Illus. 312

27.   HOW TO DRILL FOR FIGHTING FOR THE BALL

The purpose of this drill is to teach men to fight for the ball and to play the ball.

INSTRUCTIONS:

(1) Place two defensive backs seven yards apart.

(2) A coach is stationed ten yards away.

(3) The ball should be thrown between the two backs and have them fight for the ball.

(4) Throw the ball high enough so that both defenders have an equal chance for the ball.

(5) Rotate players frequently.

(6) See Illustration 314.

28. HOW TO DRILL FOR FOOTWORK

The object of this drill is to develop good footwork for the defensive backs.

INSTRUCTIONS:

(1) The defensive backs line up in single-file order and take their turn.

(2) On a signal from the coach, the players start running backward, facing the coach at all times.

(3) The coach calls out "right," "left," "back," and so on, and the defensive halfbacks react to these commands.

(4) The passer throws the ball at an opportune time and the receiver runs back to the passer with the ball.

(5) See Illustration 313.

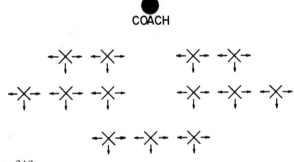

Illus. 313

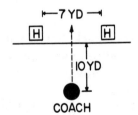

Illus. 314

29. HOW TO DRILL FOR RECOGNIZING A PASS OR RUN

This drill is designed to provide practice for recognizing a pass or run against a T formation team.

INSTRUCTIONS:

(1) Place a tackle and an end on offense.

(2) Line up a guard and a halfback on defense.

(3) Have the halfback watch both the end and the tackle.

(4) On each play, have the tackle either block the guard or give ground as if to block for a forward pass.

(5) If the tackle blocks, the halfback should come up fast to the outside.

(6) If the tackle back steps, as he would on pass protection, the defensive halfback should expect a pass.

(7) See Illustration 315.

30. HOW TO DRILL FOR BODY POSITION

This drill is designed to provide practice for two ends in receiving, while a defensive halfback attempts to break up the play.

INSTRUCTIONS:

(1) Place two ends and a halfback ten yards downfield. The halfback should be placed in the center. Allow two yards spacing between each player.

(2) Have the halfback or man in the middle line up two or three yards deeper than the other two.

(3) The coach throws the ball in the area of the three players. The ends are asked to receive and the halfback attempts to break up the play.

(4) The ball should be thrown long, short, to both sides, hard and soft. This provides training in judging and meeting all types of passes.

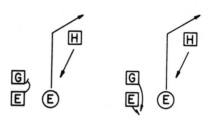

Illus. 315

(5) Use two groups of three to increase the efficiency of the drill.

(6) Assign a manager, if available, to return the footballs to the coach.

(7) Two footballs are needed in this drill.

(8) See Illustration 316.

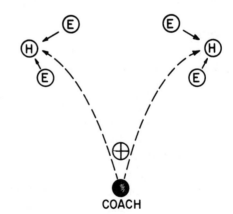

Illus. 316

31. HOW TO DRILL FOR DUMMY DEFLECTION

The purpose of this drill is to provide practice for the defensive backs in playing a deflected ball.

INSTRUCTIONS:

(1) Locate two lines of defensive backs approximately five yards behind a standing dummy in the hook zone.

(2) Place a center and quarterback on offense.

(3) Station the two linebackers on defense.

(4) As the passer indicates his intentions, the linebackers retreat and the defensive backs come forward.

(5) The linebacker deflects the ball and the defensive back attempts to intercept at its highest point.

(6) See Illustration 317.

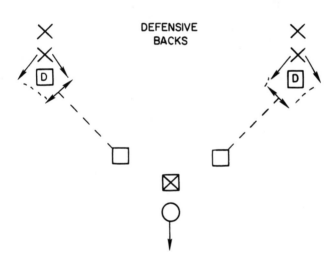

Illus. 317

32. HOW TO DRILL FOR TEN YARD PASS DEFENSE

The purpose of this drill is to begin teaching pass defense without giving the offensive man the advantage.

INSTRUCTIONS:

(1) Station a passer, center, and receiver on offense on the sideline. This is a cross field drill.

(2) Place a pass defender eight yards deep on the five-yard line.

(3) The receiver has a limited area to maneuver—between the goal line and the 10-yard line.

(4) The receiver attempts to get free and the defender works the five-yard line back and forth.

(5) This is a good drill to build confidence in the defensive man.

(6) When the defensive back improves, add five yards and then ten yards to cover and then add another defensive back.

(7) See Illustration 318.

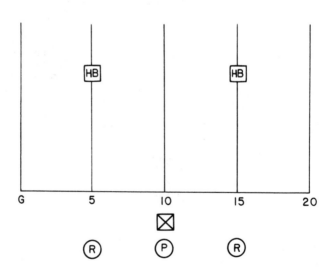

Illus. 318

33. HOW TO DRILL FOR MATCHING FEET

The purpose of this drill is to teach the fundamentals of footwork.

INSTRUCTIONS:

(1) This is a stationary drill.

(2) Line up back "A" facing back "B" with three yards between.

(3) When back "A" takes a step with his right foot to his right instruct back "B" to step with his left foot.

(4) Have "A" step to his left. Instruct back "B" to take a step with his right foot.

(5) Back "B" can see how simple it is to cover "A."

(6) Reverse the procedure.

(7) Gradually increase speed.

(8) See Illustration 319.

Illus. 319

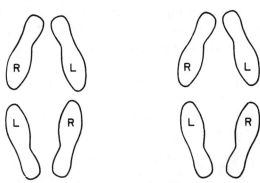

34. HOW TO DRILL FOR BEING OUTNUMBERED

The purpose of this drill is to provide practice in footwork while playing two defenders. This is a good drill for both linebackers and secondary.

INSTRUCTIONS:

(1) A defensive player is opposed by two attacking players.

(2) The defensive man must guard an area outlined between two dummies standing ten yards apart.

(3) The two offensive players try to out-maneuver the one defender by use of the lateral passes only.

(4) A clever defender can feint and stall to defeat the offense.

(5) The attacking players are given a time limit of 20 seconds to advance the ball for a point.

35. HOW TO DRILL FOR JUMPING ROPE

There is no better drill for developing footwork and coordination than rope jumping. It is also excellent for strengthening the knees and ankles.

INSTRUCTIONS:

(1) Make sure the rope is plenty long. If the players are jumping with their shoes and equipment this is essential.

(2) Have ropes for all the backs and ends. Sixteen to twenty ropes are needed. Alternate ropes with lineman.

(3) Have the backs jump for five minutes as part of their warm-up.

(4) During the last minute of jumping, jump as high off the ground as possible.

(5) We use rope jumping drills every spring practice.

(6) See Illustration 320.

Illus. 320

36. HOW TO DRILL FOR CHINA

The purpose of this drill is to teach footwork and defensive reaction.

INSTRUCTIONS:

(1) We call this the Chinese drill.

(2) Place two men in the center of a large circle.

(3) The circle may be from 10 to 15 yards in diameter.

(4) The center men try to knock down or intercept passes from the outside men.

(5) The players on the outside may fake and try to out-guess the men in the circle.

(6) See Illustration 321.

Illus. 321

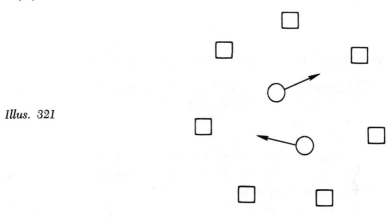

37. HOW TO DRILL FOR JUMPING

The purpose of this drill is to provide practice for the defensive backs in getting off the ground.

INSTRUCTIONS:

(1) Have the backs form a single file line.

(2) Have them run under the goal post and jump to touch the cross bar with one hand and later with both hands.

(3) This is a good morale drill.

(4) See Illustration 322.

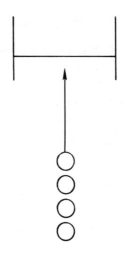

Illus. 322

38. HOW TO DRILL FOR BALL FIGHTING

The purpose of this drill is to provide practice for the defensive backs in fighting for the ball.

INSTRUCTIONS:

(1) Form small groups of two or three.

(2) Have a passer throw the football into the group.

(3) Require the defenders to fight for the ball and come forward running with it.

(4) See Illustration 323.

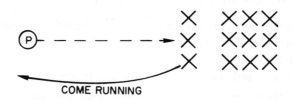

Illus. 323

39. HOW TO DRILL FOR DOUBLE PASS DEFENSE

The purpose of this drill is to work two defensive backfields at the same time.

INSTRUCTIONS:

(1) Locate two complete pass defense units on either side of a passer.

(2) Have the passer alternate throwing the ball first to one unit and then to the other.

(3) Have the passer attempt to throw the ball to open areas and make all the backs go for the ball.

(4) Encourage them to lateral and react to lead in the interference.

(5) See Illustration 324.

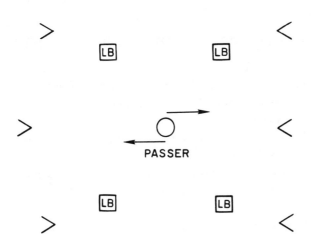

Illus. 324

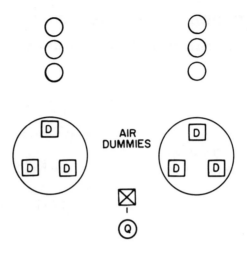

Illus. 325

40. HOW TO DRILL FOR OBSTACLE INTERCEP-TIONS

The purpose of this drill is to make the defender aggressive and create an obstacle to interception.

INSTRUCTIONS:

(1) Place several air dummies on the ground five yards in front of the defenders.

(2) Station a quarterback and a center on offense. At the exchange of the ball the quarterback drops back and throws the ball over the dummies.

(3) The defensive man must run forward and intercept while jumping over the dummies.

(4) See Illustration 325.

41. HOW TO DRILL FOR LATERAL MOVEMENT

The purpose of this drill is to improve lateral running.

INSTRUCTIONS:

(1) Place two dummies ten yards apart. Place another dummy for the defender to run around.

(2) Station two passers on offense and have a manager to feed them footballs.

(3) The defensive men run forward four steps, and upon reaching the fourth step drop back two and break off in a parallel run to the right or left as indicated by the coach.

(4) Have the defenders run in a straight line between the two dummies.

(5) See Illustration 326.

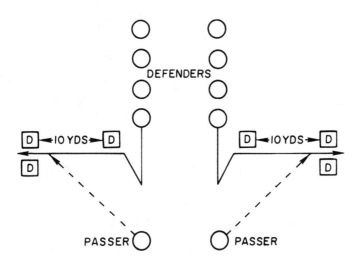

Illus. 326

42. HOW TO DRILL FOR PARALLEL—BACKWARDS

*The purpose of this drill is to combine the two previous drills
and give reaction training in running parallel and backwards.*
INSTRUCTIONS:

(1) Again, the defensive man runs forward four steps, drops
back two, moves laterally five yards, and then goes into a backward run.

(2) As the defender is running backwards, a hand signal by
the coach changes his direction to a parallel run at which time
the ball is thrown.

(3) See Illustration 327.

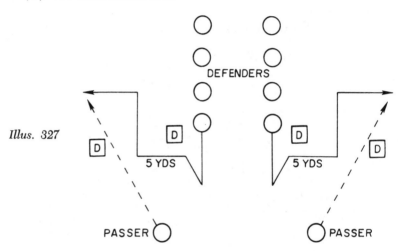

Illus. 327

43. HOW TO DRILL FOR UP-OUT-BACK

*The purpose of this drill is to improve the reactions of a
defender coming forward, moving to the outside and then going backward.*
INSTRUCTIONS:

(1) Have the defensive man run forward four steps, drop
back two, move laterally five yards, and then go into a backward run.

(2) The ball is thrown to the defender at any time during the drill to force concentration.

(3) Place one dummy to run around and one 12 yards downfield.

(4) See Illustration 328.

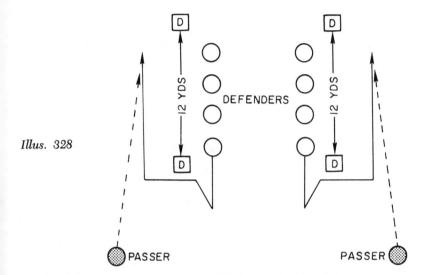

Illus. 328

44. HOW TO DRILL FOR DOUBLE ONE ON ONE

The object of this drill is to put the defensive man at a disadvantage and make the drill competitive. This is also a time saver drill when teaching pass defense.

INSTRUCTIONS:

(1) Place two quarterbacks and two centers on offense.

(2) Locate the left and right ends at their respective positions.

(3) Station two halfbacks on defense.

(4) One quarterback will throw to the left ends and one to the right ends.

(5) Play one side against the other and have a manager keep account of the number of interceptions and completions.

(6) Have groups alternate first one side and then the other. In this way it is possible for one coach to correct errors.

(7) See Illustration 329.

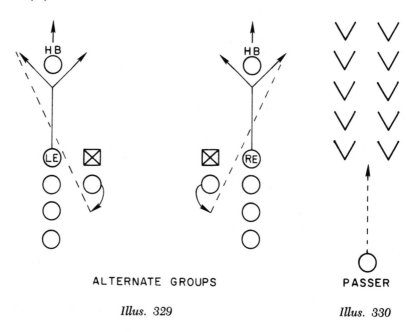

ALTERNATE GROUPS   PASSER

Illus. 329   *Illus. 330*

45. HOW TO DRILL FOR BALL FIGHTING

The purpose of this drill is to impress upon the defenders that they have as much right to get the ball as the receivers.

INSTRUCTIONS:

(1) Form two lines about one yard apart facing the passer.

(2) The passer stands ten yards away with plenty of footballs and throws as fast as possible high, low, etc.

(3) The front men in the lines try to intercept the ball. They return to the end of the line and the next two move up.

(4) This is a rapid drill.

(5) See Illustration 330.

46. HOW TO DRILL FOR COFFIN-CORNER INTER-CEPTORS

The purpose of this drill is to develop ability to cover more ground and intercept passes.

INSTRUCTIONS:

(1) Defenders line up on the goal line in front of the goal post.

(2) The passer stands in the 35-yard line at midfield. Later he moves back to the 40-yard line, and then 45-yard line.

(3) The passer throws a high, lofting pass toward either coffin corner.

(4) The players standing on the goal line attempt to intercept the ball and return up field.

(5) See Illustration 331.

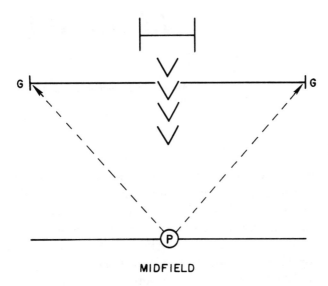

MIDFIELD

Illus. 331

12

DRILLS FOR THE LINEBACKER

An efficient linebacker is an unlicensed chiropractor.

—Tom Lieb

LINEBACKERS CAN MAKE OR BREAK A DEFENSIVE LINE. A GOOD defensive fullback is a stone wall to any offense. Usually he is in a position to meet all plays between the ends with direct contact and all plays outside the ends from a short distance, because he is very hard to block out. Properly located, he can cover flat passes and all those over the line of scrimmage, as well as block linemen under punts. He can diagnose plays and guide the line, checking the linemen when over or under shifted. He can play according to linemen's location on the line of scrimmage and their various individual and cooperative

440

charges. He must be the most deadly tackler and most efficient in diagnosing plays.

A linebacker does not necessarily have to be an offensive fullback or center. Any man might play in the line backing position if he has the qualifications.

Because there is no position that is harder to coach than linebacking, no attempt will be made here to set down definite drills for each of the linebacking maneuvers. Nevertheless several drills and techniques will be listed so that the coach may select and allot time for these various skills.

1. HOW TO DRILL FOR LEG LIFT

The purpose of this drill is to teach the linebackers the correct form, leg lift, and drive for tackling.

INSTRUCTIONS:

(1) The linebackers are divided into two groups and lined up facing each other.

(2) These lines should be five yards apart.

(3) Tackling is one-on-one at one-quarter speed.

(4) The tackler makes contact with his shoulder, lifts the opponent, carries him five yards, and sets him down on his feet.

(5) The man being tackled should use just enough evasiveness to make the tackler keep a good base with head up and alertness for the shifting of the ball carrier.

(6) This drill develops *leg lift*, drive after tackling, and eliminates going to the knees after tackling.

(7) This drill conditions the shoulder to shock and can be used every day without the danger of injury.

2. HOW TO DRILL FOR MEETING THE BLOCKER

The purpose of this drill is to improve the reactions of the linebackers when meeting a blocker.

INSTRUCTIONS:

(1) Line up four blockers and a center on offense.

(2) Place a reserve player five yards behind the center to represent a ball carrier.

(3) Place four linebackers one yard behind the line of scrimmage, and to the outside of the blocker.

(4) When the ball is snapped have the player in the backfield move in any direction or fake a pass.

(5) Instruct the linebacker to contact the blockers and react to the play.

(6) Never allow the linebacker to step around the blocker.

(7) A coach should be stationed behind the defense to provide hand signals to the blockers to take the linebacker in or out.

(8) See Illustrations 332a and 332b.

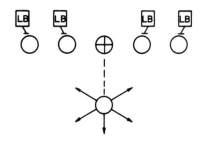

Illus. 332a

Illus. 332b

3. HOW TO DRILL FOR THE MONKEY-ROLL

The adaptation of the monkey-roll as used in gymnastics helps increase agility and reactions of the linebackers. Also learning how to fall and roll is of value to players backing up the line.

INSTRUCTIONS:

(1) Place three players on the ground in a prone position.

(2) Number the players from one to three.

(3) Have the No. 1 man roll over the No. 2 man, as the second man moves to the outside. No. 3 then rolls over No. 1.

(4) The process is then repeated.

(5) See Illustration 333.

Illus. 333

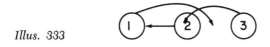

4. HOW TO DRILL FOR BACKING UP THE LINE

The object of this drill is to provide game condition practice in backing up the line.

INSTRUCTIONS:

(1) The offensive center passes the ball to the runner who, with his blockers, either tries to skirt the end or cut-back.

(2) Station a held dummy directly in front of the center for practice in check blocking.

(3) The linebacker comes up fast and tries to prevent a cut-back play.

(4) The linebacker fills to the outside but watches for cut-backs.

(5) Place a halfback and an end on defense upfield.

(6) See Illustration 334.

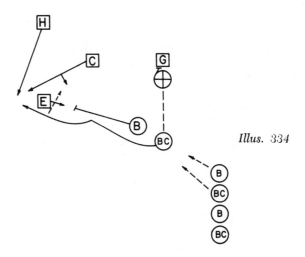

Illus. 334

5. HOW TO DRILL FOR SUPINE TACKLING

The object of this drill is to improve the tackling ability of the linebackers by a reaction drill.

INSTRUCTIONS:

(1) Place the tackler in a supine position, five yards from the ball carrier.

(2) Have a ball carrier in a reverse position with his back to the adversary. Locate a football at his feet.

(3) Station two dummies on either side of the ball carrier.

(4) On a signal from the coach, the ball carrier must pick up the ball, pivot, and attempt to avoid the tackler.

(5) The tackler must spring to his feet and meet the runner.

(6) This is an excellent drill and the players enjoy it.

(7) See Illustration 335.

Illus. 335

6. HOW TO DRILL FOR SECONDARY TACKLING

The purpose of this drill is to give the linebackers and half-backs game-condition practice in tackling a ball carrier and provide the ball carriers with practice in open field running.

INSTRUCTIONS:

(1) Centers, fullbacks, left and right halfbacks are grouped single file, in their respective defensive positions.

(2) Ball carriers line up single file behind the offensive center.

(3) The lead men in each unit take part in the play.

(4) The defensive men are instructed to perform as they would in a game: (a) Linebackers preventing the ball carriers from cutting back, and (b) Halfbacks protecting their outside and coming up fast.

(5) The ball is snapped to the lead carrier, who runs a course of his own choosing.

(6) After the ball carrier has been tackled, he drops back to the end of his respective file and the next set performs. Allow each set several chances.

7. HOW TO DRILL FOR STAYING AT HOME

The object of this drill is to train the linebackers to protect their territory.   This is an excellent drill to cure linebackers who chase faking backs.

INSTRUCTIONS:

(1) Place a complete team of eleven men on offense.

(2) Station a six man line and two linebackers on defense.

(3) Have the offense run through their regular maneuvers at half speed.

(4) Stress getting across line of scrimmage for the linemen and protection of territory for the backers.

(5) After several plays have the offense run through a play, but *without the football.*

(6)Watch the linebacker's reactions. If he does not know where the ball is he must *not* move.

(7) This drill always provides several laughs and is a good tonic for the entire squad.

8. HOW TO DRILL FOR PROTECTION OF TERRITORY

The object of this drill is to develop the linebacker in protecting his territory.

INSTRUCTIONS:

(1) Place two bags in a position to represent the off-tackle and the end-run hole.

(2) Line up a complete backfield, with a center, that can run either of these plays against a linebacker.

(3) Have the linebacker be responsible for these two holes without letting him know which place the offense is running. Then let him see if he can stop the play.

(4) Alternate a pass play to the flat once every five plays.

(5) This drill is good practice for offensive blocking, fakes, and steps. Work to the left side also.

(6) See Illustration 336.

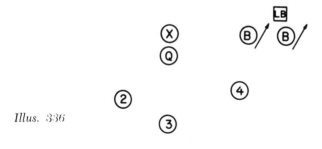

Illus. 336

9. HOW TO DRILL THE MIDDLE BACKER

This drill is designed to give the middle linebacker practice in analyzing the offensive play of a T formation team where the guards are pulling. The object is to train the linebacker in observing these guards and center so that he can fill the hole.
INSTRUCTIONS:

(1) Station two guards and a center on offense.

(2) Place a guard and middle linebacker on defense.

(3) The coach should stand behind the linebacker and signal to the offensive guards and center.

(4) If the right guard pulls right, the linebacker fills the off tackle hole.

(5) If both guards pull right, the linebacker expects an end run.

(6) If the right guard lead-posts with the center, the linebacker fills the territory of the right guard.

(7) If only the left guard pulls to his right he should expect a trap on the right side of the line.

(8) These are possibilities of the movement to the right side. The same possibilities exist to the left side.

(9) See Illustration 337.

Illus. 337

10.   HOW TO DRILL THE OUTSIDE LINEBACKER

The purpose of this drill is to provide practice for the outside linebacker in judging where the offensive will strike.

INSTRUCTIONS:

(1) Place a right tackle and right end on offense.

(2) Locate a tackle, end, and linebacker on defense.

(3) The coach should be stationed behind the linebacker to give offensive signals.

(4) If the right end blocks the defensive tackle, an off tackle play is coming over the end.

(5) If the right end blocks the linebacker, it is an off tackle play or possibly an end run.

(6) If the right end moves downfield, it is a pass or a play to opposite side.

(7) See Illustration 338.

Illus. 338
```
              OB

         T        E

       RT   RE
```

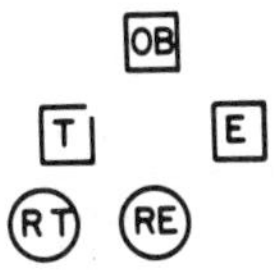

11.   HOW TO DRILL FOR CHUGGING THE END

The object of this drill is to provide practice for the line-backers in delaying receivers.

INSTRUCTIONS:

(1) Have the linebackers with the ends and backs when they are practicing pass patterns.

(2) Place the linebackers on defense and have them chug the ends on each pass.

(3) Alternate two linebackers at a time.

(4) This drill also offers practice for the ends in getting free.

(5) A five minute practice period is sufficient.

12. HOW TO DRILL FOR PASS REACTION

The object of this drill is to train the linebackers to react quickly when a pass occurs.

INSTRUCTIONS:

(1) Station two ends eight yards apart and eight yards downfield.

(2) Have the linebacker position himself two and one-half yards behind the line of scrimmage.

(3) Locate a center and passer on offense.

(4) The passer throws to either end.

(5) When the passer fades to throw, the linebacker retreats and attempts to knock down or intercept the ball.

(6) Have the passer fake a pass and run occasionally.

(7) See Illustration 339.

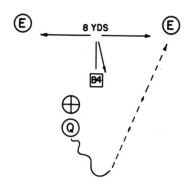

Illus. 339

13. HOW TO DRILL FOR DOUBLE LINEBACKING

The purpose of this drill is to simulate game conditions and provide practice for two linebackers.

INSTRUCTIONS:

(1) Line up a skeleton backfield, along with a pulling guard and a center, on offense.

(2) Place two linebackers and two ends on defense.

(3) Select all plays, including passes, which will give the linebackers varied defensive situations.

(4) A linebacker does not necessarily have to be an offensive fullback or center. This drill is effective in trying other men at the linebacking position to determine if they have the necessary qualifications.

(5) See Illustration 340.

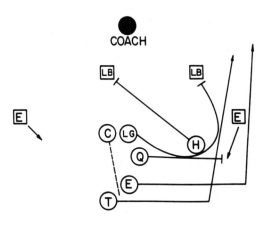

Illus. 340

14. HOW TO DRILL FOR BULL-IN-THE-RING

The object of this drill is to emphasize balanced defensive position. The player in the center of the ring learns to react quickly to the blockers coming from many angles as they attempt blocking him out of the ring.

INSTRUCTIONS:.

(1) Place a linebacker in the center of a ring of six or seven players.

(2) The ring should be fifteen feet in diameter with the players evenly spaced around it.

(3) Have the player assume his linebacking position ready for action.

(4) The coach calls out the name of one of the players in the ring who shuffles straight forward to shoulder block the "bull."

(5) Call another name after contact is made and the player has almost returned to the outer circle.

(6) Provide each player with an opportunity to block and release before changing the man in the center of the ring.

(7) Do not call the names too quickly, because the linebacker in the center will be unable to react to meet them.

(8) Start this drill at half-speed until the players understand the procedure and the man in the circle can defend himself.

(9) This reaction drill may be used for the entire squad.

(10) See Illustrations 341a and 341b.

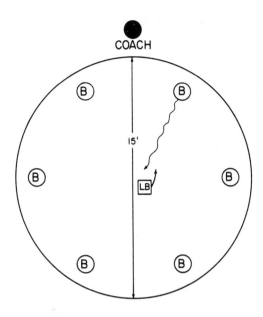

Illus. 341a

Illus. 341b

15. HOW TO DRILL FOR COMBINED TACKLING AND BLOCKING

This is a very effective all purpose blocking and tackling drill.

INSTRUCTIONS:

(1) The ball carrier stays three yards behind the blocker, and the tackler is ten yards ahead of the blocker.

(2) The tackling area should be limited in width to ten yards.

(3) As the blocker approaches, the tackler tries to ward him off with his hands and shoulders keeping him away from his legs and feet.

(4) This is a fine drill to develop linebackers.

(5) See Illustration 342.

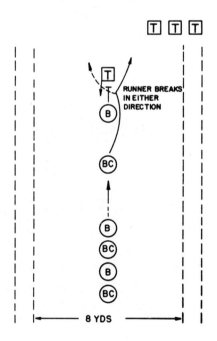

Illus. 342

16. HOW TO DRILL FOR GETTING DEPTH

The object of this drill is to show the linebackers the importance of getting depth on a pass.

INSTRUCTIONS:

(1) Place two linebackers in their normal positions on defense.

(2) Position a passer from five to seven yards from the linebackers.

(3) Have the passer throw the ball as hard as he can when the defenders are up close.

(4) Then repeat the same procedure by having the linebackers get their depth and both operate on the same plane.

(5) The linebackers will realize they can cover twice as much territory if they will retreat.

(6) See Illustration 343.

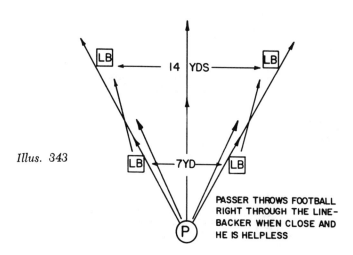

Illus. 343

PASSER THROWS FOOTBALL RIGHT THROUGH THE LINE-BACKER WHEN CLOSE AND HE IS HELPLESS

17. HOW TO DRILL FOR POSSESSION

This drill is designed to teach the linebackers to retreat and fight for possession of a thrown ball.

INSTRUCTIONS:

(1) Station two linebackers on defense five yards apart.

(2) Have another player act as a passer to throw the ball.

(3) The defensive players start back pedaling together with five yards separating them.

(4) Insist that they always watch the passer.

(5) Stress weight forward and body balance so that they can stop, come back, or move laterally to either side.

(6) After they have retreated 10 yards, the passer rifles the ball between the linebackers and they fight for possession of it.

(7) Have the passer throw the ball short so the linebackers must come forward.

(8) See Illustration 344.

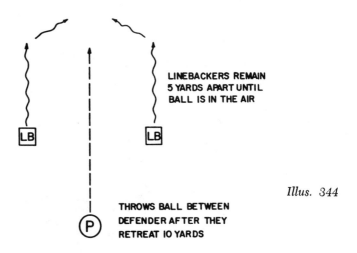

LINEBACKERS REMAIN
5 YARDS APART UNTIL
BALL IS IN THE AIR

Illus. 344

THROWS BALL BETWEEN
DEFENDER AFTER THEY
RETREAT 10 YARDS

18. HOW TO DRILL FOR POSITION

The object of this drill is to teach positions; playing as well as fighting for a thrown ball.

INSTRUCTIONS:

(1) Place two players on defense for each position.   Include three sets of linebackers.

(2) Have the coach fake in one direction and throw the ball in an area of two defenders.   Have them fight for the ball.

(3) With the assistance of a manager to feed footballs to the coach, this can be a fast-moving drill.

(4) See Illustration 345.

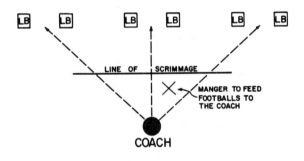

Illus. 345

19. HOW TO IMPROVE A LINEBACKER'S TIMING

The purpose of this drill is to improve a linebacker's reactions and familiarize him with a certain offense.

INSTRUCTIONS:

(1) Any linebacker could improve himself by playing linebacker while the backfield men are running plays to develop their timing.

(2) This drill would teach him not to follow fakes and to react quickly.

(3) The same idea could be incorporated with the line alone. The linebacker could be alert for pulling lineman, etc.

20. HOW TO DRILL FOR GETTING TO A SPOT

The purpose of this drill is to build confidence in the linebackers in getting to a spot as quickly as possible.

INSTRUCTIONS:

(1) Place five linemen on offense with a passer. Use freshmen linemen.

(2) Station five receivers downfield at from 12 to 15 yards.

(3) Place two linebackers and two ends on defense to cover the passes.

(4) Stress getting to a spot as quickly as possible *under control.*

(5) The five men placed behind the line, move right or left so the defenders will not know where they are.

(6) Have them react when the passer throws. They should cover the width of the field.

(7) Use a good passer for this drill.

(8) See Illustration 346.

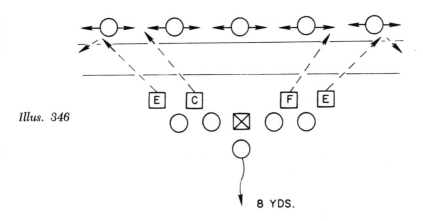

Illus. 346

21. HOW TO DRILL FOR LINEBACKER'S REACTIONS

The purpose of this drill is to train the linebacker in his reactions to the ball and not to follow fakes.

INSTRUCTIONS:

(1) Place a quarterback, center, and three backs on offense.

(2) Place four dummies on defense with one or two linebackers behind them. Space the dummies approximately four yards apart.

(3) Have the center line up three yards from the nearest bag.

(4) Have the backs practice their own offensive maneuvers or have a J.V. backfield run opposing plays.

(5) See Illustration 347.

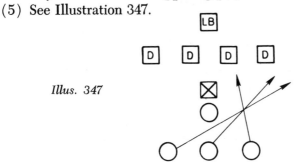

Illus. 347

22. HOW TO DRILL FOR THE TWO BAG PUNCH

This drill is designed to give the linebacker practice meeting one blocker and then a second.

INSTRUCTIONS:

(1) Station two offensive linemen side by side.

(2) Place a middle linebacker between them.

(3) The move of the middle linebacker should be short, sharp and jolting as he takes on the blockers.

(4) Contact should be made with the shoulders, upper arms, and forearms.

(5) See Illustration 348.

Illus. 348

23. HOW TO DRILL FOR GETTING DEPTH

This drill is designed for linebackers to practice running backwards. This is a fine footwork drill.

INSTRUCTIONS:

(1) Line up a complete team on offense. These men need not be regulars.

(2) Station three linebackers on defense and instruct them to "fly back" as soon as a pass shows. They may jam the ends first.

(3) They must get back to a desired depth of ten yards as quickly as possible and then slide either right or left facing the passer.

(4) See Illustration 349.

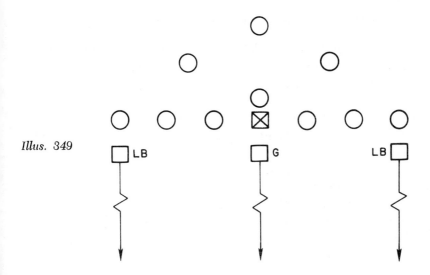

Illus. 349

24. HOW TO DRILL FOR KEYING

The purpose of this drill is to provide practice for a linebacker in keying the offensive guard.

INSTRUCTIONS:

(1) Place two dummies approximately two yards apart.

(2) Have a linebacker play one-and-a-half yard deep. This will vary with down and distance.

(3) Station a guard on offense. This guard may do the following: (a) Pull in either direction; (b) Block to either right or left; (c) Block straight ahead; (d) Pass-protection block.

(4) See Illustration 350.

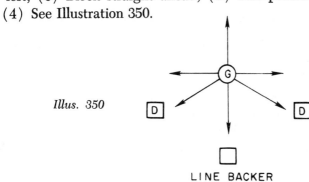

Illus. 350

25. HOW TO DRILL FOR GAME CONDITIONS

The purpose of this drill is to give the linebacker tackling practice, to ward off blockers, to observe the pulling guard, to be moving forward to meet the play at the line of scrimmage.
INSTRUCTIONS:
(1) Place four dummies in a straight line two yards apart.
(2) A pulling guard is placed between the two middle dummies.
(3) Behind this guard is a reserve back as a ball carrier.
(4) Station a linebacker three yards in front of the guard.
(5) On a signal the guard pulls either left or right to lead the ball carrier through a hole or around either end. The linebacker must get through the blocker and make the tackle.
(6) See Illustration 351.

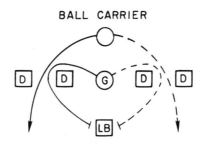

Illus. 351

26. HOW TO DRILL FOR FIGHTING OFF BLOCKERS

This drill gives the linebackers good practice in warding off three blockers.
INSTRUCTIONS:
(1) Place three linemen on offense.
(2) Alternate linebackers versus these linemen.
(3) The coach should be behind the linebacker to give signals. One finger means the left guard blocks the linebacker.

Two fingers means the right guard should do the same and three fingers means the center. A closed fist indicates all three should come out and block.

(4) See Illustration 352.

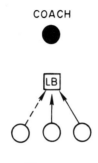

Illus. 352

27. HOW TO DRILL FOR RED DOG

The purpose of this drill is to give the linebackers practice in "red dogging."

INSTRUCTIONS:

(1) At the end of practice take the linebackers off to one side of the field versus a reserve or freshman group.

(2) The linebackers should have signals; for example, "Joe" could mean that the left linebacker will shoot.

(3) "Jim" could mean the right linebacker shoots and "let's go," could mean both linebackers shoot.

(4) Five minutes is sufficient.

(5) See Illustration 353.

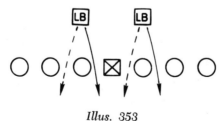

Illus. 353

28. HOW TO DRILL FOR FAKING

The purpose of this drill is to give the linebacker practice in observing who has the ball. If live he also gets tackling practice.
INSTRUCTIONS:

(1) Place either a complete or partial backfield on offense with a center.

(2) Station a linebacker on defense.

(3) The halfbacks cross and the Q.B. can either fake or give.

(4) See Illustration 354.

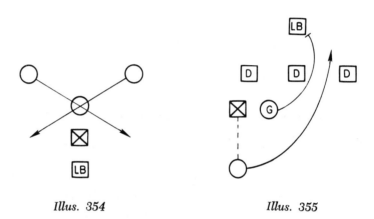

Illus. 354   *Illus. 355*

29. HOW TO DRILL FOR BACKING UP THE LINE

This in an excellent combination offensive and defensive run, but designed to provide practice for a linebacker.
INSTRUCTIONS:

(1) Place a center, an offensive guard, and a back on offense.

(2) Line up dummies and a linebacker on defense.

(3) Offensive back may cut in holes 1, 2, or 3.

(4) Linebacker comes up fast, plays guard and attempts to prevent over-running of the play which is a major fault.

(5) See Illustration 355.

30. HOW TO DRILL FOR TACKLING

The object of this drill is to improve tackling, reactions and pursuit for the linebackers.

INSTRUCTIONS:

(1) Place two standing dummies 15 yards apart.

(2) Station two linebackers between the dummies.

(3) Line up at least four or five reserve backs to act as ball carriers.

(4) See Illustration 356.

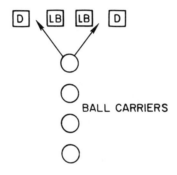

Illus. 356

31. HOW TO TRAIN A LINEBACKER TO STAY AT HOME

The best way to develop a linebacker is to have him work under game conditions. This drill is set up with that thought in mind.

INSTRUCTIONS:

(1) Select a complete backfield and one center.

(2) Have these five men execute their plays as they would in a game.

(3) Have the linebackers protect his territory and play the ball.

(4) Set up six dummies with enough spacing to allow a back to run through.

(5) This drill may be used dummy or live.

(6) See Illustration 357.

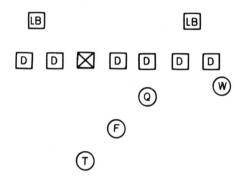

Illus. 357

32. HOW TO DRILL THE LINEBACKER ON CHUG-GING ENDS

The purpose of this drill is to develop the linebacker in his responsibilities on the passing game.

INSTRUCTIONS:

(1) Place two ends, a center, and a quarterback on offense.

(2) Place two linebackers on defense in front of the ends.

(3) When the ball is snapped, the ends try every maneuver to escape, while the backer does everything within his power to knock him off balance and prevent him from going down field.

(4) See Illustration 358.

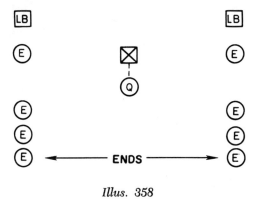

Illus. 358

13

TEAM DRILLS

*The team is the wheel, the players the
spokes, the coach, the hub.*
— G. H. A.

A DIVERSIFIED PROGRAM OF TEAM DRILLS IS A COACHING NECESSITY.
It permits the coach to direct either a large or small squad in
an efficient manner, and maintains player interest through the
rotation of drills.

Since team drills involve many players, the coach must
definitely control the practice tempo of the group. Team
drills require much more organization and discipline than do
individual drills.

The fundamentals of football are supposed to have been
carefully taught and thoroughly learned in the early training
weeks of the season. But a team oftentimes wanders away
from the first principles. This may come about through the

carelessness of either the coach or the players, or because the minds of the players and coaches have become focused on team play to such an extent that they have forgotten there is such a thing as individual play.

Accordingly, it becomes necessary at such times to go back to the grinding drills of the early season practice. At any rate some time must be taken from team maneuvers as the coach must concentrate on regaining lost individual performance. It is never safe to ease up on signal and offensive dummy drills. They are ideal drills that should be utilized at least three days a week throughout the entire season. Team drills are worthless unless the *FIRST basic fundamentals of football have been properly taught and well absorbed by the players.*

The team drills included in this chapter cover all phases of football from conditioning the players to actual body contact.

1. HOW TO DRILL FOR TEAM DUMMY SCRIMMAGE

The purpose of this drill is to allow all squad members to participate in dummy scrimmage.

INSTRUCTIONS:

(1) Organize as many teams as the size of the squad will permit.

(2) One team plays defense while the other teams run offensive plays.

(3) Each team plays on defense for ten plays.

(4) The teams alternate as follows. Team No. 1 becomes No. 4; 4 becomes 3; 3 becomes 2; and 2 takes the place of 1.

(5) See Illustration 359.

2. HOW TO DRILL FOR CADENCE CHARGING

A certain cadence and rhythm must be developed and maintained by all members of the squad in order to insure precise timing.   This drill is useful in obtaining that objective.

INSTRUCTIONS:

(1) Divide the squad into groups of eleven men.

(2) Each group should have a quarterback or signal caller.

(3) Have the players line up side by side and assume a regular offensive stance.

(4) Each signal caller then takes the responsibility of call-

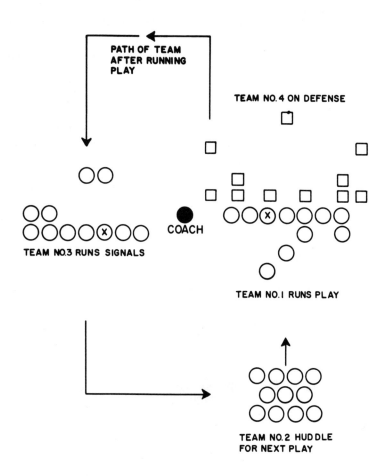

PATH OF TEAM
AFTER RUNNING
PLAY

TEAM NO. 4 ON DEFENSE

COACH

TEAM NO.3 RUNS SIGNALS

TEAM NO.I RUNS PLAY

TEAM NO.2 HUDDLE
FOR NEXT PLAY

Illus. 359

ing out the starting signal and giving the count in regular
cadence.

(5) Players charge on the number designated by the signal
caller.

(6) Have each squad charge for a distance of ten yards.

(7) Station coaches in the center of the field and the players
then proceed around the field in their respective groups.

(8) The coaches are in position to see who the high chargers
are and can offer suggestions.

(9) See Illustration 360.

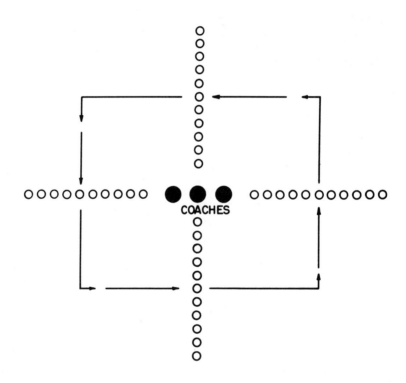

Illus. 360

3. HOW TO DRILL FOR COVERAGE AND RETURN OF PUNTS

This team drill is designed to nullify the effectiveness of a good kicking team by returning punts as well as to provide practice in punting and coverage of punts.

INSTRUCTIONS:

(1) Line up a complete kicking team with substitutes on offense.

(2) Locate a complete team with replacements on defense.

(3) Players alternate after every punt, or after every three.

(4) The coaching staff should check on the following:

    (a) Punting

    (b) Receiving and returning punts

    (c) Ends downfield

    (d) Blocking ends

    (e) Blocking punts

    (f) Protection

(5) Time should be given to this phase of the game at least once a week and any one or all of the kicking parts may be emphasized.

(6) See Illustration 361.

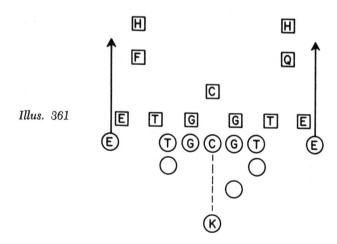

Illus. 361

4. HOW TO DRILL FOR SIGNALS

The purpose of this drill is to provide practice in starting, to improve the team's timing, and also to serve as a conditioner by running the players.

INSTRUCTIONS:

(1) Line up as many teams of eleven men as possible and have them run their regular signal pattern.

(2) Each team should have a quarterback in command.

(3) Station at least two coaches in the center of the field and have the teams run signals around the field in their respective groups.

(4) Have the players drive hard for five yards and relax for five yards; that is all that is necessary.

(5) Do not allow men to assume their stance just before the ball is snapped because this would be telegraphing the start signal. Instead, have them assume their stance just before the last series or, if in huddle, from the time they reach the line of scrimmage.

(6) Have players visualize a man in front of them on different plays in relation to the play called.

(7) On back plays, the line should drive with proper double-teaming, making holes, and so forth.

(8) Interior line should not charge on passes and kicks. Have them yell and encourage receiver to drive harder.

(9) On runs, reverses, and so on, run hard and follow possible direction of pulling men.

(10) If signal drill is long, have the men line up fast and rest on one knee, because it is possible to get in more plays.

(11) After each lineup for the next play, have absolute silence.

(12) After the ball is snapped, the men should yell out to

one another in regard to their respective weak points. (Coach should let the men know these weak points until corrected or improved.)

(13) See Illustration 362.

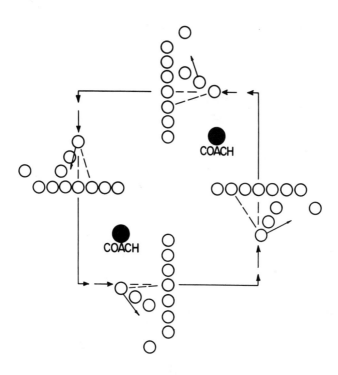

Illus. 362

5. HOW TO DRILL FOR PASSING SIGNALS

This is a combination pass drill designed to provide practice for both the offense and defense.

INSTRUCTIONS:

(1) Line up three sets of backs and ends on offense with a center.

(2) Place two linebackers, two halfbacks and a safety man on defense.

(3) Have the quarterback run all pass plays.

(4) Rotate the teams every ten plays.

(5) Have a manager record the completions and interceptions to create competition.

(6) See Illustration 363.

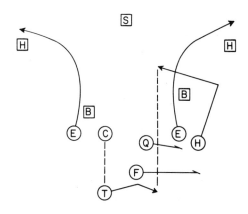

Illus. 363

6. HOW TO DRILL FOR FORWARD PASS SCRIMMAGE

The object of this drill is to have all players active in the forward passing game with emphasis on developing the passing offense.

INSTRUCTIONS:

(1) Line up a complete team on offense.

(2) Place another team of eleven men on defense.

(3) Have every player active, but allow no tackling.

(4) Instruct the members of the defensive team to tag the passer or receiver.

(5) Have the offensive team call only pass plays.

(6) The offensive team keeps the ball until it is lost on downs or intercepted, or a touchdown has been scored. Then the two teams reverse positions.

(7) See Illustration **364**.

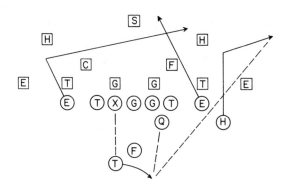

Illus. 364

7. HOW TO DRILL FOR KICK-OFF COVERAGE

*The purpose of this drill is to practice covering kick-offs with
every man on the squad getting work.*

INSTRUCTIONS:

(1) A kick-off play is considered by many as one of the
easiest plays in football on which to score a touchdown.

(2) The reasoning lies in the fact that many times a kicking team sends its men down in only one line of tacklers instead of parading the men down in waves; i.e., fast men first,
slower men in a second wave, and finally the safety men who
protect against a possible return kick or against the possibility
of a ball carrier breaking through the first two waves of defenders.

(3) Regardless of what system a team employs, time
should be allotted to this phase of the game in regular practice
sessions.

(4) This is a "tag" dummy drill.

(5) Line up a complete kick-off team on offense.

(6) Station a complete receiving team on defense.

(7) Place different colored vests on the kicking team.

(8) Drill on exact coverage by using a whistle to stop any
faulty play.

(9) Alternate teams kicking and receiving.

(10) See Illustration 365.

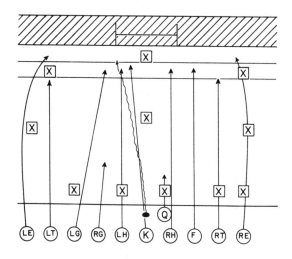

Illus. 365

8. HOW TO DRILL FOR PASS SCRIMMAGE

The purpose of this drill is to create a competitive contest whereby the pass offensive and defensive units function at the same time. It gives the offense practice in protecting the passer and the defense practice in rushing the passer.

INSTRUCTIONS:

(1) Line up the offensive and defensive teams in regular positions for a scrimmage.

(2) There is no tackling in this drill.

(3) The defensive team will *tag* the passer or pass receiver.

(4) The offensive team calls only pass plays.

(5) The offense keeps the ball until it is lost on downs or intercepted, or a touchdown is scored.

(6) The defensive linemen rush the passer to tag him.

(7) The offensive linemen attempt to protect the passer.

9. HOW TO DRILL FOR NUMBERED DOWNFIELD BLOCKING

The object of this drill is to teach downfield blocking and have fun at the same time.

INSTRUCTIONS:

(1) Place six dummies in three rows five yards apart.

(2) Assign a number to teach dummy and position a player to hold each bag.

(3) Have a coach call any number as the blocker approaches the dummies after a run of five yards.

(4) After the first block the coach calls another number so that the player may react and block that particular dummy.

(5) See Illustration 366.

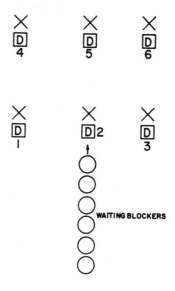

Illus. 366

10. HOW TO DRILL FOR TEAM DOWNFIELD BLOCKING

The object of this drill is to teach downfield blocking with two complete teams.

INSTRUCTIONS:

(1) Place a full team of eleven players on offense.

(2) Station a complete team of eleven men on defense.

(3) Instruct everybody on each team to remain passive except the three deep defensive secondary men.

(4) Have each coach concentrate on watching his own men and encourage them to get downfield.

(5) Insist on blocking through the defensive man.

(6) See Illustration 367.

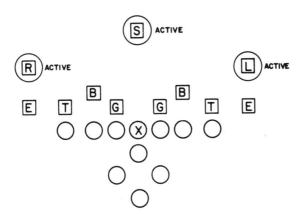

Illus. 367

11. HOW TO DRILL FOR DOWNFIELD BLOCKING AND TACKLING

This drill is designed to teach and practice downfield blocking. The drill will also improve tackling.

INSTRUCTIONS:

(1) Place three backs on offense with three blockers in two lines, four yards apart.

(2) Locate six tacklers on defensive, three in each line, four yards apart.

(3) Fifteen yards should separate the offense from the defense.

(4) Start by having the coach throw a ball to the first back in line, who follows his blocker downfield.

(5) The tacklers approach one at a time and attempt to tackle the runner.

(6) The blocker should use a shoulder block and stay on his feet to meet the second tackler.

(7) See Illustration 368.

12. HOW TO DRILL FOR DOWNFIELD BLOCKING

The object of this drill is to perfect the downfield blocking.

INSTRUCTIONS:

(1) Place three dummies in triangular position.

(2) Assign a player to hold each dummy.

(3) Locate the blockers in a line five yards from the nearest dummy.

(4) Station a coach on either side of the blocking line.

(5) The lead man in the line makes a good shoulder block on the first dummy and follows through.

(6) The coach shouts "right" or "left" and the blocker reacts accordingly. The blocker executes a running shoulder block on the dummy called.

(7) See Illustrations 369a and 369b.

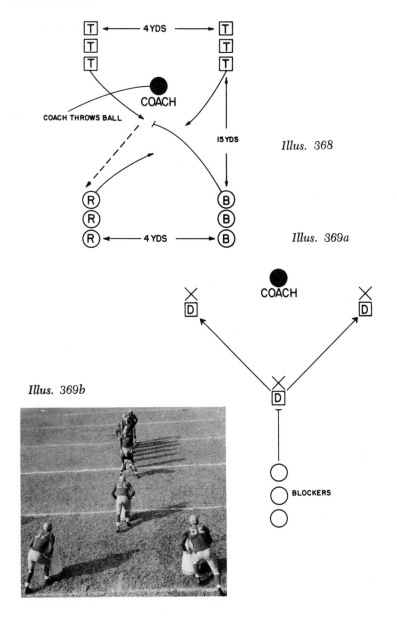

T ←—— 4 YDS ——→ T
T T T T

COACH

COACH THROWS BALL

15 YDS

Illus. 368

R B
R B
R ←—— 4 YDS ——→ B

Illus. 369a

COACH

D D

D

Illus. 369b

BLOCKERS

13. HOW TO DRILL FOR DOWNFIELD BLOCKING

This drill is designed to practice and improve downfield blocking.

INSTRUCTIONS:

(1) This drill was invented by one of the author's assistant coaches, Fred Burri.

(2) Line up five dummies in a row, five yards apart, with players holding them.

(3) Place another standing dummy approximately seven yards from the starting point.

(4) Have the players count off by five and see that each man has a different number each time.

(5) The players pull around the standing dummy and consecutively block the five bags downfield.

(6) Alternate dummy holders frequently.

(7) See Illustrations 370a, 370b, and 370c.

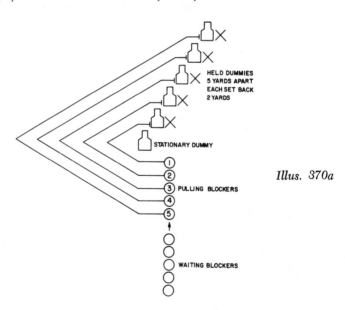

Illus. 370a

Illus. 370b   Same drill to the right with three dummies held.

Illus. 370c

14. HOW TO DRILL FOR TEAM DEFENSE

The object of this drill is to allow a reserve team to run more plays in a shorter time when preparing for an opponent.

INSTRUCTIONS:

(1) Line up a full team on offense to run opponent's plays, but emphasize only running plays.

(2) Place a skeleton team of a center, two ends, and a backfield. Have this skeleton unit throw only passes.

(3) Have both teams read their plays and passing patterns from diagrams printed on 11" x 16" tagboard.

(4) While the offensive team is running a play, the skeleton pass team is receiving a pass pattern. With this method it is possible to run off almost twice as many plays as would be possible with just one team.

(5) Assign a coach with the defensive backs. While the offensive team is running off its play, the coach can offer suggestions to the secondary.

(6) Put a coach in charge of the line. While the skeleton team is operating, have this coach offer suggestions to the linemen on possible mistakes made on the previous play.

(7) See Illustration 371.

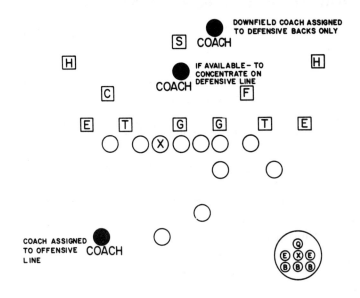

Illus. 371

15. HOW TO DRILL FOR DUMMY DEFENSIVE SCRIMMAGE

The object of this drill is to practice dummy defensive scrimmage.

INSTRUCTIONS:

(1) Place a complete team on defense against an offensive eleven.

(2) Have the offensive team run wide, right and left, slants off tackle, up the middle over the guards, or retreat to pass.

(3) Instruct the defensive team to reach and pursue these many offensive maneuvers.

(4) Note the defensive men with quick reaction.

16. HOW TO DRILL FOR RUNNING THE MAZE

The object of this drill is to test each member of the squad for agility.

INSTRUCTIONS:

(1) Place five bell bottom dummies ten yards apart.

(2) Have each player run and weave through the positioned dummies.

(3) Time each man and post his performance on the bulletin board.

(4) A back should be able to run the course under 12 seconds.

(5) A lineman should be able to run the course under 13 seconds.

(6) See Illustrations 372a and 372b.

Illus. 372a

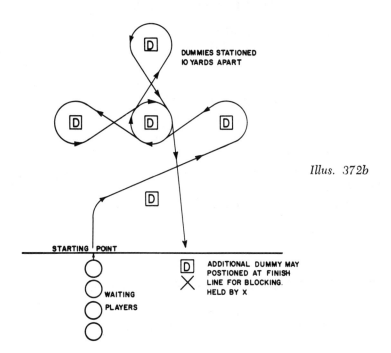

DUMMIES STATIONED
IO YARDS APART

Illus. 372b

STARTING POINT

WAITING

PLAYERS

ADDITIONAL DUMMY MAY
POSTIONED AT FINISH
LINE FOR BLOCKING.
HELD BY X

17. HOW TO DRILL FOR PLAY RECOGNITION

This drill is designed to allow the defensive team to become familiar with an opponent's offense.

INSTRUCTIONS:

(1) Select a complete reserve team to run the opponent's plays.

(2) Place a complete team on defense.

(3) Have the defensive line hit hard for contact, and then pursue the runner, but without tackling.

(4) This drill allows the defensive team to carry out its assignments comparable to game conditions.

18. HOW TO DRILL FOR GAME SIGNALS

The object of this drill is to have several teams run signals before the game begins so that they become accustomed to the crowd.

INSTRUCTIONS:

(1) Select two or three teams to run signals on the field.

(2) Have them run straight up and down the field near one sideline.   Use the hash marks as a guide for the center to position the ball.

(3) Instruct the quarterback to employ running, passing, and kicking plays.

(4) Five minutes for game signals is sufficient.

19. HOW TO DRILL FOR STRATEGY SIGNALS

The purpose of this drill is to acquaint the quarterback with tactical situations on the field while running signals.

INSTRUCTIONS:

(1) Line up one complete offensive team.

(2) Have the quarterback take one team up and down the field.

(3) The coach creates tactical situations and allows the quarterback to call the play.

(4) If the quarterback calls the right play, the coach will say "second down and four."   This gives the quarterback credit for a good call before the entire team.

(5) When in the area of increased resistance, the coach tells the quarterback to anticipate an eight man line.

(6) If the quarterback calls the right play, he gets a touchdown.

(7) After much training, the quarterback's signal calling gets to be a matter of reflex action.   When he reaches a certain area on the field, he knows what to do.

20. HOW TO DRILL FOR THE INDIAN WAR DANCE

This drill is designed to train the players for proper body position and foot work agility.

INSTRUCTIONS:

(1) Line up the entire squad in rows six deep.

(2) Have the players assume a semi-erect football position. The players must have a bend at the knees, elbows at thigh level, head up, and tail low with weight forward.

(3) At a signal from the coach the players commence to move their feet by running in place with quick short steps.

(4) The players while running in place may be given a signal to use half turns while performing the "War Dance."

(5) After three minutes, have the players by positions compete against each other to see who reacts the fastest.

(6) See Illustration 373.

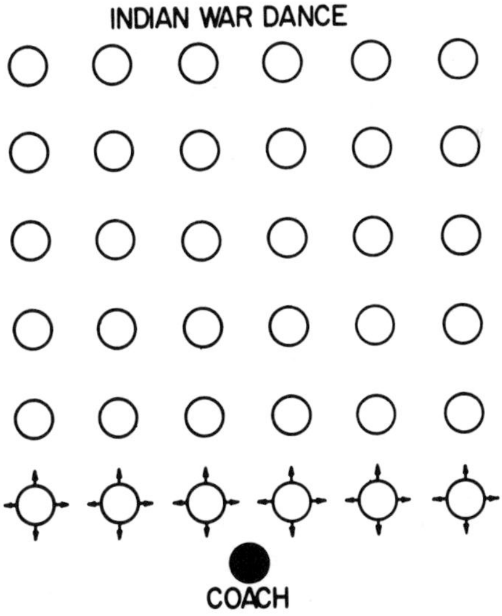

Illus. 373

21. HOW TO DRILL FOR WIND SPRINTS

The object of this drill is to provide variation in wind sprints at the conclusion of practice.

INSTRUCTIONS:

(1) Line up three or four teams (depending upon the size of the squad) on the sideline.

(2) Start them off one at a time with a running play and have them go full speed for 30 yards.

(3) They must continue until they get to the other side. Then they turn around and go back.

(4) Have each team run this sequence until one team is rewarded by being sent to the showers first.

(5) If the teams are sluggish in wind sprints, ask for three consecutive long beat hold plays.

22. HOW TO DRILL FOR "BURMA ROAD"

The purpose of this drill is to practice downfield blocking. This is also an excellent conditioning drill for early season work.

INSTRUCTIONS:

(1) Place eight dummies staggered in a diamond formation. The dummies are positioned ten yards apart.

(2) Assign a player to hold each dummy.

(3) Line up the remainder of the squad facing the first dummy.

(4) On a whistle, the first player starts fast, runs ten yards and executes a right shoulder block.

(5) Next he scrambles to his feet and continues to the second dummy using a left shoulder block, and so on.

(6) After the lead man has cleared the first dummy, the

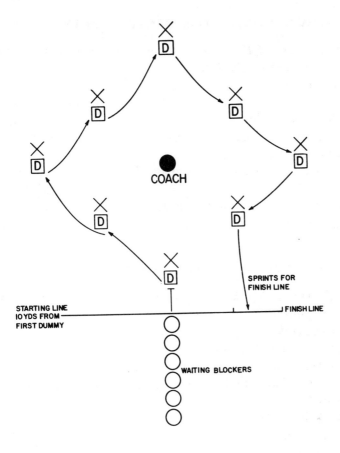

Illus. 374

second man starts and this continues until the entire squad has blocked the eight dummies.

(7) Replace the men holding the dummies after three blocks, or use members of the freshman team.

(8) This drill is an excellent conditioner for the entire squad.

(9) See Illustration 374.

23. HOW TO DRILL FOR PERFECT PLAYS

The purpose of this drill is to see how many perfect plays can be run in two minutes.

INSTRUCTIONS:

(1) Line up three teams and have them break from the huddle to run a play.

(2) Place coaches in positions indicated to observe each player's actions.

(3) See how many perfect plays each team can run in two minutes.

(4) Allow the winning team to go in early.

(5) See Illustration 376.

24. HOW TO DRILL FOR SHORT PULLING

The purpose of this drill is to provide practice for linemen on short pulling.

INSTRUCTIONS:

(1) Place eight linemen in a straight line.

(2) Have the linemen count off by two's.

(3) Then have the No. 1 men pull around the 2's, all at the same time.

(4) When the No. 1 men return, have the No. 2 men pull around them.

(5) This drill gives the linemen work on the shorter pulls.

(6) See Illustrations 375a and 375b.

Illus. 375a

Illus. 375b

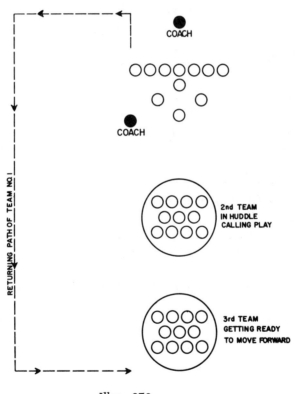

Illus. 376

25. HOW TO DRILL FOR SCRAMBLED EGGS

This drill is designed to complete the practice session by providing the men with a review of the essential fundamentals of football. The fundamentals involved in this drill are: running, pulling, blocking, tackling, dodging, and falling on a loose football.

INSTRUCTIONS:

(1) Divide the entire squad into two equal teams.

(2) Assign two players from each squad to hold dummies. The holders rotate after each turn.

(3) Position dummies as indicated in diagram.   Insist that all players run, block, and tackle at full speed.

(4) Anyone knocking down a standing dummy must run the course over.

(5) Begin by having the lead men from each file "crab" for 10 yards.   They come to a complete stop and assume their stance on a signal from the coach.

(6) Next have them run laterally for 5 yards, pull around a standing dummy, and block a held dummy.

(7) Then they run for 15 yards and tackle another held dummy.   Continuing they dodge three more standing dummies, being careful not to bump any of them.

(8) To complete the drill they sprint ten yards and recover a thrown ball.

(9) Create competition between the two groups by observing which unit can make the best blocks, tackles, and so forth, in the shortest possible time.   Insist on performance.

(10) See Illustration 377.

26. HOW TO DRILL FOR INDIVIDUAL WIND SPRINTS

The object of this drill is to run wind sprints by grouping the men in positions.

INSTRUCTIONS:

(1) Just running wind sprints with nothing gained is drudgery, even if you win.

(2) Group the men by positions and try to find the fastest man for each position.

(3) Then run the winners for each position in two or three races.

(4) This method provides the players with an extra reward while running.

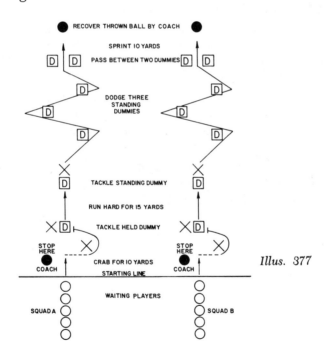

Illus. 377

27. HOW TO DRILL FOR SET-UP BLOCKING AND TACKLING

The purpose of this drill is threefold: to practice tackling, to train the ball carriers in setting up their blocks, and to develop the linemen in blocking.

INSTRUCTIONS:

(1) Place three dummies in a triangle five yards apart.

(2) Assign three reserve players to hold these dummies.

(3) Have three files of players. Two files act as blockers and the other as ball carriers.

(4) Position tacklers five yards downfield and have them alternate one at a time.

(5) The blockers may block any of the three dummies, except that one blocker must always block the lead dummy.

(6) Have the runner break, off the blocker's tail, and cut sharply. This maneuver will improve the reactions of the ball carriers because they never know which way the blocker will contact the dummy.

(7) The tackler downfield approaches as far as the lead dummy and attempts to tackle the runner.

(8) Insist on the blockers driving for five yards after contact.

(9) This drill was originated by Harold Jones, one of our assistant football coaches.

(10) See Illustration 378.

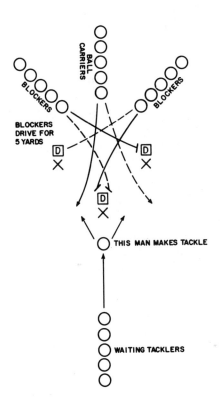

Illus. 378

28. HOW TO DRILL FOR PRE-GAME RELAXATION

This drill is designed to control and possibly eliminate the effects of pre-competition tension. The drill can be of great aid to the tense coach.

INSTRUCTIONS:

(1) May be done either standing, sitting or even lying down.

(2) Have the players take a deep breath, hold it for a moment and then *slightly* tense all the muscles in the body—legs, stomach, arms, shoulders, neck and jaw.

(3) Keep them holding their breath for five or six seconds as the muscles are tensed. Then have them exhale slowly, letting the muscles go as limp as possible on the exhale.

(4) Repeat this procedure nine or ten times, trying to go more limp each time.

(5) Associate the relaxation with a word or idea, e.g., "Let go," "Loose and easy," "Relax!"

(6) Ask the players to picture themselves hanging on a nail like dishrags.

29. HOW TO DRILL FOR CHAMPS AND CHUMPS

The purpose of this drill is to provide another method of conditioning wtih variation.

INSTRUCTIONS:

(1) Line up seven players on the 10-yard line with two yards spacing between each player.

(2) Have the players run 10 yards and do 15 push ups on the 20-yard line.

(3) Next they run to the 30-yard line and do 15 set-ups.

(4) Upon competion of the set-ups they sprint back to the starting line.

(5) Any number of push-ups or set-ups may be used. Alter exercises and obstacles may be substituted.

(6) The chumps have to run the entire length of the field and back while the champs cheer.

(7) See Illustration 379.

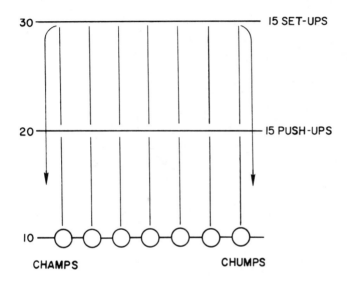

Illus. 379

30. HOW TO DRILL FOR THE SEVEN-MAN DUMMY

The object of this drill is to train the men to move as a unit. It requires constant drilling.

INSTRUCTIONS:

(1) Line up seven dummies on defense. Each dummy is to be held by members of the reserve squad.

(2) Position a dummy over every offensive lineman. Place the dummies two feet from the offensive linemen. Go on a quick count.

(3) Next, move the dummies a yard and a half from the line of scrimmage. This provides training in applying blocks with men off set.

(4) Third, with the dummies off the line at least one yard have the men holding the dummies move them in the direction indicated by the coach.

(5) Drilling against moving men enables the offense to gain confidence against stunting defenses.

(6) See Illustration 380.

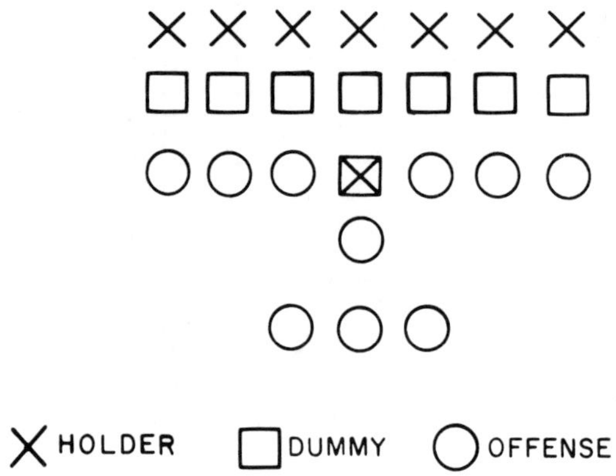

Illus. 380

31. HOW TO DRILL FOR THE CAROUSEL

The object of this drill is to relax the players and have fun when warming up before practice.

INSTRUCTIONS:

(1) Place nine dummies in a large circle five yards apart.

(2) As the players reach the practice field have them run in and around the dummies at half speed prior to calisthenics.

(3) See Illustration 381.

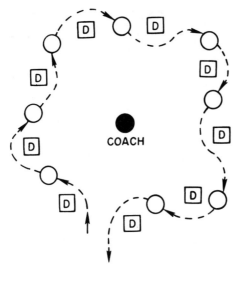

Illus. 381

32. HOW TO DRILL FOR THE THREE MAN LATERAL

The purpose of this drill is to provide conditioning and ball handling for all members of the team.

INSTRUCTIONS:

(1) Divide the squad into two complete teams with half of each team on the two goal lines.

(2) Three men run at the same time from one goal line to the other lateraling the ball back and forth.

(3) This is an excellent drill for ball handling, since the lateral is almost as important as the individual's speed.

(4) See Illustration 382.

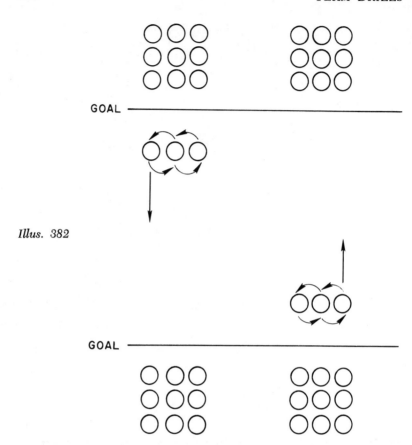

Illus. 382

33. HOW TO DRILL FOR ONE STEP SIGNALS

The purpose of this drill is to practice team takeoff and assignments, yet not run the play.

INSTRUCTIONS:

(1) Line up four complete offensive teams in a square formation.

(2) Place one coach in the center of the square. If more coaches are available, assign one to each team.

(3) Have quarterbacks alternate calling plays for the four teams as well as the cadence. This is also good practice in voice control for the quarterbacks, since they must "sing-out" to be heard by all four units.

(4) Each team takes only the first step in the execution of individual assignment on the play called.

(5) All four teams should go off in unison. If one team, or an individual, is late in executing his assignment, it is quite obvious.

(6) See Illustration 383.

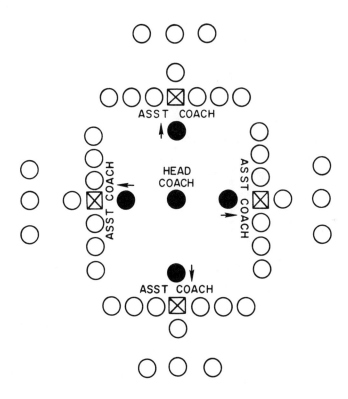

Illus. 383

34. HOW TO DRILL FOR GOAL TO GOAL RELAY

The purpose of this drill is to provide running for condition-ing with competition.

INSTRUCTIONS:

(1) Divide the squad into two complete teams with half of each team on the two goal lines.

(2) Each player runs a sprint relay race from one goal line to the other.

(3) Have each runner carry a ball and hand-off to the front man in line at the other end of the field.

(4) This drill provides wind sprint practice without drudgery.

(5) See Illustration 384.

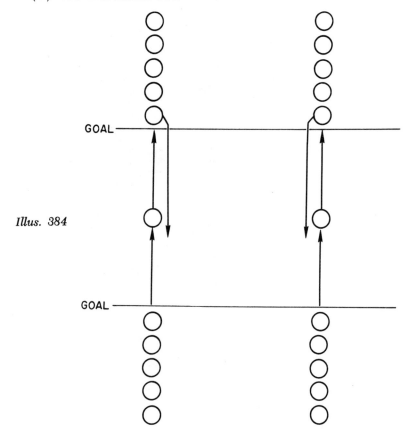

Illus. 384

35. HOW TO IMPROVE TEAM TAKE-OFF

The idea here is to do something different and yet effective to impress importance of team takeoff.

INSTRUCTIONS:

(1) Simply use a regular track-starter's gun with blank shells.

(2) Have all the men count together at first and then use the gun to impress on the team the importance of the takeoff.

36. HOW TO DRILL FOR KICKING ORGANIZATION

The purpose of this drill is to organize the team so that no time is wasted and no one is idle while practicing punting, covering, conditioning, centering, and receiving.

INSTRUCTIONS:

(1) Place the interior linemen in two lines and have them alternate sides in covering.

(2) Place the ends on their respective sides and have them alternate sides in covering.

(3) Locate a center and several punters on offense. Use an assistant center to hand the balls to the active center. If several centers are available station them downfield to act as assistants to return the footballs.

(4) Station several receivers in single file order to catch and *field* every kicked ball. They return the kick approximately 20 yards and then throw the ball to an assistant.

(5) See Illustration 385.

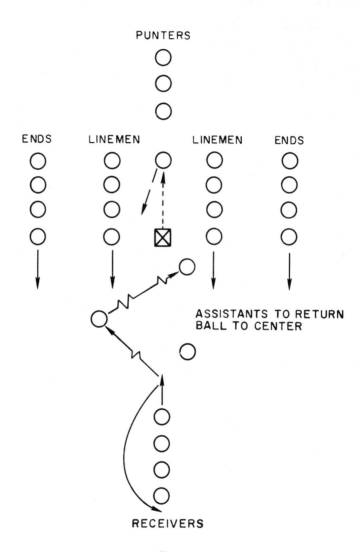

Illus. 385

37. HOW TO DRILL FOR THE CANVAS STRIP

The purpose of this drill is to give the offensive team something to align themselves on and also to drill on staying low after the takeoff.

INSTRUCTIONS:

(1) Place an entire team on offense and have them line up on the canvas strip.

(2) Locate a long piece of rope approximately one yard away from the initial starting point. Use the sled or stakes driven in the ground to fasten the rope.

(3) The team charges on a pre-determined snap signal by the quarterback and they must stay low to get under the rope. See Illustration 386a.

(4) The same canvas strip may be used as a dividing line for offense and defense. See Illustration 386b.

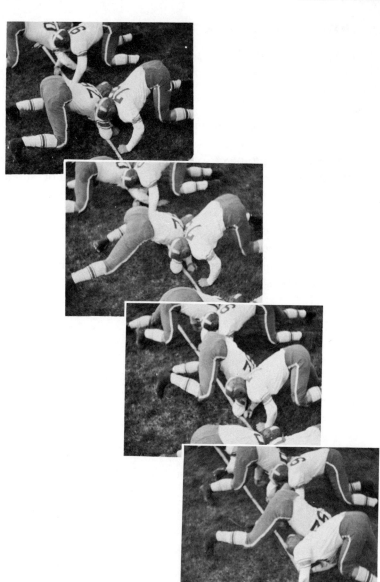

Illus. 386a

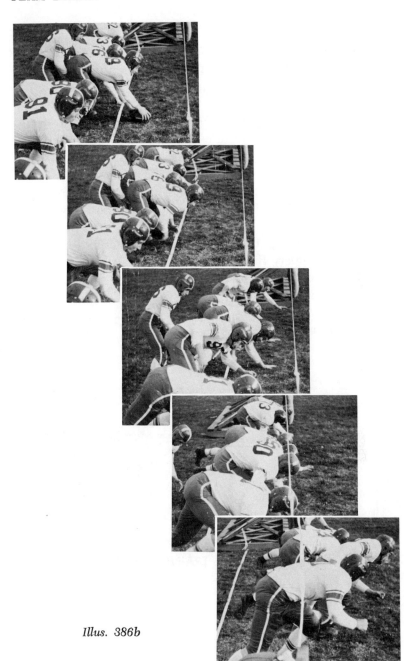

Illus. 386b

38. HOW TO DRILL FOR HIT AND GO

The purpose of this team training sled is that it allows full team signal drills without anyone holding the dummies. Each player may block and then go downfield.

INSTRUCTIONS:

(1) Line up the complete offensive eleven versus the training sled.

(2) Have the center vary his position of alignment, so that the linemen can practice against different defenses.

(3) The quarterback calls the play and the players block and then release downfield. Backs may run almost any course they desire.

(4) This hit-and-go training sled is manufactured by Track and Field of Slippery Rock, Penna.

(5) The sled may be used for conventional things such as body toughening, rip up, pursuit, slanting, hitting on the count, etc.

(6) See Illustration 387.

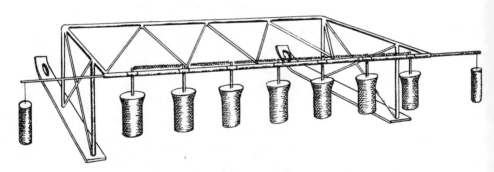

HIT-AND-GO TEAM TRAINING SLED

Illus. 387

39. HOW TO DRILL FOR MASS BLOCKING

The object of this drill is to provide blocking practice for the entire squad in the shortest possible time.

INSTRUCTIONS:

(1) Line up the entire squad in separate files according to positions.

(2) Station eleven blocking dummies five yards downfield. Allow four yards spacing between each dummy.

(3) Assign eleven freshmen players to hold the dummies. Have seven linemen and four backs from the frosh squad. The freshmen backs hold the bags for the varsity backs and the linemen do likewise.

(4) The players run five yards and block with either a right or left shoulder block according to the coach's signals.

(5) Have the coaches positioned in the areas represented so that every detail can be observed.

(6) Make this a fast moving drill with plenty of noise.

(7) See Illustration 388.

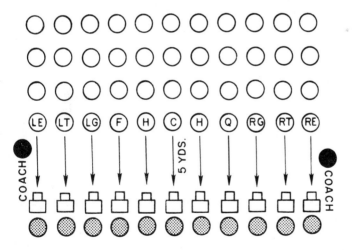

Illus. 388

Part IV

THE CONDITIONING GAME

14

ORGANIZING THE

CONDITIONING DRILLS

BEFORE STARTING THE CONDITIONING DRILL THE COACH SHOULD have his squad report to a specific place and at a given time. The drills should commence *exactly on time*. Use either end zone for your conditioning exercises. This is desirable if the practice session takes place on the same field where scheduled games are played.

Have all the coaches out in front of the group. Each coach does the preliminary exercise to help get the men started with enthusiasm. After the players are off to a good start, only the captain and the coach assigned to lead the drill continue movements. The others walk among the men and offer encouragement. Informality is desirable at this time.

Each exercise should have a name. This helps the men to remember the drill. The name should be called out in a loud clear voice and followed by a brief demonstration. Use football terminology whenever possible. The conditioning period can become dull and monotonous if the coach is careless. Therefore everyone should make an effort to see that plenty of enthusiasm and pep are put into each drill. Have the men count cadence whenever possible. The coach may have the entire squad chant a slogan about defeating that week's opponent.

This chant may be used all during the week. A constant flow of chatter should come from the coach leading the squad. Always change from one exercise to another without a waste of time. Do not overdo one exercise, but cover all of them on the program with fewer repetitions. Exercises named after squad members have *great appeal* and each coach should have at least two. Do everything possible to keep this period moving fast. Get plenty of work done by having fun.

As previously mentioned, the squad should know the value of each drill and its relation to particular aspects of football. In this method, each member of the squad becomes responsible for applying the drill to his particular shortcomings.

The coach is the key to a successful conditioning program. His pep, enthusiasm and spirit will determine how well the exercises are performed and the values derived by the men.

Circle formation

Circle formations may be used to vary the conditioning procedure. They are excellent for a strenuous workout. Players are required to jog in a clockwise direction, while the exercises are being taught, except the stationary drills. Instructions should be simple and direct. Succeeding exercises are explained while the players continue to jog. Use a stationary exercise and follow it with a running drill. The alternating procedure allows a maximum amount of conditioning in a minimum amount of time. If the squad numbers over fifty men, it is better to employ two circles. See Illustration 389.

As shown in Illustration 390, the square formation is also popularly used in conditioning workouts.

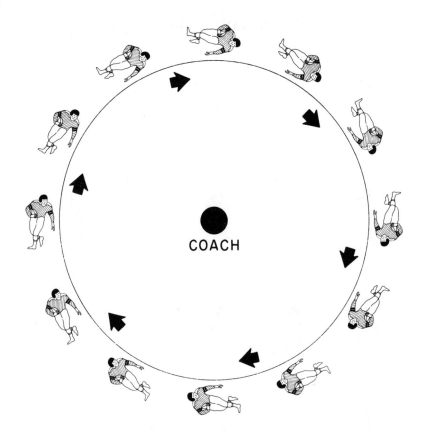

Illus. 389

THE SQUARE FORMATION

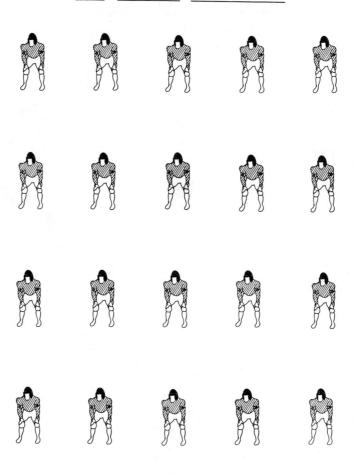

Illus. 390

COACH

15

PRE-GAME WARM-UP DRILL

> *Now is the time to warm-up, not condition*
> G.H.A.

IN DOING RESEARCH ON PRE-GAME WARM-UP, THE AUTHOR DIS-
covered a lack of description of specific warm-up exercises.
However, all coaches mention the importance of the pre-game
warm-up. It is possible that coaches assume the warm-up
should be discussed in the study of physiology, which is an
integral part of the professional training of the coach. We
think perhaps the absence of written material on the warm-up
accounts for the lack of uniformity in its use. In other words,
available publications have not treated the warm-up with the
same degree of clarity and exactness that they have the tech-
nical aspects of football.

In discussing the warm-up, physiologists state that the first
responses at the beginning of any activity are irregular and
indicate erratic performance. This tendency toward erratic
performance is ever present and is to be avoided in practice as
well as in competition. Authorities say the cause of irregular
responses at the beginning of exercise is the lack of uniform

optimum conditions for the best muscular contractions. In warming up, these conditions are adjusted. Since there is an increase in body temperature, there is an improvement in the tonus of muscle (its readiness to respond). Through an improvement in circulation and respiration, a uniformity of temperature is brought about. Thus, the ability to respond is equalized in the muscles of the body.

Concerning the question of the warm-up, the position which the physiologists take is as follows: If the temperature of the body rises only slightly it will increase the efficiency of the muscles. Furthermore, it is said that warming up of an athlete increases the secretion of adrenalin and accounts in part for the beneficial influences obtained. This secretion increases with activity and varies with severity. The adrenalin increase re-enforces the nervous stimulations. The adrenalin mechanism seems to call forth a better distribution of blood to active muscles, nerve centers, heart and lungs, with an increased oxygen-carrying capacity of the blood through an increase in the number of red corpuscles.

One can readily conclude that the pre-game warm-up is regarded by both the coach and the physiologist as a *positive* procedure to be stressed prior to all vigorous competition.

Organization

A very definite warm-up plan should be prepared for the squad. This should be rehearsed prior to the day of the game. However, we do not believe in a highly organized pre-game warm-up. We prefer a specific procedure to be followed, but allowing flexibility for the men to relax. We believe this warm-up period can be overdone and that it has been in many instances. We have watched teams with warm-up drills that were so precise and militant that they appeared to have played at least a quarter of the game in warming up.

We like to appear on the field early. In other words we always want to be the first team on the field. There are many reasons for this. We like to take our time and eliminate the rush period. We want every kicker and receiver to be given several opportunities to kick and catch the ball and not have to quit on a poor punt or dropped pass. We want to have plenty of time when we return to the dressing room for relaxation, equipment repairs or adjustments, and final instructions.

We like to return to the field, if possible, before our opponents after the pre-game talk. We attempt to be one jump ahead of the opposing team psychologically, and yet we are taking our time because of an early appearance. We like to use the entire field for certain maneuvers; to select the end zone of our choice for calisthenics; to take advantage of tardy scouts, etc. We prefer to appear on the field 35 minutes before game time. Our pre-game drill will consume 15 minutes of that time. It requires approximately two minutes to return the entire team to the dressing room and the same time to appear on the field prior to the kick-off. This gives us ten minutes in the dressing room for announcing starting line-ups and presenting final instructions. We send the starting eleven on the field five minutes before game time and the others follow.

Equipment

There should be plenty of footballs available so that the work may be highly concentrated in the short time permitted. We want nine footballs, two kick-off tees and two conversion tees. Each player must keep his helmet on during the entire warm-up. The sideline coats should be draped over the bench. The team trainer is responsible for his sideline supplies.

The Warm-up

The procedure outlined in detail pertains only to calisthenic program.

We prefer to have the captain lead the team onto the field at a jogging pace. We designate him as the leader of the

warm-up period. The five exercises we use for warm-up are:
(1) Coordinator.
(2) Inguinal Roll.
(3) Cross Bending.
(4) High Bounding.
(5) Grass Drill.
The inguinal roll and the cross bend were discussed in chapter five. The grass drill was explained in chapter four. The pre-game grass drill is very *brief*, consisting of five commands; we are not conditioning now.

Game Skills

After the calisthenics the backs and line separate. The ends remain with the linemen for starts and signals before commencing their drills. Below is a brief breakdown of the game skills for the line, ends, and backfield men:

LINE

(1) Team Starts   (Six for each line.)
(2) Signals   (Four plays for each line.)
(3) Bang Shoulders   (On all fours.)
(4) Form Tackling   (Three each.)
(5) Passing Game   (With lineman throwing and two receivers crossing.)

ENDS

(1) Team Starts   (With line six for each line.)
(2) Signals   (With line four plays for each line.)
(3) Pitch and Catch   (Playing catch eight to 10 yards apart.)
(4) Footwork Drill   (Defensive drill meeting interference.)
(5) Receiving   (With backfield running patterns.)

BACKS

(1) Kicking (two centers and two kickers alternating.)

(2) Returning kicks (Each back has opportunity.)

(3) Long passing (Each passer throws until warm—every man has opportunity to receive—begin with hook pass.)

(4) Long passing (Each passer throws three long passes.)

(5) Interceptions (Reserve back throws balls directly to defensive backs and line-backers.)

SPECIALISTS

(1) Kick-offs (three to six kick-offs of each type.)

(2) Conversions (Six conversions; alternate centers and holders.)

(3) Field Goals (three field goals—one each from right, center and left positions on field.)

The entire pre-game warm-up should consume not more than 15 minutes.

COORDINATOR

The purpose of this drill is to stimulate circulation, respiration, and start the all-around body warm-up. To relax the men and relieve tension.

INSTRUCTIONS:

(1) Stand with feet together and the arms down at the sides.

(2) Jump to stride with the arms sideward and upward. Keep jumping, returning to the starting position, bringing arms sideward and downward. As the arms come downward kick one leg forward and touch the hands together under the leg. Alternate this forward kick with the other leg. Actually this exercise is the jumping jack with a forward leg kick.

(3) 15 to 20 repetitions.

(4) See Illustration 391.

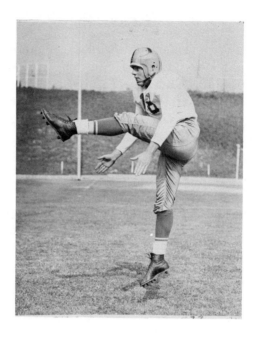

Illus. 391

HIGH BOUNDING

The purpose of this drill is to stretch the muscles of legs, knees, and ankles, to stimulate circulation in the lower extremities, and to develop balance.

INSTRUCTIONS:

(1) Stand erect with arms at side with body weight forward on toes.

(2) Jump straight upward as high as possible. Keep jumping with weight on balls of feet. Repeat in rhythm with the entire squad. One leg at a time may be used for variation.

(3) 10 to 20 repetitions.

(4) See Illustrations 392-393.

Illus. 392

Illus. 393

16
GRASS DRILL

"The Core of Conditioning"

It has always been our theory to organize the practice so that as many details as possible are patterned after things that actually occur in a game. If we had only time to teach one conditioning item it would be grass drills, which do more to promote condition, agility, and hardening of the body than any calisthenics that exist.

A very common mistake among football coaches is to devote a substantial amount of time at the start of the season to conditioning, then allow this amount to decrease when he becomes involved with the apparent need to improve skills, tactics, and strategy. Eventually the level of condition his squad attained declines and he loses the strongest weapon of all. Grass drills are the core of our early season training as well as pre-practice sessions after the schedule has commenced. We employ them every day during the entire season, but never for more than two minutes duration. As beneficial as they are, the coach must be careful not to overdo them. With grass drill overdoing is worse than underdoing.

The grass drill teaches immediate response to an oral signal. The oral command is far better than a whistle (which some coaches use) because it stimulates demands by the voice and that is what the men go on in a game. Consequently, there are mental as well as physical benefits. The grass drill demands ability to think with speed as the pace is increased.

The drill is excellent for all members of the team, regardless of size. It is especially advantageous to the slow, awkward players and improvement can soon be seen in these men.

Motivation for the grass drill may be obtained by having two linemen or two backs perform before the entire squad. Competition by positions (guards, ends, etc.) also develops interest and allows the coach to obtain maximum results. If the squad contains well over fifty men, have them form two large circles of approximately equal numbers to stimulate competition. If there are co-captains, place one in each formation to lead calisthenics and set the pace.

Always remember to adjust the grass drills according to the condition of the squad. They should be given only on a turfed area and when the ground is dry.

THE GRASS DRILL

The purpose of the grass drill is to teach body control when falling, to harden the body by contact with the ground, and to develop agility and endurance.

INSTRUCTIONS:

(1) Line up the entire squad in a standing position in several files seven feet apart, with the men seven feet apart in each file. The men begin by using the "stationary run" as a general warm up. Emphasize high knee lift with feet well spread and running on the toes. See Illustrations 394-400.

(2) At the command "front," the men fall to the ground quickly, face down, breaking the fall with the hands. Abdominal region should contact the ground. On the command "up," they leap to feet and run in place with knee action. On

command "back," they bend forward and roll back, breaking the fall by rolling to seat, and lie on the back. If the next command is "front," they revolve the body in the fastest possible manner, without rising to feet except at the command of "up." On the command "right," the men roll over one complete revolution, toward the right, on the command "left," they roll over one complete revolution toward the left. If the command "back" is given when the men are in a prone position, they squat through by supporting the weight on the hands and extending the legs between the arms and lie down. If the command "right" is given when the men are in an "up" position, they fall sideward to the right breaking the fall with the hands. On the command "faster," (which is given only in the "up" position) the men exaggerate the leg lift and stationary run as fast as possible.

After the men become accustomed to the drill, ask them to use the hands as little as possible. The order of the commands should be varied so the men cannot anticipate the next movement.

(3) Limit grass drills to one to two minutes. This is vigorous exercise and can be overdone.

(4) See Illustrations 394-400.

Illus. 394

Illus. 395

Illus. 396

Illus. 397

Illus. 398

Illus. 399

Illus. 400

17

PRE-PRACTICE DRILLS

Stretch and over-stretch

CERTAIN STRETCHING EXERCISES ARE ABSOLUTELY ESSENTIAL before each practice session. If a proper warm-up procedure is followed, the athlete cannot help but be more ready to practice and less likely to become injured. Too many football teams do not use an organized warm-up except during early-season practice when working out twice daily. After the season begins each man is allowed to warm up on his own. *We believe this is a serious mistake* and that organized "pre-practice stretching drills" are a necessity for an efficient warm-up program.

By using the term *over-stretching* we hope to gain something psychologically by making the players feel loose, relaxed, and ready for competition. These drills are designed to get the blood circulating freely throughout the entire body and prepare the heart and lungs for hard action, so that the discomfort of body adjustment can be eliminated. The body contains key areas and key muscles that need overstretching to prevent pulls. Every exercise should be purposeful with a definite

533

objective in mind. We have found that the players will perform these exercises more effectively if they know why each exercise is being given and what the coach expects to accomplish.

1. JUMPING JACK

The purpose of this drill is to stimulate circulation, respiration, and start the all-around body warm-up.

INSTRUCTIONS:

(1) Stand with feet together and the arms down at the side.

(2) Jump to stride with the arms sideward and upward. Keep jumping, returning to the starting position, bringing the arms sideward and downward with the feet together. Stress jumping on the balls of the feet.

(3) Repeat 15 to 25 times.

(Note) It is advisable that the "Jumping Jack" be used as a single, brisk exercise without over-stretching. The entire body must get up steam—the joints must be lubricated. Start perspiration before over-stretching is safe.

(4) See Illustrations 401-403.

Illus. 401

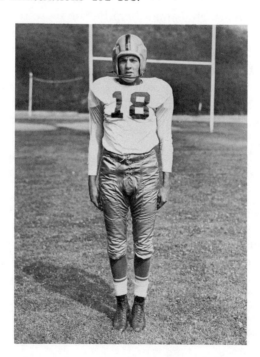

Illus. 402

Illus. 403

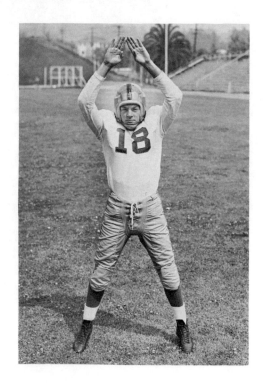

2. TRUNK ROLL

The purpose of this drill is to stretch the neck, back, legs, and shoulders and abdominal muscles.

INSTRUCTIONS:

(1) Stand with feet shoulder width apart and hands clasped behind the head.

(2) Rotate the trunk of the body in a large circle in all directions. After a while reverse the movement. Over-stretching is desirable in this exercise.

(3) Make 10-15 circles in each direction.

(4) See Illustrations 404-405.

Illus. 404

Illus. 405

Illus. 406

3. CROSS BEND

The purpose is to stretch the lateral muscles of the trunk, legs, back and shoulders.

INSTRUCTIONS:

(1) Stand erect with legs spread wide and arms extended laterally.

(2) Cross bend sideward and downward, twisting the trunk to the left, touching the far side of the left foot with the finger tips of the right hand, while extending the left arm backward and upward so that both arms are in line. Return to the starting position and reverse the procedure. Keep the knees and elbows straight.

(3) Time allowance: 10 to 15 repetitions.

(4) See Illustration 406.

4. INGUINAL ROLL

The purpose is to stretch and strengthen all the muscles in the pelvic girdle.

INSTRUCTIONS:

(1) Stand with legs spread apart.

(2) Rotate the hip outward and inward. Bend the trunk forward and downward. Repeat the process on the other side. This is an excellent exercise and if performed slowly will eliminate strain in the inguinal region.

(3) Repeat 10 to 20 times, alternating legs.

(4) See Illustration 407.

Illus. 407

5. THE ROW BOAT

The purpose of this drill is to have fun while stretching the muscles of the back and buttocks.

INSTRUCTIONS:

(1) Two players face each other sitting on the ground.

(2) The two players clasp hands or wrists to pull back and forth.

(3) Repeat six to eight times.

(4) See Illustrations 408-409.

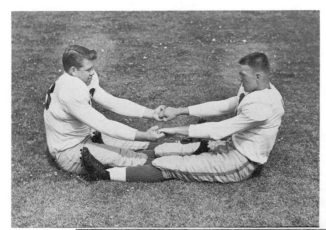

Illus. 408

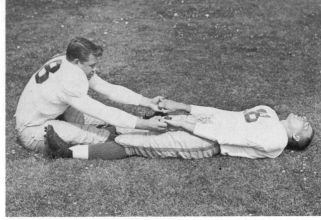

Illus. 409

6. THE BICYCLE

The purpose of this drill is to stretch the lower back, loosen the hip muscles and strengthen the neck.

INSTRUCTIONS:

(1) Assume a supine position on the ground with the feet raised over head, without the use of hands for support.

(2) Rotate the feet in a large circle. Make this exercise short and snappy.

(3) Repeat 15 to 20 times.

(4) See Illustration 410.

Illus. 410

Illus. 411

7. ABDOMINAL RAISE

The purpose of this drill is to strengthen the abdominal wall and to stretch the long muscles of the entire back.

INSTRUCTIONS:

(1) Lie on the back with the hands clasped behind the head.

(2) Raise the trunk and twist so that the left elbow touches the right knee. Return to lying position. Repeat with the right elbow touching the left knee.

(3) 5 to 10 repetitions.

(4) See Illustration 411.

8. THE JACKNIFE

The purpose of this drill is to develop the abdominal muscles and the flexors of the hip.

INSTRUCTIONS:

(1) Sit with the legs extended, hands on hips.

(2) Snap both legs off the ground, at the same time attempt to touch the toes. Return to starting position with legs on the ground and hands on hips.

(3) Repeat five to eight times.

(4) See Illustrations 412-413.

Illus. 412

Illus. 413

9. THE CAN-CAN

The purpose of this drill is to stretch the lumbar region of the low back.

INSTRUCTIONS:

(1) Lie on the ground in a supine position with arms sideward.

(2) Kick right foot to left hand and return. Kick left foot to right hand and return. Keep shoulders on ground, use a twisting movement of trunk and thighs.

(3) Repeat four to six times with each leg.

(4) See Illustrations 414-415.

Illus. 414

Illus. 415

10. BOTTOMS UP

The purpose of this drill is to stretch all the back muscles, especially the lower back, and to pull the vertebrae apart. To strengthen the muscles of the hips and buttocks.

INSTRUCTIONS:

(1) Lie on the back with arms at sides.

(2) Raise legs upward and attempt to touch toes to the ground behind the head. Keep the legs straight and touch the toes to the ground alternately.

(3) Repeat 10 to 15 times.

(4) See Illustration 416.

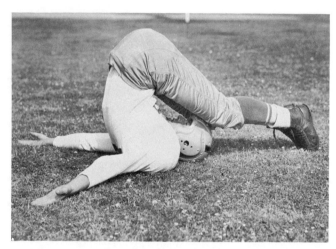

Illus. 416

11. THE BUTT BUSTER

The purpose of this drill is to strengthen the muscles of the arm and shoulder joint, to stretch the muscles of the hip joint, and to have fun. This is a morale exercise and we usually name it after one of the players. ("The Nielson special," etc.)

INSTRUCTIONS:

(1) Lean in a supine position with hands supporting body weight. The body should be kept in a straight line from the

Illus. 417

Illus. 418

shoulders to the heels. Emphasis: no body sag at the hips.

(2) Bring both legs under the body as in Illustration 428 and then return to original position. Repeat on numbered cadence or chant name of particular rival ("Beat Santa Barbara," etc.) See Illustration 429.

(3) Repeat 10 to 15 times.

(4) See Illustrations 417-418.

12. THE ROCKING CHAIR

The purpose of this drill is to strengthen the abdominal and back muscles.

INSTRUCTIONS:

(1) Lie face down with arms stretched overhead or clasped behind the neck.

(2) Raise arms, chest, head, and legs off the ground. This is followed by a rocking motion on the abdomen. Return to starting position. Repeat.

(3) Exercise for 30 seconds.

(4) See Illustrations 419-420.

Illus. 419

Illus. 420

Illus. 421

Illus. 422

13. THE PUSH UP

The purpose is to strengthen the back, chest and arms.

INSTRUCTIONS:

(1) Lie face downward. Place hands on ground shoulder width apart. Keep legs straight and together.

(2) Dip and barely touch chest (not knees or abdomen) to ground. Keep back straight and tail down. Perform slowly. Repeat.

(3) Repeat five to ten times.

(4) See Illustrations 421-422.

14. THE BRIDGE

The purpose is to strengthen the muscles of the back of the neck.

INSTRUCTIONS:

(1) Lie in a supine position, arms at side, knees bent, heels on the ground.

(2) Raise the shoulders and hips off the ground by pressing on the arms. Body weight rests on back of head and heels. Return to original position, and repeat.

(3) Repeat 5 to 10 times.

(4) See Illustration 423.

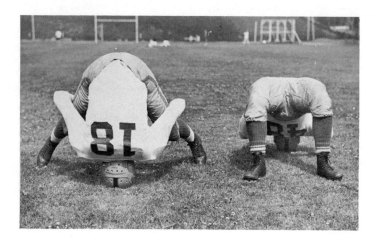

Illus. 423

15. STARTS

The purpose is to complete the warm-up cycle after calisthenics and prepare the players for contact, to improve individual takeoff ability, and to stretch the muscles (anterior and posterior) in the legs.

INSTRUCTIONS:

(1) Have the men assume a good offensive stance.

(2) On the snap of the ball the men forward as fast and hard as possible for five yards.

(3) Do eight to 15 starts.

(4) See Illustration 424.

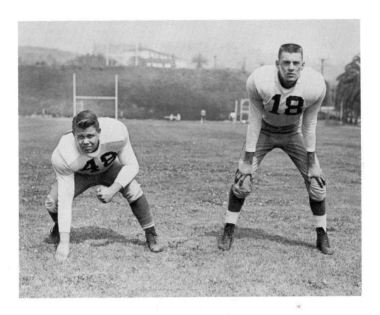

Illus. 424

OTHER DRILLS

We have omitted many drills from our pre-practice conditioning program. We do not recommend any type of squatting exercise. We favor exercises for limbering and stretching rather than the tightening and restricting type that curtail circulation. Furthermore, we believe many exercises require more expenditure of time than the benefits seem to justify. The following exercises were omitted:

1. The "duck walk" is executed by squatting down as low as possible and then walking forward or backward. The hips of the player should be as close to the heels as possible.

2. The "deep knee bend" is executed by standing erect and squatting as far down as possible.

3. The "co-ordinator" is executed by assuming a squatting position with hands on ground outside of feet. Then extend legs to a prone position and dip chest to ground. Spring to erect position.

4. In the "rope skip," each player has a rope and should attempt to jump as fast as possible. This is a good spring practice drill.

5. The "leg lifter" is executed by lying on the back with the hands under the hips. The legs are held still and raised off the ground.

6. "Pushing" is any drill that is executed by two players facing each other. Their hands are placed under each other's shoulders with the idea of attempting to push each other back.

7. "Forward on the inside" and "backward on the outside" are used to strengthen the ankles. See Illustration 425.

Illus. 425

Strenuous work during summer

One of the common beliefs regarding conditioning is that shoveling concrete, construction work, section work and such forms of strenuous labor are essential to good physical condition. Heavy work hardens the players, but in many cases drains too much on their reserve, and every football player needs some reserve strength. In addition, too much strenuous labor of this type tends to slow down the athlete rather than develop speed and quickness which are vital to success. Some heavy labor is desirable, but it can be overdone and if overdone may develop the piano-mover type of athlete.

18

REACTION DRILLS

Reaction makes position

G. H. A.

FOLLOWING THE IDEA THAT CONDITIONING EXERCISES SHOULD simulate things actually done in scrimmage and games, we employ reaction drills. The drills are therefore valuable for development of skills which are needed and used in game conditions. Reaction drills are superior for improving reaction time and developing co-ordination and agility in the awkward players. These drills develop an ability to respond quickly and accurately to verbal commands. The time between signals must be varied to develop the quick reactions desired. Reaction drills do not demand the same precision which should characterize the conditioning exercises. The following movements suggest some of the possibilities for reaction drills.

552

1. THE CRAB

The purpose is to develop agility and co-ordination.

INSTRUCTIONS:

(1) On all fours, face down, on hands and feet.

(2) At the command "go," the men crab quickly forward. At the command "left," they crab laterally to the left. "Rear" means reverse the direction. "Drop" means fall to the ground face down. "Go," in each case means to crab straight forward. "Roll over" means to revolve the entire body and return to original position. Other possibilities are: 1. Crab 10 yards forward; 2. crab 20 yards backward; 3. roll 10 yards, etc.

(3) Exercise one to two minutes.

(4) See Illustration 426.

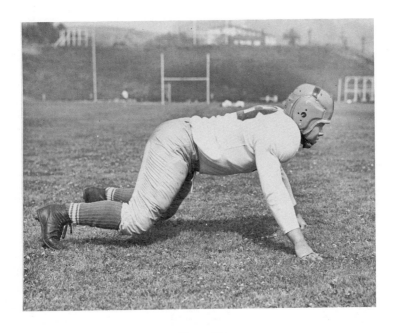

Illus. 426

2. HIKE AND DROP

The purpose is to develop co-ordination and harden the body.
INSTRUCTIONS:

(1) Linemen and backs assume their offense stance.

(2) At the command "hike," the men run forward. At the command "drop," they drop to the ground face down as in the grass drill. At the command "right," they turn and sprint to the right at an angle of 45 degrees. If the command is "left," they run to the left at a 45 degree angle. At the command "rear," they run backwards. "Go" in each case means to sprint straight ahead.

(3) Exercise one to two minutes.

3. INVERTED WALK

The purpose is to stretch the chest muscles and strengthen the upper back and to develop co-ordination.
INSTRUCTIONS:

(1) Sit with the hands on the ground.

(2) From the sitting position lift the hips to a back leaning rest. At the command "forward" walk straight ahead. At the command "rear" walk backward. At the command "right" proceed to walk to the right and on the command "left" walk to the left. Men should move as quickly as possible.

(3) Exercise 15-25 seconds.

(4) See Illustrations 427-428.

Illus. 427

Illus. 428

4. BEAR WALK

The purpose of this drill is to develop co-ordination and to stretch the hamstring muscles.

INSTRUCTIONS:

(1) Face down on hands and feet.

(2) Travel forward by moving the right arm and right leg simultaneously and then the left arm and left leg simultaneously. At the command "rear", the men travel backward by using the same movement in reverse.

(3) Exercise 10-15 seconds.

(4) See Illustrations 429-431.

Illus. 429

Illus. 430

Illus. 431

5. THE Z RUN

The purpose is to develop speed and endurance and to harden the body by contact with the ground.

INSTRUCTIONS:

(1) Linemen and backs assume their offensive stance.

(2) Upon the signal to go, the men run fast at an angle of about 45 degrees to the right; on the whistle they drop to the ground. At the next whistle they spring to their feet and repeat the Z run to the left and drop. This continues until the command is given to stop.

(3) Exercise 1-2 minutes.

19

SECOND HALF

WARM-UP DRILLS

Make it a rule to warm-up

IT HAS LONG BEEN OUR OPINION THAT INADEQUATE WARMING UP
occurs after halftime activities. The coach usually keeps the
players in the locker room as long as possible while reviewing
details of the first half and discussing strategy for the second
half. He realizes the need for adequate warming up, but is
usually pressed for time during the intermission.

It has been our policy to attempt to dismiss the men from
the locker room at least five minutes prior to the second half
kick-off. By the time all the players file out and are on the field
approximately two minutes will have elapsed. (Depending
upon location of dressing quarters) We believe we have accomplished little by using almost all of the time allotted between halves and then forcing the players to rush out on the
field with practically no warm-up. We know that without a
specific warm-up period that we are being unfair to every man
on the team by subjecting him to possible injury.

558

Dr. Floyd R. Eastwood has been compiling research for twenty-one years on football injuries and fatalities. His research indicates that evidence accumulated during the past years verifies the early football injury studies (1931-1935), that injuries and fatalities occur more frequently soon after an individual enters a game or starts a practice period. *Inadequate warm-up* is a more important contributing cause than is fatigue. The first five minutes of activity are the most hazardous.

With the above considerations in mind the five following exercises are designed as an adequate third quarter warm-up:

1. Jumping Jack
2. Inguinal Roll
3. Cross Bend
4. The Stretcher
5. Starts (Both individual and team)

Of the above five exercises, only the stretcher is presented here for the first time. The others were described in Chapter 17.

THE STRETCHER

The purpose of this drill is to stretch as many muscles as possible in the entire body. To develop flexibility in the hip and lower back area.

INSTRUCTIONS:

(1) Standing position with the feet well spread and grasping the ankles with the hands.

(2) Lean the upper extremity over slowly and attempt to touch the head to the ground. Stand up, relax and repeat procedure.

(3) Repeat six to eight times.

(4) See Illustration 432.

Illus. 432

20

RECOMMENDED CONDITIONING PROGRAM

No one should play or practice without warming up

IN THIS CHAPTER IS OUTLINED A SERIES OF EXERCISES AND MOVE-ments which we have successfully used for ten years. We do not claim this program of drills is the best developed, but it has accomplished our purpose. Any exercise that will help prevent an injury, regardless of how silly it may look, is the exercise to use. The objective of our recommended conditioning program which we refer to follows:

(1) Use of preliminary exercises for *stretching* the muscles for warm-up and relaxation.

(2) Use of specific exercise for *strengthening* and *developing* groups of muscles necessary in football.

(3) Use of grass drill for conditioning and *hardening* of the body.

(4) Use of individual and team starts to increase *speed* and *takeoff* ability.

As a rule, we always spend from eight to ten minutes before

each practice session, whether spring or fall, in some form of stretching exercises. We have found it advisable to use what we term, "exercise for coordination." This has been forced on us in view of the number of boys who reach college without certain fundamental training. In addition to the above we use game skills such as kicking, passing, running, etc. as conditioners. In general, we aim to limber up, co-ordinate, condition, improve wind, and harden the body before we call upon the player for any strenuous effort.

Since these drills have been explained in Chapter 17, we will only list them here. They should be performed in the following order:

   (1) Jumping Jack (15 to 25 repetitions).
   (2) Inguinal Roll (10 to 20 times each leg).
   (3) Cross Bend (10 to 15 repetitions).
   (4) The Can Can (4 to 6 repetitions with each leg).
   (5) The Old Rocking Chair (20 to 30 seconds).
   (6) The Butt Buster (10 to 15 repetitions).
   (7) The Jack Knife (5 to 8 times).
   (8) The Crab (30 to 45 seconds).
   (9) Grass Drill (1 to 2 minutes).
(10) Starts (8 to 15 starts).

INDEX